PLACES

ALSO BY PHILIP SHABECOFF

A Fierce Green Fire

A New Name for Peace

Earth Rising

Poisoned for Profit (with Alice Shabecoff)

ABOUT THE AUTHOR

Philip Shabecoff was a reporter for *The New York Times* for over three decades. He served as a foreign correspondent in Europe and Asia, as White House correspondent during the Nixon and Ford administrations and, for his last fourteen years with the Times as its chief environmental correspondent. After leaving the paper, he founded and published *Greenwire*, the daily online news report. He has written four previous books (one with his wife Alice Shabecoff), one of which, *A Fierce Green Fire*, was the subject of a recent documentary film by the same title. He lives in Massachusetts with his wife. They have two children and five grandchildren.

PLACES

Habitats of a Human Lifetime

Philip Shabecoff

Becket Mountain Books

ISBN: 978-0615686189

Printed in the United States

Book design by Carr-Jones, Inc.
Cover photo by Alan Jones

To Alice,
again and always

A place that ever was lived in
is like a fire that never goes out.

Eudora Welty

CONTENTS

INTRODUCTION

This is a memoir, but its principal subject is not my life. It is instead a memoir about *places*—places where I lived or worked or visited, some just briefly. I wrote this book with the hindsight of all I have learned about the environment, a field I followed closely for nearly half a century in the latter part of a long career as a reporter, publisher, and author. Unlike most memoirs, this is a work of extrospection rather than introspection, of looking at the external world rather than the inner self.

Many elements make and enrich a lifetime: people, things, events, ideas, art, experience—and places. In our civilization, at least in America, we have become excessively preoccupied with things—cars, clothes, computers, houses, toys—some useful, some not, but most basically ephemera. Things, however, are not what we are or who we are. They are not the stuff of memory; they do not inspire loyalty or love or passion—at least they should not.

Of all the other elements that build a lifetime, place is perhaps the most neglected. In this country at least, we are so mobile, blown about by the vagaries of the economy and careers, so enticed by the superhighways and the friendly skies that attachment to places is, for many, fragile to non-existent. We have become modern nomads, gypsies who move our wagons to wherever jobs or preferences take us. Through our televisions, our movies, our Facebooks, our YouTubes, our Blackberries, we inhabit virtual places and lose sight of the real places around us and how they affect our lives.

In part this may be an extension of the frontier tradition of a relatively new people on what was, within memory of relatively recent generations, a fresh new continent that invited exploration, new experience, and moving on. In larger part it is because our civilization treats places so badly, so indifferently that we fear becoming attached to any single place. Ancient forests are leveled and converted into pulp and plywood. Pastures and wheat fields vanish, replaced by tracts of suburban development. Towering machines slice mountains to the valley floor.

Vital, multicultural city neighborhoods suddenly become abandoned, burnt-out slums. Bustling small industrial cities molder into decaying tenements, foreclosed homes, rusting factories, contaminated brownfields, and populations of idle workers, as corporations pull out without a thought for the places they leave behind. Our friendly, comfortable small bakeries, butcher shops, and grocery stores go out of business, unable to compete with the mega-market at the mall a few miles away. Multilane highways bisect our old playing fields. Our swimming holes are rendered malodorous dead pools by chemicals dumped into the water a hundred miles upriver.

Here in the United States, we have gotten off relatively lightly, thanks in part to the short-lived environmental enlightenment in the latter part of the twentieth century. In other parts of the world, industrialized warfare has transformed lush, productive landscapes into moonscapes. Misguided economic development has drained living seas and turned day into black night with industrial fumes. Pollution of the air and water has made some regions virtually uninhabitable, inhabited only by those who have nowhere else to go. In poor countries, the pressure of too many people struggling to exist on too few resources strips their places of the basics of life.

As a professional journalist, I have been perhaps even more nomadic than most contemporary Americans. I have lived on three continents and traveled on two more. Writing assignments have taken me to every region of the United States. I always appreciated the opportunity to experience new places and was invariably excited by the aesthetic, cultural, and social encounters each place afforded. Over the past forty years or so, however, as I concentrated on environmental issues, I began to think about, and more recently grasp, I hope, the relationship of place with the content and quality of my life and the lives of others.

The basic premise of ecology, the science that underlies environmentalism, is that all organisms—and the air, soil, and water that support them—are indivisibly linked in a community of life. As I assimilated this premise, I began to see the places I was in and had occupied previously in a new light. I saw how they had shaped and enriched my life. I saw, too, how in a very small way my life had shaped the places I had inhabited. Finally, I learned how humans, collectively, are radically altering those places, in some cases for the better but more often for the worse in ways that bode ill for our posterity.

In recent years we have begun to understand our social ecology—the way human communities live in and affect their ecological niches. Many of us are becoming alert to the reality that our social, political, and economic relationships can radically affect the natural community of life in which we dwell. Most of us, I think, are less aware of how those places affect our lives, but we neglect them at our rapidly increasing peril.

This memoir describes the places in which my life has been lived as natural and social ecologies. It will includes places where I have dwelled or worked—the Bronx; Manhattan; Westchester County; Washington, D.C.; the Berkshire Hills of Western Massachusetts; a small village and a small city in Germany; and Tokyo—and some of the places I have visited for work or pleasure—the Catskill Mountains, the American West, Vietnam, Bali, East Africa, France, and England.

Personal relationships are crucial to how comfortably and happily we fit into our community and ecological niche. Many of these places have been inhabited by people I have known intimately as family, friends, neighbors, and colleagues, or briefly as news sources—presidents, premiers, billionaires, peasants, workers, corporate executives, welfare mothers, teamster thugs, environmentalists. They appear in the places I describe. There are also many stories, such as the one about the mayor of a fought-over Vietnamese village who told me he no longer wanted to be a mayor but instead an astronaut because there are no wars on the moon. Or about Richard Nixon standing in the brilliant sunshine of San Clemente, backing away with fear in his eyes like a cornered animal as a circle of reporters closed in around him, launching questions about the Watergate cover-up.

This book, however, essentially is about the places of my life and what thinking about them from an ecological perspective has taught me about my world and my relationship with it. It is also about the collective relationship of my fellow homo sapiens on this planet, which is our only home.

PLACES

CHAPTER 1

THE BEST PLACE

The Barn on Becket Mountain

The best place is the place where I am now. It is a house that stands in a small clearing in a second- or third-growth forest near the top of Becket Mountain in the Berkshire Hills of Western Massachusetts.

It is late afternoon in late summer as I sit here. The sunlight moves across the top of the big ash tree just outside the window in front of me, turning its compound leaves into a mosaic of light and dark green. Below it a greensward in need of mowing slopes downhill to an old stone wall that we restored to its original orderliness many years ago. Next to the ash tree, a large boulder, deeply split along one edge, looks as if it were struggling to free itself from the earth. Many years ago my children named it Giant Rock, but to me it looks more like the head of a snapping turtle rising out of the water or even the head of a whale breaching from a sea of fern and mountain laurel.

If I look over my shoulder through the screened porch to my right, I can see down another gentle slope about a thousand feet long, to a corner of the swimming pond we had dug out of a swampy meadow many years ago. From the kitchen window on the opposite side of the room, I see our small vegetable garden and behind it a wildflower meadow blossoming atop our septic field. At the edge of this acre or so of cleared land, the forest crowds in so thickly that we can see into it barely one hundred or two hundred feet. We could have a long view of the hills if we cleared a few more acres, but we are happy to remain in the close embrace of our trees.

Some other mountain, some other land, some other house could just as easily have been the best place for us. We have seen more beautiful, quiet, and interesting places around the country and the world. But this place—this house, this land, this pond—is our place, our own small corner of the universe. We have shaped it, lived on it, labored on it, and loved it for more than forty years. Over that time we have wooed our acres to create a landscape that merges gently and almost imperceptibly with the natural world around us. It is our middle landscape, our compromise between the wild and the cultivated. This is our familiar habitat, a place we know intimately, where we feel comfortable, safe, at home. The tension that subtly but inevitably grips us in the noisy, frantic, machine-driven city ebbs after a few days here. We are at peace, a rare thing in our age.

When we are here, we feel we are in the real world, a world very different from the artificial environment and virtual reality in which we spend so much of our lives. Often, usually several times a day, I walk slowly around our clearing, grateful and astonished that I possess such beauty.

We chose the house site and helped clear the land around it. We chose the house when it was no more than bare oaken beams, all that was left of a barn erected by some Yankee farmer more than a century-and-a-half ago, more than thirty miles away in another state. We watched and helped every step of the way as it was rebuilt on our land. We have harvested and eaten food from our own garden. Our small children scooped tadpoles from the pond with kitchen strainers, and their children did the same before they too grew up and away. My mother, Sylvia, never saw this place, but my father, Sidney, and my wife Alice's parents, Henry and Elsie, visited every summer. They are all long gone, but for many years they ate with us at the picnic table beneath the pine tree and in the warm evening sat at their ease on the Adirondack chairs in front of the house, talking to their grandchildren and watching the changing colors of the evening sky.

If we have helped shape the land here, it also has helped shape us, as have many of the places in which we have lived and worked. Being here has given us a vivid sense of the world in which we live; it has encouraged us to attune ourselves as much as possible to the rhythms of the natural world that surrounds us. Our lives feel more vital and immediate here, a feeling we try to take with us when we return to our urban habitat and one that helps sustain us throughout the year.

We now have nearly sixty acres of land. We bought the first parcel, about twenty-seven acres, in 1968 when I was a foreign correspondent for *The New York Times* in the process of transferring from Germany to Japan. My mother died that year, the same year in which Dr. Martin Luther King and Robert Kennedy were assassinated. Those events left me with a panicky feeling. I felt adrift in a strange and hostile world that contained no place to which I belonged, no portion of the Earth to which I could return and claim as refuge.

I did not even see the land before I became its part owner. I was already in Tokyo when Alice and her sister, Susan, with whom we share the property, bought it from Walter Wilson. A radical socialist who had fled New York City with his wife Fanny in the 1930s in despair over the failure of the capitalist system, Wilson had then become a millionaire speculating in Berkshire real estate. He had an eye for landscapes and a feel for what people like us wanted: trees, stone walls, water, and solitude.

We were able to acquire our property fairly cheaply because there was a lot of empty land available in the Berkshires for many years after World War II. Most of the farms, pastures, and orchards had been abandoned. Small agricultural holdings in New England provided an increasingly scant, hardscrabble living, particularly in the face of overwhelming competition by giant agribusiness companies and the inrush of produce from abroad. Young people, often better educated than their parents, left for the higher paying jobs and more exciting lifestyle of the cities. Where there had been cornfields, apple orchards, and dairy herds, a tangle of mostly young trees and thick brush took possession of the land. Moreover, New Yorkers and Bostonians fleeing the summer heat had not yet rediscovered the Berkshires.

In the nineteenth century, the Berkshires had been the fashionable place to be. The rich built big elaborate mansions, which they called, I think without irony, "cottages," some of which can still be seen in Lenox and Stockbridge. The area was also popular with artists and writers. Herman Melville had a house in Lenox. So did Nathaniel Hawthorne, whose former house stands

3

next to the grounds of the Tanglewood Music Festival. William Cullen Bryant was a frequent visitor who liked to take friends to the top of Monument Mountain in Great Barrington, a small but precipitous peak that commands a sweeping view of Berkshire County from its summit.

The Berkshires, however, fell out of fashion. The city people preferred Cape Cod or the Hamptons or to spend their money on trips to Europe and Asia rather than on summer houses.

The land we bought is off a dirt road about a mile from the Jacob's Pillow Dance Festival. When we arrived only three other houses stood along the road. One of those was a small eighteenth-century gray-shingled cottage (without the quotation marks), belonging to a friend of Susan's named Bertha Hatvary, a large, witty, and gregarious divorcée who soon became a friend of ours. It was called Porcupine House, because when Bertha bought it, the floors and siding had been partially eaten away by marauding porcupines with a taste for weathered shingles and old pine flooring. Like Bertha, the house had character but not too many frills. We had rented it once while on home leave from Germany and immediately recognized the Berkshires as our ideal habitat.

We found the land thickly wooded, with only one small, open, wet meadow. The trees were mostly medium-size old growth, less than a hundred years old we thought, but there were many forest giants—white pines, beeches, and black cherries—that towered imposingly over the canopy. The land sloped gently upward from the meadow on the flank of the mountain. Fern and bracken, mountain laurel, and wild azaleas grew profusely wherever the sun touched the forest floor. It was a landscape into which we could burrow and insulate ourselves from the noisy, busy, concrete-covered world of our working lives.

The first thing we did when we arrived on our own land in the summer of 1970 was to hire a local contractor to dig a pond for us in the wet meadow. Alice must have a place to swim; we think she may have been a river otter in a previous life. When we built the pond, the Commonwealth of Massachusetts encouraged the conversion of wetlands to ponds as sources of water in case fires broke out in forests, and an employee of the state agriculture department designed it for us. The contractor, however, pretty much ignored the plan and dug a big hole in the ground. Shortly after the pond was completed, the land around it began to flood, and we had to threaten to withhold payment to get him to dig the diversion ditch around the pond called for in the plan.

Over the years the ditch has become a delightful stream that rushes and gurgles after a rain. We had the contractor lay down sand for a small beach and extend the sand area out into about fifty feet of shallow water to where several flat boulders had been stacked. We call it Diving Rock because directly in front it, the pond dips to its deepest point, some six feet, so we can dive headfirst into the water. We have given names to a number of the rocks on our land that we think have personalities. In one section of the pond a boulder comes up to within a few inches of the surface but cannot be seen from the bank. Anyone standing on it looks as if he or she is walking on water. Someone dubbed it Jesus Rock.

For the first couple of years, the banks of the pond were bare of vegetation and as barren as a desert. We called it the Negev. Over the years, however, the edges of the pond grew lush and lovely with grass and wildflowers: daisies and Black-eyed Susans, dianthus, forget-me-nots, hawkweed, purple vetch, milkweed, goldenrod, tansy, and many others that I cannot name. The outer edges of the bank gradually became lined with slender white birch trees punctuated by a few larches and with swamp maples that blaze into a rich red in late summer. I built a rudimentary wooden bridge to let us cross the ditch. In summer the Joe-Pye weed and sumac, daisies, Johnny-Jump-Ups, and blackberry bushes crowd around it, creating an enchanting water garden.

The pond has been the source of endless problems, a deep, water-filled pit into which we have thrown thousands upon thousands of dollars. One of the problems is beavers. Every few years, in the early spring, a new family of beavers decides that the place would make a nice homestead and proceeds to build an elaborate dam across the narrowest part of the stream— formerly the diversion ditch. I have nothing against beavers per se. In fact I admire them. I just don't want them to mess with our pond and trees. After all, this is our pond not theirs. It wouldn't be here if we hadn't built it. If a young beaver family wants to set up housekeeping in a new location, it should respect our property rights and find some natural pond or stream to start construction. If all the decent ponds are taken because there are too many beavers, maybe it is time for the beaver community to start seriously considering family planning.

We love our pond, despite the considerable expense it requires to maintain. We call it "The Center of the Universe." Each year its edges are covered with a foot-wide black band of miniscule tadpoles that, through some conjurer's trick, transform themselves later in the summer into thousands of tiny frogs. The little tadpoles are a bit disconcerting when we are swimming and feel them bump against our skin, but we are glad to see them each spring because their appearance means our pond has not been assailed by the acid rain that has destroyed life in many bodies of water in the Northeast.

We stocked the pond several times, first with brown trout and then with hardier large-mouthed bass. We did it for my young son who liked to fish, and we hoped he would use the pond as an adult. He does not, but for a number of years prehistoric-looking great blue herons visited the pond almost daily to try their luck at fishing, rising ponderously out of the water when we approached, then flying slowly off on their great wings. The herons may be partly responsible for emptying the pond of fish every couple of years, but we think poachers from the neighborhood are the more likely culprits.

The decline of farming has destroyed a traditional way of life for many Berkshire families. It has been good, however, for wildlife, which is returning in growing numbers to the woodland that not long ago had been fields, pastures, and orchards. When we first came here, there were no wild turkeys, but now every summer large flocks of the handsome birds walk insouciantly across our lawns. We have not yet seen any coyotes but occasionally hear their wild howls in the middle of the night. One night when we were driving home from dinner at a friend's house, we turned onto our road and saw a tall shape a few hundred feet in front of us. At first we thought it might be a very tall man, but when we got close we saw in our headlights, to our surprise and delight, that it was a moose. It was a huge creature-

—as big as a moose in fact. We followed closely behind as the moose, unperturbed, trotted slowly ahead of us on the road for about a mile, turning its head back occasionally to look at that bright light behind him.

We are regularly visited by black bears, which tear down and destroy our birdfeeders and rummage through our compost heap. Once we were sitting on our porch in mid-afternoon when a young bear came up the slope from the pond, climbed a big birch tree a few feet away, and crawled out on the limb to knock down the birdfeeder. When it climbed down to begin its snack, I shouted loudly and clapped my hands and the bear scuttled a few feet off into the woods. Less than a minute later, it returned and, ignoring my shouts, settled down to eat. A few moments later, the bear lifted its head, sniffed, and then moved rapidly off into the woods. We didn't understand why until shortly afterward a second, larger bear came quickly up the slope and disappeared into the woods in the direction of the first one.

Until recently, we took pleasure from our bear visits. One summer, however, a sizable ursine tried to break through one of our doors while we were in the house. It was a bit frightening, even though we knew it was just trying to get at food. We called the state's environmental police, but the bear, unable to get in, had left by the time they arrived. They told us that if they had found the bear inside our house, their regulations required that they shoot it. We were glad they didn't, but it is clear that humans have to establish some better modus vivendi with wildlife. We want to share the land with bears and beavers, porcupines, and moose, but we don't want them to threaten our grandchildren's safety or damage our house and gardens—or our pond. How this can be done, I cannot see. It is clear that we humans still have not learned how to coexist comfortably with the other life with which we share the planet. Our approach to the dilemma is to wipe out species, both plant and animal, that get in our way. Perhaps our inability to get along with other life is a clue to why humans have so much trouble getting along with one another.

On the shore of the pond opposite the beach is a large boulder shaped like a miniature Alp that we call Mansfield Park. It got its name this way: One morning, when my daughter,

Alexa, was about thirteen years old—a beautiful, spirited child still in long pigtails—she plucked Jane Austen's novel from our bookshelves and sat down to read it. At lunchtime I asked her how far she had gotten in the book. She replied that she had finished it. I said she couldn't possibly have read the whole thing in just a couple of hours, but she had. We went down to the pond, and while the two of us sat on top of the boulder in the warm sunshine, she proceeded to tell me the entire story of Mansfield Park, with details, from first chapter to last. The telling took about an hour, but it is a memory I continue to think about and cherish now that my daughter is in her fifties. The boulder has been called Mansfield Park ever since.

We camped on the edge of the pond for several weeks each summer waiting for the house to go up. Alice and I slept in a large tent ornately furnished with cots for sleeping and orange crates for end tables and chests. Alexa and her brother, Peter, had a slightly smaller tent and Susan had a pup tent, which was promptly dubbed The Grand Hotel. Our dog, Tagalong, an affectionate, fun-loving mixed golden retriever border collie rescued as a small ball of fur from an animal shelter, slept under the canopy in front of our tent. A large canvas served as our kitchen. We cooked our meals on an open fire or a little two-burner propane camping stove. The food was simple: bacon and eggs or cold cereal and milk for breakfast; sandwiches for lunch; broiled steak, hamburgers, or chicken, with potatoes roasted in the fire or sometimes spaghetti with bottled sauce for dinner. Everything seemed delicious. Our toilet was a portable commode, filled with chemicals and placed about fifty feet behind the tents—an okay arrangement, except when it rained and water ran down the back of our necks as we sat.

We spent our days swimming in the pond, watching the kids paddle around in small inflatable canoes, tossing baseballs and Frisbees, collecting firewood, and tramping through our woods. We made excursions into the town of Lee for supplies and to Bertha's house to fill plastic jugs with water from her well. On rainy days, we stayed in the big tent and played Go Fish or I Doubt It and endless games of Monopoly. When we grew tired of games, we read by the light of kerosene lamps. In the evening, after cleaning our dinner dishes, we sat around the fire telling stories and singing songs; sometimes the children fell asleep on our laps. On clear nights we could look up through the clear sky at an infinity of stars. We did not think about much except living. As a reporter for a daily newspaper, I did not have to worry about long-term projects I would have to face when our vacation ended. Each day existed for itself. That is, I believe, an unusual luxury in the contemporary world.

Thinking back decades later about those long, relaxed summer weeks camping around the pond, with Peter and Alexa as lively companions all day long, Alice and I agreed that those were probably the best days of our lives. We thought the kids loved it as much as we did. But when they were grown they told us that they had not been all that happy; they would have preferred to be with other boys and girls their own age. Ah well, their loss was our gain.

The slope between the pond and the house site we had selected next to Giant Rock was so thick with trees and brush that we had to blaze a trail to be able to make the thousand-foot round trip without getting lost each time. The four of us—Alice, the kids, and I—used hand axes and saws to cut away small trees, tough tangles of blueberry and blackberry bushes, and other woody shrubs to clear an opening about thirty feet by thirty feet approximately where we wanted the foundation. We wanted the western side of the house to face the pond, but when we stood at the house site, we could not see the pond through the barrier of crowding trees. The only way we could orient ourselves in the proper direction was for Alice to stand down near the pond and shout so we could lay out pegs and string in the proper direction. The children groused a bit about the hard work, but after it was done, they took great satisfaction in our mutual achievement.

I had thought about a small cottage, perhaps a log cabin, for our home here, but Alice and Susan had their hearts set on reconstructing an old barn. We found, through a journalist colleague who had grown up in the Berkshires, a young builder named Al Sommers who never had put up a barn but was eager to try. He had his eye on an old barn with rotting siding in his hometown of Chatham, New York. When we asked him to rebuild it for us, he ripped off the old siding, exposing the massive posts and beams, still held together by their original wooden pegs and still showing the marks of the adze with which they were shaped a century-and-a-half earlier.

Al let the beams weather in the open air for a couple of months. While we were waiting, we got another contractor to build a curved driveway, more than six hundred feet long, from the town road to our home site. The men who worked on it let us know they thought we were foolish for building so far from the road, in an area where several feet of snow accumulates each winter. Local people built close to the road to minimize the plowing they would have to do. The road is gracefully curved, hiding the house from the road, and is overarched with trees that turn the approach into a green tunnel.

We hired another company to dig our well. They only had to go down sixty feet to hit the aquifer, which gives us all the bracingly cool water we need, even in the driest summers. To bring a pipe from the well to our house thirty feet away, however, they had to use dynamite to blast through the solid gneiss shelf a few inches beneath the scant topsoil. Another reason our land was so cheap is that it never could have been used for farming because the soil is too thin and stony. Several times we have seen wind and ice storms uproot sixty-foot-tall spruce trees, leaving a root system only several inches thick but twenty or more feet in diameter. We discovered an old cistern in the woods near the road, a graceful circle of moss-covered stone about five feet in diameter, so the land once may have supported a small dairy herd. Perhaps there had been a small orchard as well; there are a couple of gnarled old apple trees near the pond that still bear small, leathery skinned but sweet apples.

Most of the house went up during the summers we were camping by the pond. Al and his crew took stones from some of the many stone walls that crisscrossed our land—all in perfect north-south or east-west alignment—to build the foundation. We had used some of the lumber intended for the flooring joists to build platforms for our tents, but Al came in the middle of our vacation to take them away; it was time to build the floors. He had numbered the beams before dismantling the barn in Chatham and reassembled them, with a few changes, as they had been placed originally. Alice and I think the house was at its most beautiful when it was a skeleton of oak beams outlined against a blue sky.

Al had a natural eye for design. He took the sturdy ladder—once used to reach the hayloft—that had been in the middle of the barn and moved it to the south wall, where it became a fifteen-foot floor-to-ceiling window that provided light to our kitchen and dining room. He built an earthen ramp up to where the old barn doors had been and then installed heavy, sliding plate-glass doors that faced down to the pond. The living room ceiling is twenty-six feet high with the oak beams exposed. Alice, Susan, and I spent hours scrubbing the accumulated grime from thick oak floorboards salvaged from the old barn, and Al used them to form one wall of the living room where they glow warmly in lamplight. Old stalls and storage rooms were converted into five bedrooms and two bathrooms. Four of the bedrooms are only eight-by-twelve feet in size, small but big enough. Susan's bedroom, under the eaves on the third level, is substantially larger. Alice and Susan insisted on windows everywhere, so, unlike many barns, the interior is light and airy.

Al indulged his own playfulness with a few eccentric touches, including a door that opens out from what was to be Peter's bedroom on the second floor to empty space seven feet above the living room floor. He attached a thick rope to a beam in the room, and Peter and his visiting friends as well as energetic adults used it to climb down from the room and, those with enough strength, back up. I was able to climb up in my younger days but no longer. Now my grandchildren and their friends scamper up and down the rope like squirrels.

One of Al's crew, an athletic, sweet-tempered young man named Jed Lipsky, volunteered to make the stone chimney we wanted to go up through the center of our barn. Again using stones gleaned from the walls on our land, he took a couple of months to build us a formidable structure six feet wide and rising twenty-six feet to the ceiling of our living room and a couple of feet more above the roof. Jed had built one stone chimney before, a small affair for a log cabin he had constructed for himself. After completing ours he said he never would do another. "The strain was too much," he explained. "Not the physical strain but the mental strain of deciding which stones to use and where to place each one." We think what he made for us is a textured work of art, like some of the stone walls in Japan that are considered national treasures.

While Al and his crew were putting up the siding, the interior walls, and the roof, I began to clear the land between the house and the pond. In that first year, I used only axes. I did not know how to operate a chainsaw, was more than a little afraid of them, and regard them as one of the more destructive technologies of the twentieth century. By the end of the summer, I had opened enough of the woods to get a partial view of the pond, but it was slow work. A big black cherry, sixteen or more inches in diameter, took me the better part of a day to fell and even more than that to cut into pieces that I could use in the fireplace or carry away into the forest.

We used a lot of wood for the stove and fireplace, and I also wanted to clear more land around the house. So the following summer, with some trepidation, I drove to Sears in Pittsfield and bought a chainsaw. In the more than forty years since, I have felled a substantial number of trees but always with mixed feelings. Last September, for example, I cut down a sizable ash tree I'd had my eye on all summer as a candidate for felling— both for firewood and to make room for a graceful young beech growing beneath its branches. Even so, I held off for months before taking the chainsaw to the ash.

Choosing a tree for cutting takes a lot of thought and soul searching. Trees are important, valuable forms of life, undoubtedly more important and valuable to the planet than imperial, destructive humans. Cutting down a big tree changes the way the land will look, so I have to think about aesthetics before I turn on the saw. Living among the trees, surrounded by their beauty and calmed by their dignity and permanence, knowing that most of them will still be here when I am gone, is one of the great joys of living at the Barn. Although we have thousands of trees of various species on our property—white, gray, and yellow birches; red maples; swamp oaks; beeches; ashes; white pines; hemlocks; spruce; poplar; black cherry; larches; and others—I hesitate to cut any of them down (except for the striped maples, which I regard as trashy weeds).

Trees, I've found, are tough critters that do not give up on life easily. Each spring when we return to the Barn, I find that young trees that I had cut to within a few inches of the ground are already putting out long new shoots. One tree, the big black cherry I had cut to open the slope to the pond, taught me indelibly where the word "stumped" came from. After I felled the cherry, I let the stump, about twenty inches in diameter and two feet high, sit on the slope and waited for the roots to decay. Three years later I decided the time had come to remove the stump, which marred the view to the pond. With an axe I cut all the un-decayed roots I could and then tried to push it over. It wouldn't budge. I cleared some of the dirt around the base then hacked away at more roots, and then Alice and I pushed together. Nothing. I dug underneath the root system, got the jack from the car, and tried jacking the stump out of the ground. The stump won clearly over the jack. I was stumped. The stump stayed where it was until the following summer when our friends, Bill and Mil Duncan, and their teenage sons, Graham and Ian, came to visit. The four of them joined Alice and me in pushing and tugging and lifting until, after about forty-five minutes, the stubborn stump finally came out of the ground and we rolled it into the woods.

Some trees I just became fond of; they are friends. My favorite is the ash tree next to Giant Rock. I like it just because it is so big and solid, a commanding presence. Its compound leaves fill the sky when I look out the window. About fifteen years ago, a forester who looked at our trees said that the ash was sick and probably would die in a few years, but it continues to flourish. Another of my favorites is a spruce that stands next to our kitchen garden. Alice and Susan have asked me a number of times to cut it down to allow more sun to shine on the garden, but I wouldn't think of it. It was a slender, graceful little creature when we first cleared the land and tagged it as one of the trees we wanted to remain. Now the tree is a towering presence some sixty feet tall, shapely and strong. When we walk in from our driveway, it frames and gives proportion to our house. Right outside our porch, which we built a few years ago when we expanded the Barn to accommodate our growing family, stands a burly white birch, already old when we took over the land. Parts of it have succumbed to age and weather, but every year when we come up to open the house for the summer, we give thanks to see it is still there.

Our trees are alive with birds, although not as many birds as there should be. With continuing deforestation and pesticide contamination of their winter habitat to the south, particularly in Central America, fewer birds return to our Massachusetts woods in spring and summer. Before the bears forced us to give up our birdfeeders, their sunflower and thistle seeds attracted enthusiastic throngs of cheerful black-capped chickadees, as well as goldfinches, purple finches, and a reliable contingent of red-breasted grosbeaks that speckle the dark-green forest with flashes of color. No matter how often they suddenly materialize, we are always thrilled to hear the supersonic wing beats of the ruby-throated hummingbirds as they flit from blossom to blossom of the bright-red bee balm growing outside our bedroom window. For several years we were awakened at dawn by a loud *rat—tat-tat* on the side of the house. It was a handsome yellow-breasted sapsucker pecking repeatedly at the metal frame of a dining room window, displaying a woodpecker machismo intended to attract a mate. After a couple of weeks, the pecking stopped, so we assumed he found a bride. Sometimes a dense crowd of grackles descends on our blueberry bushes when the berries are ripe, and we rush outside banging pots and pans to chase them away, feeling a bit guilty as we do so.

We have, over the years, cleared enough trees to give us a broad view of the pond. When clearing, we left a few of the statelier pines, birches, and maples, which create a park-like, grassy slope dotted with mountain laurel and wild azalea beneath the trees. The laurel and the azalea, locally called swamp pinks, fill the long slope with splashes of white and pink and an intoxicating spicy scent in the springtime. About twenty blueberry bushes punctuate the wildflower meadow on the far side of the house. In a good year, the bushes yield twenty to thirty quarts of berries. We eat many of them fresh from the bush; the rest Alice and Susan preserve as spiced blueberry jam or freeze for use in cakes and pancakes over the winter. We also have a small, cultivated raspberry patch that yields enough berries each summer for a few weeks of eating with sugar and cream, or ice cream, or just browsing straight from the bushes.

Alice, Susan, and I all wanted a vegetable garden. I suspect the impulse to commit agriculture continues to smolder even inside urbanized humans such as we are, who approached middle age without ever having planted a seed or harvested a bean. Grubbing around in the dirt with bare fingers is elementally satisfying, especially with the optimistic belief that such grubbing will be reward in due course with delicious food. Alice longed for a kitchen garden she could look at while standing at the sink washing dishes. A paltry, cosmetic layer of soil that barely could sustain grass and shrubs, however, covered the land around our house. A shovel poked into the soil bangs against solid gneiss shelf after an inch or two. Our problem was solved when one of our construction workers brought in a couple of truckloads of loam; he claimed it was his grandmother's old potato patch.

We were innocent of any knowledge of how to garden when we first started. So we did what we always do when we need to learn something—we read books and magazines. Rachel Carson's *Silent Spring* had been published a decade earlier, and the environmental revolution was picking up momentum, so we knew we should not use fertilizers and pesticides made with synthetic chemicals. Books like Helen and Scott Nearings' *The Good Life* alerted us to the joys of growing and eating our own food. Rodale's *Organic Gardening* magazine was our sacred text, and we found further details in *The Complete Encyclopedia of Gardening* and at least a dozen other how-to books.

We were ambitious vegetable gardeners at first. The loam covered an area of thirty by fifty feet, which we surrounded with a low electrified fence to discourage rabbits, raccoons, and porcupines from using the garden as a cafeteria. I came up a few days in early spring every year to break the soil and dig in manure. For many years I used an implement called a Missouri Mule, a device with a big metal front wheel and behind it a pair of handle bars from which hung a metal shaft with metal tines at its foot. Pushing it through soil compacted by the winter's frost was hard work, especially when the sun was hot and black flies were swarming. I was relatively young and energetic, however, and convinced myself that I enjoyed the work. We grew herbs, lettuce, and other greens; tomatoes; peas; green beans; pump-kins; squash; and several varieties of sweet corn and cucumbers for pickling, using my Grandmother Minnie's recipe for kosher dill pickles. Over the years we also tried onions, potatoes, car-rots and salsify, but though we pile on hundreds of pounds of manure and compost every spring, we never have had enough soil to grow decent root crops.

Gradually our agricultural ambitions narrowed. We had planted a sour cherry sapling named Montmorency in the woods, where it stayed five years, barely gaining any height or girth. When we moved it to a corner of our sunny, fertilized vegetable garden, however, it sprang skyward like Jack's bean-stalk, and within two years we were picking cherries for pies and jam.

During a hard winter, porcupines or deer gnawed most of the bark off the cherry tree and it died within a year. We mourned it as if it were a family pet. The size of the garden shrank to about thirty by twenty feet, and now we grow mostly salads, tomatoes, green beans, and, of course, pickling cucum-bers. I stopped using the Missouri mule in my mid-fifties. Now we pay local Boy Scouts to rototill the land each spring, and af-terward I throw down bags of organic manure (can there really be such a thing as organic manure?) and use a small, motorized tiller to finish preparing the soil. In the meantime, we have found another outlet for our horticultural energies. We discov-ered a late-blooming passion for cultivating flowers.

We enlarged the Barn in 1996 to accommodate the growing size of our family. By then we had four grandchildren, and there would be a fifth to come. So we built a new wing with two large bedrooms, another bathroom, and a laundry room. We also added the screened porch and an entrance mudroom and tool shed. Around the wing we stacked four-inch-by-four-inch tim-bers to construct raised flowerbeds. Into those beds we have poured large quantities of topsoil, money, and effort. The results probably would not pass muster for a photo spread in *House and Garden* magazine, but we find them very appealing to our eyes, nose, and soul.

The bed on the east side of the Barn, Susan's responsibility, is mostly herbs, with some bee balm for hummingbirds, and nasturtiums and moonbeam coreopsis for bright color. Alice and I built a trellis out of green saplings, nailed it above Susan's border, and planted a climbing rose beneath it. In a little more than a year, the bush grew in a lavish eight-foot-high display of shining dark-green leaves and lush pink roses that bloom all summer and into fall. Susan also takes care of the north border, which is filled with shade-tolerant plants such as monk's hood, bleeding heart, and snakeroot. The west border is mostly Alice's, and she has had a hard time controlling her impulse to try every possible annual and perennial. In season it is crowded with delphinium, hollyhocks, gaillardia, campanula, rudbeckia, coreopsis, cosmos, lobelia, mallow, primrose, aster, perennial geranium, mugwort, and others that I cannot keep track of. We put up another trellis with a climbing rose on that side of the house as well.

Across from the north side of the Barn is a sunny patch in which grows a vigorous clump of volunteer tiger lilies. I decided it would be a nice place for spring bulbs, so I planted about fifty daffodils, hyacinth, and tulips in front of the lilies. The tulips died out after one year, but the other bulbs are flourishing. When the spring flowers fade, however, and their green arms droop to the ground, the bed begins to look somewhat depressing.

In gardening, one thing always seems to lead to another, and soon I was adding dahlias, lilies, irises, anemones, foxglove, and Helenium to the bed. Therefore I began to add annuals, including zinnia, snapdragon, and cleome. Soon thereafter I experimented with perennials native to the Berkshires. Then, after spending a summer month exploring the English countryside a few years ago and inspecting with some awe the gardens of some of the stately homes, I determined I would also have a small rose garden. After much work and expense preparing the ground, I planted some fifteen rosebushes—hybrid teas, English, and floribunda roses in shades of white, pink, and red. They take far more effort than I had imagined. To preserve them I abandoned in this one place my resolution not to use chemical pesticides on my land. Even in the first year, gorgeous, fragrant flowers on which to feed my senses amply rewarded me.

I retired from daily journalism some years ago, and since then we spend much of the year, May to mid-October, at the Barn. Many days I spend at my desk working on books or articles. Several times a day, however, either alone or with Alice, I go outside to walk around the house, inspecting the flowerbeds to see what is blooming, to cut some flowers for our rooms, to pluck Japanese beetles from the roses and raspberry bushes, and just to enjoy the clean air, the scent of blossoms, and the sense of having created in an inexpert fashion something that is, to us at least, miraculous and beautiful. Those little walks envelop us in peace and quietude, mental states rarely experienced in our world of urban work and living. Gardening does not help my back, which is frequently sore, or my knees that now go "click" every time I walk down stairs. Each day, however, I go out for my hour or two of stoop work in our flower and vegetable beds without thinking about it. I may have a twinge of regret prompted by twinges of physical pain when I get out of bed the next morning, but I am back in the garden almost every day.

My enthusiasm for gardening seems to increase with age, and I suspect that many people moving toward the end of life feel the same way. There is something about creating and nurturing new life and beauty that is deeply satisfying and consoling, an affirmation of faith in the future, even though we will not be present in that future.

We tend to stick close to the Barn when we are up there, but we do make excursions. Best of all, we like to load our dented old Grumman aluminum canoe on the top of the car and explore lakes we locate on the detailed maps put out by the US Geological Survey. Of course we have to venture outside several times a week to the market or to run other errands. Several times each summer, we throw a picnic into the car and drive a half-hour away for concerts at Tanglewood in Lenox. (We have an old *New Yorker* cartoon pasted to our kitchen cupboard that shows a man and woman standing in front of their vacation home and saying to a visiting couple, "The great thing about this place is that it is far enough from Lenox so that we don't have to go to Tanglewood if we don't want to." Another cartoon shows two farmers leaning on a fence looking at a distant barn where a cocktail party is in progress and one is saying, "Say, Ed, remember my barn when it had cows in it?")

After we discovered skiing, we retrofitted the Barn with an oil-fired forced air-heating system so we could come up in the winter. The house is not well insulated and difficult to warm. Winter there, however, provides us with new pleasures. When there is fresh powder on the thick blanket of snow, the world is a brilliant white in every direction, flashing with blue diamonds as sunlight refracts off the surface. Unlike in the summer, when the thick foliage of our temperate rain forest restricts our depth of vision, the bare trees and bushes allow us to see hundreds of yards into the woods and to groove on the asymmetric pattern of tree trunks that stand dark and bare against the snow. The cold air is as bracing and intoxicating as a vodka martini. Walking through the snow, our feet make a satisfying crunch, and it seems we are putting footprints on one of the few substances on this planet unsullied by human activity. Of course that is not really true. Every snowflake, like every drop of rain and virtually every molecule of matter, bears the residue of fossil fuel combustion, chemicals released into the ambient air, and other detritus of our careless, wasteful, dangerous industrialized civilization. But walking across the shimmering expanse of our fields and down to our dazzling white pond, I feel as if I am an explorer in an undiscovered, pristine landscape.

One year we decided we would have a Christmas tree in the barn. We are both Jewish, but while Alice's parents had a tree every year, my family never did and I never could bring myself to break the faith. But Alexa's husband, Roger Bertling, comes from a Roman Catholic family, so he was my excuse to agree to have a tree.

Alice and I came up a day before Christmas to open the Barn. The grass still showed intensely green where the snow had blown aside, and the sky alternated between bright blue and sudden dark-gray clouds that sent down swirls of fresh snow. That evening I built a fire, and before dinner we sat next to it in our armchairs, books and whisky in hand, and our two cats, Juba and Nabi, then still alive, settled beside us. The wind whistled outdoors, and snow splattered against the windows, but we were warm and comfortable by the fire.

19

The next day, Susan, Alexa, and her husband, Roger, with their children, Adam and Sophia, arrived, and the seven of us went into the woods to find a suitable tree. We found a fragrant young spruce near the pond, and I cut it down with an axe. Then six of us carried it up to the house through the snowy woods. I felt as if I were inside a Grandma Moses painting. The tree was about twelve feet tall, fitting nicely in our living room. We decorated it with ornaments that Alice had collected over the years in the hope I would someday give in and permit a tree. We added ribbons made by our small granddaughter and some popcorn strings and then piled our presents beneath it. Afterward we all sat down for a dinner of steak broiled over the fire and potatoes baked in its coals—except for Alexa, a vegetarian since she was fourteen years old, who had a bowl of pasta. The evening was a great pleasure, but because of the forbidden tree, a somewhat guilty pleasure for me.

I am probably making the Barn sound too much like an earthly paradise, but we sort of feel that way about it. There are, however, a number of serpents in our Eden. The longest of these snakes is the Massachusetts Turnpike. It is some two miles from our property, but we can always hear it, especially when eighteen-wheelers grind up the steep grade of Becket Mountain, which is most of the time, day and night. Often this is merely white noise, but sometimes it intrudes on our peace and isolation.

There are a lot of tormenting insects in the woods to remind us that this is not quite heaven. In May, when we are getting our garden in, black flies swarm so thickly that we wear long-sleeved shirts and beekeepers' hats to hold them at bay, lest we be sucked dry. Later the deer flies emerge to attack us from the rear and take vicious bites out of any exposed flesh. Mosquitoes are the worst because they sometimes get into the house and whine around our ears at night as they look for delicate morsels of prime human to nibble. We have a friend from India who is a Jainist, and once, when I was about to swat a mosquito on my arm, she mildly suggested I just brush it aside. I whacked it anyway. Once I was pruning a swamp pink when yellow jackets nesting in the ground beneath it attacked me en masse. I escaped by jumping into the pond fully clothed, including hat and work gloves, but not before they had inflicted a half-dozen painful stings. I believe in the sanctity of life, but I make exceptions for biting insects. While I admire the iridescent copper and green beauty of Japanese beetles, I get a frisson of pleasure every time I sweep a clump of them off my rosebushes, which they busily chew into shreds, and into a coffee can filled with soapy water.

We are not pleased, either, with the moles that throw up unsightly mounds on our lawns and destroy many of our plants. I personally think field mice are cute little creatures, but I wish they would stay outside and not leave a thick sprinkling of turds inside our kitchen drawers and cabinets and chew our furniture when we are away over the winter. We warily welcome visits from the black bears in our neighborhood but cannot convince them not to play demolition derby with our birdfeeders and compost bins.

A habitat is not just a physical place but also a community of life that occupies it, including—overwhelmingly in the modern world—human life. In that respect the Barn is increasingly distant from Eden.

One of the reasons we loved this property was its privacy, its sense of isolation from the built, crowded, industrialized, anxious modern world. With many trees and few other people around, we could imagine we were on a frontier, living a simpler, more direct life while we were here. Of course that was always an illusion, as the noise from the turnpike reminded us. We are linked by phone lines and electric cable, by car and radio, and by heating oil supplies from the Arabian Peninsula to the workaday world, captives to its economics and its conveniences, and dependent on the supermarket a fifteen-minute drive away. In the quiet of our clearing, though, we could at least play at being intrepid, hardworking homesteaders.

Over the years, however, the woods around us have begun to fill up. There are now a score of houses around us, some of them second homes but most occupied by local families who are transforming our pastoral fantasy into suburbia. The narrow dirt town road that used to be a tunnel through an arch of trees has been widened to accommodate increased traffic and the snow plows that now clear out for new homes and a fishing camp. We often pick up beer and soda cans and fast food wrappers when we take our daily walk along the lane. At night we can see the lights from other houses when we look out our windows. The Jacob's Pillow Dance Festival a mile away has expanded its activities, and we often hear music from its outdoor performances. The glaring sodium lamps in its parking lot dim the stars. More is to come. A developer from Long Island acquired property next to ours and, the last we heard, was planning to build twenty or more homes around a ring road. Another developer from Belgium filed plans to erect condominiums at the end of our road and is looking for more property near us. The Massachusetts Turnpike Authority recently raised again a proposal for building a cloverleaf in Becket, a project that town residents successfully resisted some years ago.

It is inevitable, I think, that many more people will move in. The woods around our property will thin, the wild turkeys, bears, and foxes will once more retreat, and we will hear other people's radios blaring music we do not want to hear. It will be increasingly hard for us to cling to our foolish myth of homesteading in a fresh countryside.

Yes, of course others have a right to live here in the woods. We have no right to close the door behind us. Even so, we cannot help regret our lost solitude, the mystery of a landscape where the imprint of human activity is light.

The world is becoming too full. Since I was born some nearly eighty years ago, the population of the United States has more than doubled and that of the world has more than tripled. This swelling mass of human animals places enormous and increasing pressure on the systems and resources that sustain life on Earth—the land, the water, the air, the trees, and the rest of life with which we share the planet. All of the empty and useful and secluded places are being filled up. For the poorest of our species, the pressure of human numbers is adding to hunger, thirst, disease, and the murderous competition for the basics of survival. In the affluent world, it means traffic jams and air pollution, global warming and acid rain, and the toxification of our environment. It means more misery for the urban poor and a vanishing way of rural life of farms and small towns and villages.

Although we feel as if we are part of the natural community on Becket Mountain, we do not feel all that much at home among the human community. We did have some friends and neighbors about whom we cared. Shortly after we arrived, Joe and Helen Walker, a couple in their fifties who had been managing an alms house in Danbury, Connecticut, moved to the property across the road. With Helen's help, Joe, a robust, handsome man who had grown up on a farm and had held a number of jobs requiring manual skill and practical knowledge, built his own house, a neat, comfortable yellow-painted cottage decorated with many of Helen's paintings and floral arrangements. Helen, a cheerful, endlessly optimistic woman, despite losing several of her children and, later, her beloved husband, was a superb cook and baker and is a natural genius at gardening. She was also a talented artist. Joe and Helen taught us many useful lessons about country living and bailed us out of a few emergencies. Joe died a few years ago and Helen badly missed him, but she continued to live by herself at home, providing cookies, flowers, and a warm welcome to everyone who showed up at her door until she died peacefully at age ninety.

Joe Marx, a lean, taciturn man who lived just down the road, also helped us cope with our land and house problems and occasionally came to our house for dinner, where he put away astonishing amounts of food in silence. He looked and sounded like the archetypical rural Yankee, but in fact came from Kansas, had once danced at Jacob's Pillow, was gay and died mysteriously in middle age, possibly of AIDS.

Ken and Ann Smith, a young couple fresh out of prestigious colleges, moved in down the road a few years after we moved here, built their own house and started to raise a family. Ken taught himself cabinetmaking, and now his joinery creates exquisite pieces for wealthy clients. Ann has worked for years as a paralegal for a law firm in nearby Pittsfield. She is undoubtedly much smarter than any lawyer in the firm but chose not to go to law school in order to spend enough time with her daughter and son, both of whom grew up wonderfully in their little house in the forest. The Smiths have become bulwarks of the community, performing many public services, including running the Becket Land Trust, which acquired for the town a big, abandoned gran-

23

ite quarry, now turned into a nature preserve and museum. Ken and Ann grew close to Joe and Helen Walker; their kids called Joe and Helen Grandpa and Grandpa. The Smiths kept a careful eye on Helen and helped her out with various chores. So did some of Helen's other neighbors, including us.

But we who have been coming to Becket for more than four decades and now spend half the year there are still regarded by most of the local residents with whom we come in contact as "summer people," outsiders who have no part in the community. As "temporary" residents, we have to pay a personal property tax not imposed on year-round residents. Although summer people outnumber the twelve hundred full-time inhabitants and contribute a lion's share of the town's revenues, they cannot vote for selectmen or participate in any decisions made by the town affecting them or their properties. Massachusetts may have been the "cradle of liberty," but Becket, at least, does not consider taxation without representation to be tyranny—or it doesn't care if it is.

The village of Becket is a pleasant enough place, with some big old houses, a post office, and a garage. An old-fashioned general store with a lunch counter shut down a few years ago but, to the surprise of many, reopened a few years later. There is also an arts center, well used by the summer people, and a pretty, nicely stocked library. We do not think of it as our town, however, and seldom go there except to bring our trash to the transfer station once a week. Instead we head in the opposite direction to Lee, a working town with several mills and factories that supported the papermaking industry that once was the economic backbone of the area and still employs many of its men and women. A handsome, white-painted Congregational Church, which boasts the tallest wooden spire in New England, dominates the attractive village green. Lee has not yet been yuppified like nearby Stockbridge and Lenox, which have sprouted boutiques, shops, and pricey bistros and attract busloads of tourists. Even so, there have been ominous signs of late, including the opening of a large outlet mall on the outskirts of town. The pandemic of commercialization that is metastasizing throughout the Western world (and increasingly the Eastern) is already casting its shadow, in the form of real estate developers, over our little corner of the forest. Of course, this is a selfish and misanthropic point of view. The Berkshires have long been a somewhat depressed region, and many of the people who live here barely scrape by. The area can use a healthy dose of economic development. Still, we wish it would not come at the expense of the rural character of the place that somehow continues to linger.

The town, the Barn, and the land around it seem to me so immediate, so real—real in a way that it is far different from the virtual reality of our urbanized, technocratic, IT civilization. John Muir, a founding father of the American conservation movement, once observed, "Most people live on the world, not in it—have no conscious sympathy or relationship to anything about them." And that was a century ago. Today's computers and television, air conditioning, DVDs and SUVs, jet planes and cell phones, reliance on far distant food and energy producers, strip malls and mega cities thrust us even further outside the world. But when I am cutting wood for the fireplace, digging in our gardens, picking berries from our bushes, hanging wash on our line; when I watch a family of turkeys strut through our meadow; or when I sit on our porch in a thunderstorm and the spray from the rain touches my face, it seems to me that I am in the world and intimately attached to it. I myself feel more real, more at home, more a part of the life around me, more linked to the past, more...American.

In truth, of course, the deeper reason I am happy here is that this place is not the real world at all. It is a place apart from the everyday world of work and cares and pressures and deadlines. It is not the usual world of concrete and steel and glass, of noise and dirt and crowded sidewalks in which I have spent much of my life. What I love about this place is really an echo of a vanished, or at least rapidly vanishing, world. More than a half-century ago, another of environmentalism's patron saints, Aldo Leopold, wrote, "Like winds and sunsets, wild things were taken for granted until progress began to do away with them." Far more of the wild things and wild places have been done away by progress, or what passes for progress, since then, and the pace of their loss is rapidly accelerating.

In reality this place is an illusion, a created fragment of an earlier time when most people lived on the land or in small towns. It is our theme park, our Disneyland. Although we spend half a year here now, this place is not the way we live; it is the way we vacation, the way we escape. We could buy the land and build our Barn only because we earned a living in other places doing other things.

Maintaining the illusion can be difficult. On September 11, 2001, I was sitting at my desk writing and listening to the radio when the first news came of the attacks on the World Trade Center and the Pentagon. We do not have a television set here, but after a while we walked over to Helen Walker's house and arrived in time to see the towers, filled with humanity, melt to the ground like dying candles. After a while I went back to my desk, but I could not write. So I went outside and sat on the chair and looked down to the pond. Sitting there with the trees and grass and water around me usually makes me feel peaceful and contented. Yet at that time, I felt only grief and anger and numbness. The mountain, the land, the house, I knew, were no refuge from the real world and its horrors.

It was many days before I could write again.

CHAPTER 2

THE FIRST PLACE

Pelham Bay, the Bronx, New York City

All places are memory, except this one here, this one now.

My own first place is a memory once removed. I remember when I was about eight years old, lying almost asleep in bed in our rather dreary apartment in the mid-Bronx, watching the mysterious gliding patterns on my bedroom ceiling created by the headlights of passing cars filtered through the slatted blinds. Suddenly an image flashed vividly into my mind like a slide on a screen. It was of a tall white column viewed through a small oval opening.

I know, I know. That sounds like the hoariest, most embarrassing of Freudian clichés, but sometimes a column is just a column. When I told my mother about that flash of memory the next morning, she said yes, I had probably recalled lying stomach down in my baby carriage when I was an infant, looking out a small oval window in its blue canvas hood at a commemorative marble column that rose in the middle of Pelham Bay Park. The park is near the apartment house in the far northeastern Bronx where we lived for my first seven years. My mother was a sophisticated woman, who, like many children of immigrants from the Old World, prided herself on being thoroughly modern. She knew her Freud. But I recall no trace of amusement in her face as she explained the image. I was able to verify the baby carriage with the oval window for myself because it was still in use for my sister, who is six years younger than I. I saw the column several times later in my childhood and youth while visiting the park. Some seventy years later, that earliest image remains vivid.

Pelham Bay Park, one of the largest open spaces in New York City, was my first close encounter with the world of nature. I played on the ground at the feet of my mother as she sat on the park benches talking to other young wives of the neighborhood. I gazed with fascination and, I like to think, inherent appreciation, at the glowing clusters of violets and buttercups that sprung from the fragrant springtime earth. The water of Long Island Sound, which licks the southern edge of the park; the tang of salt air; and the freshness of the breeze blowing inland were my first experiences of the ocean. We walked across broad lawns kept trimmed and crisply green by the "parkies," the city employees who tended the grounds and kept an eye on visitors, and through groves of tall, mature trees. It would be many years before I could call trees by their given names, but as I re-grow them now in my mind, they are all deciduous: white and black oaks, red maples, European lindens, locusts, and horse chestnuts.

There also were a number of useful and ornamental created structures scattered through the park—statues, a stadium with a track, a pavilion, that commemorative column. The effect, as I think of it now, was of a kind of Bronx Arcadia, or Virgil's middle landscape set down at the edge of Metropolis. Ever since that is the kind of landscape in which I feel most at ease, most happy. Over the years I came to love the forest wilderness, the grandeur of high mountains, the austere beauty of the desert. Like Thoreau, however, I like my wilderness not too wild; I grow a bit edgy when I am surrounded by nature that appears untouched by humanity—although in reality there is no such place on the planet at the beginning of the twenty-first century. Even the depths of the ocean feel the impact of human activity. Still, I am most comfortable, most at home, in a landscape that has been lightly altered—parks, open woods, meadows, and gardens, our forest in the Berkshires, which I have thinned and built a home upon.

One of the structures in the park was a large square of concrete raised two or three feet above the lawn, probably a stage or a bandstand. Another of my earliest memories is of my mother, Sylvia, roller-skating by herself around the square while I played on the grass below. Sylvia has been dead for over fifty years, but then she was still a girl in her twenties, a happy young mother, still full of life and joy, an inward smile on her face as she whirled around the makeshift skating rink in the springtime sunshine.

My mother was an intelligent, interesting, complex woman. I never had a chance to ask her because we were adults together for only a brief time, but I think that by the end she felt she had made some bad choices in life. Short and rather plain of face and figure, she was nonetheless an attractive woman because of her vivacity, her love of fun, and her wit. She had grown up in Manhattan—in Harlem, actually, then a way station for Jewish families scratching their way out of the slums of the Lower East Side—the daughter of a reasonably well-to-do baker. She graduated from New York University, the first in her family to go to college and then, in the late 1920s, received a law degree from St. John's University, one of the first women to graduate from that law school. She practiced with a corporate law firm for several years, contributed to a well-received text on business law, and then quit to become a full-time mother after I arrived on the scene. In those days—I was born in 1934—married women, mothers in particular, were expected to stay at home. My arrival transformed a free-spirited flapper and liberated college girl, a young professional on the rise, into a more or less conventional and growingly depressed housewife.

Although I did not realize it until I was older, my parents were an unusual and, in important ways, ill-fitting couple. Sidney, my father, was a tall, broad-shouldered, athletic, fair-haired, handsome man. In his younger days, people said he looked like the actor Richard Dix, a matinee idol who late in his career played the mysterious Whistler in a series of B movies. Born in 1900, Sidney grew up in the gritty mill town of Norwich, Connecticut, to which his parents had emigrated from St. Petersburg in Russia in 1888, the year of the Great Blizzard in the Northeast. He was the youngest of five children raised by his parents, Philip and Bessie—Feyvel and Bosha to Yiddish-speaking members of the family—two gentle souls, according to family accounts, who died before I was born.

Sidney was and remained throughout the many years he lived in New York City, a small-town boy who relied on his good looks, good nature, and enormous charm to carry him smoothly through life. His boyhood escapades, recounted with

29

relish in his old age—apple stealing, barrel burnings, mass snowball fights—could have come straight out of *Penrod* or *The Story of a Bad Boy*. He had been a mildly dissipate young man who liked his liquor and was, according to his own accounts, much involved with the willing young girls of the town. One year he won the duckpin bowling championship of the State of Connecticut. Although naturally talented in mathematics, he had no overt intellectual aspirations or accomplishments. When I was young, my parents told me he had attended Storrs College, now the University of Connecticut, for a couple of years. Late in life, however, Sidney admitted that he had dropped out of high school and never attended college. "I fell in with a bad crowd," he said by way of explanation. This was one of the lies they occasionally told my sister and me, not so much to deceive us, I think, but because lying was more pleasant than facing the reality of their lives and failures. It was a habit easy to fall into, and I had to work hard at teaching myself not to lie as I was growing up.

Sylvia and Sidney met when her father, Abe, moved his family to Norwich from Harlem to open a bakery. It is easy to see how the teenage girl fell for the tall, handsome, and, to her, worldly and a bit dangerous young man seven years her senior. He was already in the adult world, earning a wage from his job in one of the textile-processing plants in a nearby town. It is also easy to understand why he was attracted to this small, lively, intense, sharp-tongued girl from the big city who read books and had strong opinions but who shared his sense of fun and mischief.

The business in Norwich did not go well, and Abe moved his family back to New York after a couple of years, this time to the Bronx, where he opened still another bakery. Sylvia and Sidney's courtship went on sporadically by long distance for the next ten years. They saw each other only a few times a year, although they usually managed to spend New Year's Eve together. I am not sure what their courtship entailed, although sometimes I caught them glancing conspiratorially at each other after talking about "that cabin on Lake Oxaboxa." While he loved Sylvia, Sidney clearly had what we would now call a commitment problem. They finally married only after Sylvia delivered an ultimatum; she had received a proposal from another man and would accept it unless Sidney agreed to marry her at once.

Sidney moved to New York, where he went to work for a wool-reprocessing plant in Lower Manhattan. Every morning he shaved and put on a suit and tie and left our apartment before seven to take the subway to his place of work on Vesey Street, but he was by no means a white-collar worker. His title was production manager, but in fact he was simply a foreman, supervising a group of about a dozen African-American women who sorted the woolen rags that would be reconverted into a cloth called shoddy, a cheap material that had a market before the onset of synthetic fibers. The suit and tie were, I suppose, another of their self-comforting lies.

I think my mother and father were in love with each other throughout their marriage. They were an openly affectionate couple, often holding hands as they sat side by side in our living room. When I was in my teens, friends I brought to the house were surprised and a bit shocked to see my mother sitting on my father's lap. As far as I know, neither of them ever strayed from fidelity, although women were clearly attracted to my father, and after my mother died I came across a love letter written to her by a friend of her younger brother, a man many years her junior. But it was also a marriage punctuated by frequent quarrels and, on my mother's part, bouts of depression.

Part of the difficulty was the intellectual distance between them, but the great problem was money. The wage Sidney brought home in cash each Friday evening was barely enough to keep the family at the lower edge of the middle class. Sidney possessed little ambition and, for most of his life, less initiative. Even during World War II, when there were plenty of jobs and new business opportunities to be had for the taking, he didn't look around for better work than his dead-end position at the wool-reprocessing plant. As long as he made enough money to pay the rent and keep food on the table, he was more or less content. Sometimes there was not enough money even for those necessities. I still feel a twinge of empathy recalling my mother's embarrassment when the building superintendent came to the door of our apartment to remind us that we were late with the rent. Occasionally I left the dinner table wishing there had been more to eat, although we never were really hungry. There was always bread and cake, milk and eggs from my grandfather's bakery.

Sylvia kept the cash Sidney brought home in his Friday pay envelope in a collection of yellowing envelopes labeled "rent," "groceries," "clothing," "insurance," and so forth. On the frequent occasions when there was not enough in the envelopes to pay the bills, she would bitterly scold Sidney for not earning more money. Then Sidney would stalk out the door and go for a walk, often to the Brighton Cafeteria on Fordham Road for a consoling cup of coffee and wedge of pie. The next day the argument would be forgotten, but Sylvia was not happy and was frequently ill. She often stayed in bed in the mornings after Sidney had gone to work and left me to make breakfast for my younger sister, Phyllis, and myself. She did a lot of reading, mostly books from the bestseller list—books on that list were not quite as inane as today's bestsellers—kept our apartment spotlessly clean, hooked rugs, and had endless coffees and games of mah-jongg with her friends and her sister, Dora, called Dodo by all of us, who lived with her husband and two sons a few blocks away. Sylvia's rebellion against her narrowed life manifested only in her frequent illnesses and her terrible cookery—with specialties such as creamed canned tuna and spaghetti served with ketchup for sauce. Her salads were chunks of iceberg lettuce and slices of unripe tomatoes drenched in bottled dressing, her vegetables were gray peas and sodden carrot slices dumped from a can, and her desserts ran to JELL-O and instant tapioca out of boxes.

Still, I thought of them then, and still do, as wonderful parents. Starting from my early preschool days, Sylvia read random passages to me from our encyclopedia while I curled up against her on the living room couch. She encouraged me to read and instilled in me a love of books and learning that continues to this day. She was always interested in my schoolwork, my friends, and all aspects of my life. When I came home for lunch or after school, she sat down with me at the kitchen table and we talked about our day. When I reached my teens, my friends often came over to have long conversations with Sylvia about their own lives and problems, conversations they could not have with their own parents. She was also as generous as she could be with her children. Although I had few toys, she always made sure I was decently clothed. Every September, just before school started, she took me to Alexander's department store on Fordham Road and the Grand Concourse and bought me new shoes, pants, a shirt or two, socks, and underwear, and occasionally a new sweater. (When I was fitted for my shoes, incidentally, my feet were placed under a kind of X-ray machine to obtain an accurate size. I assume no one was aware of the potential dangers posed by X-rays to the health of young children.) For my winter coats and rare suits, we went once every few years to the Manhattan loft where my Uncle Jack (not actually a relative but a close family friend), who worked as a garment cutter, could get us the clothing at wholesale prices. Once Sylvia pawned her diamond engagement ring—one of several times the ring was hocked—to send me for a month to a summer camp in the Catskill Mountains. That ring now graces my beautiful, middle-aged daughter's small hand and will one day adorn the hand of her daughter, now a winsome if occasionally surly teen.

Sidney was as much a playmate as a parent. He had a goofy, preadolescent sense of humor. He would make me a sandwich for lunch and then, saying that it was too thick to eat, would sit on it to flatten it. He had a collection of stock phrases that were made hilarious by their predictability and repetition. When anyone in the family dropped something on the floor, he could be counted on to say the obvious: "You dropped something." If somebody did something awkward or foolish, like walking into a door, he would say, "Anybody could do that." When asked for a decision about taking some action in the near future, he could be relied on to temporize with a "We'll see what's what." Although Sidney is long gone, those phrases remain in use by his children, his grandchildren, and even his great grandchildren. He knew only two songs—"The Animal Fair" and "The Boston Burglar"—but enjoyed singing them with his children at any opportunity. All children adored Sidney; they sensed he was one of them. He spoke to them in double talk, pretended to pull coins out of their ears, and always kept them amused and interested. He was the member of the family to organize excursions such as hikes and picnics.

A lot of my time with my dad, who was a superb athlete, involved sports. He enjoyed teaching me the basics of baseball and football and spent hours tossing a ball around with me or hitting ground balls for me to field. One early spring when I was about twelve or thirteen years old, he went with me and a group of my friends to Harris Field, a nearby city ball field, where we intended to start practicing our baseball for the upcoming season. When we got there, we found that the gate in the high chain-link fence that surrounded the field was locked. The parkies apparently had decided that the turf was still too wet from the winter snows and spring rains. My friends and I groaned with disappointment, but Sidney said, "Come on" and started to climb the fence. We followed and made it over without mishap, but Sidney tore a large hole in the seat of his pants as he scaled the fence. Undaunted, he scampered around the soggy field with us for the rest of the chilly late afternoon.

Several years earlier, Sidney took me to my first professional baseball game. He was a New York Giants fan, so we went to the late and much-lamented Polo Grounds, a long, narrow, appealing anachronism perched on Coogan's Bluff above the Harlem River. He bought us tickets in the upper grandstand, which, if I remember correctly, cost $1.25 each. To reach our seats, we walked up what seemed to my short legs like an endless series of steep gray ramps. When we emerged from the gloom of the tunnel, however, it seemed to me we had stumbled on to a particularly glorious corner of heaven. The field shimmered in brilliant sunshine, and the infield and outfield grass was a sparkling emerald green. The red clay base paths and chalked foul lines were outlined against the grass with geometric precision. Although they were far below where we sat, the ballplayers taking batting and fielding practice appeared to me as godlike, larger-than life figures. The sharp crack of the bat and the thud of hard-thrown balls smacking into leather gloves were sounds very different from those I was used to from my sandlot games. The packed stands, buzzing with excited anticipation, were filled mostly with men in white shirtsleeves, many of them wearing fedora hats, and were hazy with cigarette and cigar smoke and flickering with the brief flames of hundreds of matches being struck; every adult male seemed to smoke in those days. My dad bought us hot dogs and peanuts. Although it was wartime and the players were mostly older or somewhat infirm athletes, the game, in which the Giants were pitted against the Pittsburgh Pirates, was exciting. The Giants won in the bottom of the eleventh inning when their legendary player-manager, Mel Ott, hit a home run. The ball he hit landed very near where we sat, just beyond the right field foul pole, and my father tried to catch it. In the more than sixty years since, I have been to many games in many ballparks, but that is still the closest I ever came to a batted ball, fair or foul. Although I later deserted my father to become a fan of the New York Yankees, that first trip to the Polo Grounds hooked me as a baseball enthusiast for life. It was the experience of the place, even more than the game itself, that captured me.

We had moved to Pelham Bay just after I was born, into a one-bedroom apartment on Roberts Avenue, the same building that housed my Grandfather Abe, my Grandmother Minnie, and my great-grandmother, Minnie's tiny, sweet-tempered mother, then in her seventies, whom we all called Bubbie, who lived with them. In the mid and late thirties, Pelham Bay was a quiet neighborhood with a low population density. It was a blue-collar neighborhood, and during the Depression, few cars were on the streets. No one worried about crime. By the time I was six, I was allowed to play outside by myself and even to cross the street. Across one street was a vacant lot about a quarter-of-a-mile long choked with weeds and shrubs. Across the lateral street was another vacant lot, smaller but dotted with sizable old trees. Diagonally across from the apartment building was the red brick public school where I would attend kindergarten and part of first grade. The sidewalks, the three-sided courtyard of our apartment building, and the vacant lots were my playgrounds. The trees and the tall weeds on the lots were ideal settings for games of hide-and-seek, cops and robbers and cowboys and Indians—the last often featuring heroes from my favorite radio program, *The Lone Ranger*. (I was not the only child who loved that show. To start our first ever music appreciation lesson, Miss Horan, our first grade teacher, played a scratchy 78 rpm record of a movement of Gioachino Rossini's "William Tell Overture," which was the theme music of *The Lone Ranger* program. It was a brilliant stroke. The class went wild with excitement. I am probably not the only member of that class for whom that lesson was the start of a lifelong love of classical music.)

Some of my playmates in the vacant lots were Irish boys who taught me to roast potatoes—we called them "mickies"— by putting them in a large can with burning newspaper. Most of the residents of Pelham Bay were Irish and Italian Catholics. There were only a handful of Jewish families. Early on I experienced one of the few overt anti-Semitic encounters of my life. One afternoon when I was six years old, I went down the hall from our apartment to ring the doorbell of my friend, Billy, who lived on the same floor. As I stood at the door, Billy's father, a policeman, came up from the elevator. His face was red, and his eyes seemed unfocused when he looked at me. He must have been drinking heavily. Unlike the author of *Angela's Ashes*, I cannot remember lengthy conversations from my early childhood verbatim, but more than seven decades later I remember the words of Billy's father with absolute clarity. *"Get away from here you, little Christ killer,"* he said gruffly. I didn't know what all of his words meant, but there was no mistaking his tone, and I beat a hasty retreat. That night at supper I asked my parents what "Christ killer" meant. With raised eyebrows they asked where I had heard those words, and when I told them, my father rose angrily from his chair and walked out the door. He returned a few minutes later and said, "He won't talk to you like that again." Somehow, however, I didn't get to play with Billy very much after that.

My only friend was Theodora, a girl my age who lived in the apartment across the hall from us. I recall Teddy as a beautiful black-haired, violet-eyed little girl, although my memory may be confusing her with the very young Elizabeth Taylor as she appeared in the movie *Lassie Come Home*. Teddy's family soon moved away, and for a while, I was a rather lonely child.

There was really little anti-Semitism. Once or twice I got pushed around as I walked to school and heard the word "Jew" spoken as an epithet, but I pushed back and wasn't much bothered. What was difficult for a little child in that environment was the constant feeling of being the *other*—of living in a culture I could not share and, in fact, was strictly off limits. During one

Christmas season, a friendly neighbor invited me in to see their decorated Christmas tree. Looking at the fragrant tree, aglow with multicolored lights and covered with shining tinsel, with beautifully wrapped gifts piled on the artificial snow beneath it, made me feel as if I had stepped into one of the fairy tales my mother read to me. Even so, I knew this was not mine and never could be mine. When we sang carols in school, I joined in and loved the music but was always uncomfortably aware that I was singing under false pretenses. On Sunday mornings I watched my neighbors head off for church in their best clothes while I stayed behind. My parents were not very religious, and we did not go to synagogue except on the High Holy days.

It was in Pelham Bay in my sixth year that I acquired my lifelong political allegiance. During the 1940 presidential contest between President Roosevelt and Wendell Willkie, I was playing by myself in front of our house when a big, redheaded Irish boy from the neighborhood came up to me. He must have been all of twelve or thirteen years old, but he looked enormous. In a challenging, threatening tone, he demanded, "Are you Democrat or Republican?" He was wearing a blue metal badge with the word—although I was just learning to read—I recognized as "Roosevelt," but I did not know if Roosevelt was a Democrat or Republican. I had to guess, and I knew the wrong guess would have unpleasant consequences. "Democrat," I said with hope and fear. To my inexpressible relief, the boy said, "That's right" and patted me on the shoulder before walking away. I have been a Democrat ever since. (Well, the fact that both my parents were Democrats may have had something to do with it.)

In those years, some parts of the Bronx, Pelham Bay being one of them, were still not densely settled. Many years later, when I was covering the labor beat out of the Washington, DC bureau of *The New York Times*, I interviewed George Meany, then in his mid-eighties but still head of the AFL-CIO, about his boyhood in the South Bronx. A testy old man who did not suffer reporters gladly, Meany obviously enjoyed this interview, for once letting his omnipresent cigar burn out in the ashtray as he leaned back in his chair and spoke with fondness and nostalgia of the landscape of his youth. As a small boy, Meany moved with his family from Harlem in the 1890s; the Irish had preceded the Jews in the mass migration from Manhattan to the Bronx. The Bronx that Meany recalled was mostly farmland and pasture, interspersed with small villages, with names like West Farms, Morrisania, and Kingsbridge. The Grand Concourse and Boulevard, now a heavily trafficked thoroughfare down the spine of the borough, was then a grandiose (or highly optimistic) name for what was a grassy road used principally for carriage races. Sitting on the porch of his family home, young Meany was able to see the heavy ship traffic on the East River and once watched with horror as a crowded excursion boat caught fire, killing many of its passengers. A few days after the interview—this was around 1980—I drove down the street where Meany had lived. It was a grubby, claustrophobic, and menacing-feeling passage lined by mostly abandoned tenements and shuttered stores with graffiti scrawled on the plywood boards and metal shutters covering their fronts.

The Bronx, as its residents liked to brag to relatives and friends from other parts of the city, is the only borough of New York City that is on the North American mainland. The other boroughs are on islands. Remains left by hunters indicate a human presence on the land there since about 5000 B.C., according to Bronx County Historian Lloyd Ultan. When the Europeans arrived, several indigenous tribes, all of them speaking variations of the Algonquin language, occupied what is now the Bronx. The first European settler in the Bronx was Jonas Bronck, a native of Sweden then working as sea captain out of Amsterdam, who arrived in 1639. He brought with him a number of indentured servants who cleared the land and began to grow crops.

I grew up believing that my native borough was called the Bronx because when visitors to Jonas and his family ventured north of the Harlem River, they said they were going to see "the Broncks." However, when Jonas died in 1643, the only thing that was named after him was the Bronx River. According to historian Ultan, when New York City annexed all the remaining boroughs in 1898, the city fathers looked at a map, saw that the Bronx River ran through it, and named it "The Borough of the Bronx" after the river, not the family. It has been The Bronx ever since.

Most of the Bronx was filled in by the 1930s, but Pelham Bay still had a small-town feel to it. There were a few new apartment houses and several more going up, but most of the homes in the community were modest, bungalows. There were no supermarkets and, of course, no shopping malls in the community—or anywhere else for that matter. A milkman who went around the neighborhood in a horse-drawn van delivered milk in bottles to our doorstep every day, the clop-clop of hooves often the first sound I heard in the early morning. One of the great thrills of my young life was when the milkman invited me on to the van and let me briefly take the reins. Once a week in season, another horse-drawn vehicle pulled up to the sidewalk outside our building and displayed inviting boxes of fresh fruits and vegetables. A visitor to our courtyard was the Old Clothes Man, who appeared periodically and chanted, "I cash, I cash, I cash old clothes." Almost invariably, one or two people from our building would go down with a small bundle of clothes for which they would receive a couple of dimes and nickels. This was during the heart of the Depression, and every now and again men—never a woman—appeared in the courtyard playing a violin or accordion or singing popular ballads. Then residents of the building—a few of them anyway—would lean out their windows and drop a few coins that tinkled loudly when they hit the concrete below. The nights were quiet. Lying in bed in our fourth-floor apartment, I easily heard conversations among people walking on the sidewalk below. Few cars drove by. On nights the Sea Scouts met in the school across the street, I would listen to them singing when they emerged at the end of their meeting:

> Over the seas let's go, men.
> We're shoving right off.
> We're shoving right off again.

I lay there hoping that someday I would do that—not sail the seas but be out in the street, singing in the quiet night.

We did our shopping a few blocks away on Buhre Avenue, almost under the shadow of the El, the elevated train that roared by every few minutes on tracks held high overhead by iron columns. We bought many of our staples at a grocery store where a clerk behind a counter asked us what we wanted and then proceeded to pick them off the shelves behind him, sometimes using a long pole with an adjustable clamp at the end to reach for something on a high shelf. If we wanted butter or cheese, we went to the dairy store, where the clerk would cut a quarter- or half-pound of butter for us from a round wooden tub and use a wire knife to slice cheese—invariably cheddar, Swiss, or Muenster—off big rectangular loaves. There was a pork store into whose window I would stare for minutes at a time at the display of hams, bacon, and sausage, which were of course forbidden fruit for a supposedly kosher household.

I had my first ham sandwich when Theodora's parents took me to the Heinz 59 Varieties restaurant at the 1939 World's Fair. It was delicious, and with my sandwich I also received a small lapel pin shaped like a pickle. Very satisfying! More than sixty years later in fact, scenes from the fair are still vivid in my memory: the ride on moving seats through the General Motors vision of the future, Frank Buck's wild animal exhibit, radio's Edgar Bergen and Charley McCarthy performing more or less live on stage, the Trylon and Perisphere, winning a walking stick covered with gold glitter when the man in the booth did not guess my age, and thrill of thrills, actually meeting the Lone Ranger—or at any rate, the actor who played him—in person and shaking his hand.

Next to the pork store was an ice cream parlor, the old-fashioned kind with dark wood paneling, a marble counter, and round black-marble tables with wire-back chairs, where my mother occasionally took me for a chocolate malted or an ice cream soda served in tall glasses with a metal holder and handle. Directly next to the El was the Pilgrim movie theater where, when we could afford the modest admission price, we would go see the feature movie, a B movie, a cartoon, a "short subject," and a newsreel, and often receive free plates and bowls to boot. The first movie I recall seeing there was about the construction of the Suez Canal, with Tyrone Power starring as Ferdinand de Lesseps, the canal's designer. (I saw my second movie when my mother took me to the then fairly new Radio City Music Hall to see *Snow White*. Waiting for admission, we stood in a long line that stretched around the corner. When the wicked witch with her hooked, pimpled nose, long fingernails, and evil, whiny voice appeared on the screen, I hid under my seat. Many years later I told my wife about that act of five-year-old cowardice, and she told me she had done the same thing.)

My favorite place, except, of course, for my grandfather's bakery, was the candy store. There I would stand before the lavish penny candy display in indecisive agony before almost invariably spending my penny on two root beer barrels. It was at this store that I bought my first comic books, my balsawood gliders, and five-cent rubber balls. My stock of toys, incidentally, sparsely lined a couple of shelves of my parents' bookcase. I was not particularly deprived. It was a much different era of child-raising from today's ad-driven orgy of consumption, when the shelves and closets in my grandchildren's rooms are crammed with toys they rarely play with more than once.

The second home of my early childhood was the S&B Bakery, which also stood on Buhre Avenue. The "S" was for my grandfather, Abraham Spindler, and the "B" was for his son-in-law and partner, Morris Bardach, Aunt Dodo's husband. The front of the store was a long narrow space with high glass counters filled with tempting displays of frosted layer cakes; pound cakes; coffee rings; fruit pies; chocolate, coconut, and banana cream pies; mounds of cookies; fruit and cheese buns; Danish pastries; doughnuts; cream puffs; napoleons; and éclairs. On the back wall, interrupted by the big brass cash register, were shelves stacked with loaves of bread—rye, white, pumpernickel, and challah—and bins of seeded hard rolls, Kaiser rolls, onion rolls, bagels, and bialys. Through a pair of swinging doors was another long narrow room with long, deep wooden counters on each side separated by an aisle. Enticing smells of hot yeast bread, cinnamon and sugar, and chocolate that had just been slathered on yellow layer cakes saturated the warm air. On the left-hand counter, my grandfather pounded and shaped the dough into bread and rolls. Abe was a short, stocky, powerful man with a bald head surrounded by strands of black hair topping a homely but expressive face. An orphan, he had left his home in Romania in his early teens and joined the ranks of the *fussganger* who walked across Europe to find boats to America. He was very strong and was still able in his seventies to carry hundred-pound sacks of flour up the cellar stairs. At the back of the store was a wider room, which contained the two deep coal ovens for baking the bread and cakes. Once, three men broke into the store to rob it after retail hours only to be sent fleeing by Abe, who attacked them furiously with a long metal poker still red hot from the oven.

Abe was a loving man and a physical clown with a rubber face who could send his grandchildren into spasms of laughter. He also had a nasty temper that could terrorize small children and led to frequent fights with my grandmother, Minnie. She was the spoiled beauty of the family, a buxom woman with bright-blue eyes and a peaches-and-cream complexion. She had a clear, lovely singing voice, and in my mind's ear, I can still hear her in her kitchen singing Yiddish songs like *"In Tel Aviv"* and *"Belz, Mein Shetele Belz."* She married at age sixteen, a young beauty who wed a short homely man and expected to be pampered by him for the rest of her life. While Abe adored Minnie, he was not a pampering sort of man, and there were frequent days of silence between them.

On the right-hand counter, my Uncle Morris shaped and decorated the cakes and pastries. He did it with considerable artistry and was eagerly enlisted to prepare birthday, confirmation, and wedding cakes. Morris was a quiet, tired man who had been born into an affluent merchant family in Vienna. He fled Austria's anti-Semitism in the 1920s, married my Aunt Dodo, and was taken into my grandfather's business. His father and sisters belatedly escaped, penniless, to America in the late 1930s, just as the maw of Nazi genocide was about to swallow them. Throughout his long life, Morris was invariably kind and considerate to all about him. When as a small child I stood by his side watching him decorate a cake with whipped cream squeezed out of a cloth bag with a metal nozzle, he would say, "Open your mouth" and proceed to deposit a generous helping of cream into it. I would invariably be handed a small paper cup filled with chocolate sprinkles ("jimmies" was a word I did not hear until later in life). Once in a while, Abe would bring a thick steak to the bakery, lay it on top of a slab of rye dough, cover it with sliced onions, and shove it into the bread oven. When it came out of the oven, the meat was succulent and the bread chewy and moist from the juices.

I was a somewhat chubby little boy.

Morris always deferred in everything to his wife, who was also a blue-eyed beauty and who ruled him and her two sons with an iron hand. Dodo regarded herself as the autocrat of our family and brooked no insubordination. Although she and Sylvia were inseparable, frequent quarrels and constant bickering arose between the two strong-willed women. Her younger son Robert, "Robby" to me, two years older than I, was my friend and playmate throughout our childhood. Robby and I never fought, but I was a klutzy kid and repeatedly if inadvertently caused him injury. Once I threw a brick just before he ran into my line of vision and hit him on the head, opening a nasty gash. Another time we were climbing a fence and I accidentally grabbed his arm and made him fall to the ground, giving him a concussion. My pièce de résistance with Robby took place when we were spear fishing in a stream behind our bungalow colony in the Catskills, using a homemade spear consisting of a nail embedded in a broomstick. We came to a fallen tree over the stream, and Robby went over first. When I started over, I said, "Take the spear" and unthinkingly dropped it over the tree. The point went right through Robby's hand. Robby yelled with pain and said, "Goddamn it, Phil," but then, as always, was forbearing with my destructive klutziness.

Dodo and Morris's older child, Stanley, was the acknowledged star of our family. To me, he was a kind of demigod— handsome, athletic, kind, resourceful, and very smart. Once, when we were at our summer bungalow colony in the Catskills, I was in tears because Robby had abandoned me to play with other boys his age. Stanley, nine years my senior, took me for a walk through the fields and consoled me. I would have laid down my life for him. Another time Stanley, Robby, and I went for a ride in the car of my Uncle Harold, the youngest of Minnie and Abe's children, a pleasant-faced, easygoing young man. Harold parked on a hill to go into a store, leaving me in the front seat and Robby and Stanley in the rear. I played at driving and released the hand brake and the car started to roll downhill.

Stanley, who must have been about fourteen at the time, had the presence of mind to jump to the front and pull the brake on.

The family and all our friends knew Stanley would have a brilliant career and happy life. He went to Townsend Harris High School, a school for academically advanced students, and then began to study engineering at the City College of New York. Then the war came, and he was drafted into the Army. Before he shipped out for Europe, he had a quarrel with his mother, who disapproved of the girl he was seeing. They had not spoken to each other for weeks when he sailed for France. Early in 1945, when the Allies were resuming the offensive in the Battle of the Bulge, Stanley was in the van of a unit of the US Seventh Army when his jeep hit a mine. He died a few days later. He was twenty years old.

Upon hearing the news of Stanley's death, Dora immediately took to her bed and stayed there for more than a month. She slowly recovered from her grief, but I never thereafter heard her speak of what had happened to her son.

My extended family also included my father's family in Norwich, a rather strange lot, but that is a story for another chapter. In the Bronx we were augmented by close friends, among them Uncle Jack and his wife, Aunt Fanny; Aunt Bea and Aunt Lil, spinster sisters who were not related to us but were counted as family; Syd and Sol Gross, who lived in a neighboring apartment building and whose son Richie was a younger playmate and who would come to an early, tragic end; our family doctor, Henry Fink and his wife Edith, who also were refugees from Hitler's Germany; and my Uncle Harold's "gang" of friends, who also became close to Sidney and Sylvia.

We would get together for holidays such as Passover, breaking the Yom Kippur fast, and Thanksgiving dinner of course, but we also saw one another several times each week. We would visit each other's houses, and the children, sometimes in glassy-eyed boredom, played while the adults, both men and women, drank coffee and gossiped. Robby and I were often sent on Saturdays to have lunch at the home of Aunt Fanny, a gentle, self-effacing woman who invariably gave us boiled chicken served in a broth, on the top of which swam round globules of fat. (This was not our most hated meal. That honor was reserved for the dry spinach omelet prepared for us by Aunt Dodo's maid, Mamie. It is legendary in our family that Robby, forced to eat a few mouthfuls of the hideous dish, awakened the next morning with at least some of the omelet still in his mouth.) On many Friday evenings, my Uncle Harold showed up with two or three of his friends, and they sat around the kitchen table with my father, playing gin rummy, smoking cigarettes, drinking rye and ginger ale, and eating cold-cut sandwiches prepared by my mother. Most Sunday evenings, friends and family dropped in casually at our apartment or Dodo's place for cold cuts and smoked fish and ample supplies of our bakery's bread and cake and an evening of conversation, cards, and communal radio listening. We bickered and sometimes yelled and fought and hurt each other, but we formed a warm, secure circle of love and comfort—at least it seemed that way to me.

My sister Phyllis (who now goes by "Lis") was born when I was six years old, and life began to change shortly thereafter, not particularly for the better. Lis was a pretty little baby, and we all adored her, although my adoration waned a bit when I realized she was a serious competitor for my parents' attention. The last time I remember seeing my great-grandmother, her tiny figure stood on tiptoe, looking over the bars of my sister's crib, while she jangled a set of keys over the baby's face and cooed in Yiddish. Soon after, Bubbie caught pneumonia and died in Fordham Hospital. I had never had a conversation with her— she spoke no English and I spoke no Yiddish—but she was a loving presence in my early life as well as a surreptitious source of forbidden pre-dinner candy.

Within a few months of my sister's birth, we moved away from Pelham Bay to a dark apartment in the mid-Bronx. My father wanted a shorter subway ride to work and also, perhaps, to create a little distance from his in-laws. There was now also a second bedroom, although the apartment felt more claustrophobic. The building was on Morris Avenue, a narrow street lined with six-story brick houses. I was not happy in that place. Sylvia became seriously ill with a breast infection. She was hospitalized for several weeks and then had to make frequent visits to the hospital to have her breast drained. Some years later she would develop the cancer in that breast that

45

ended her life at age sixty-one. We did not know that, of course, but it was a gloomy enough period. My baby sister was sent to live with Aunt Dodo and I, given a key to our apartment to wear on a string around my neck, was frequently left to my own devices after coming home from school. As a new boy in the neighborhood, I had few friends, and some afternoons I found myself sitting alone on the curb in front of our apartment house, desperately wishing for someone to play with. I did well enough in school, although I grew uncharacteristically pugnacious and, for the first time started fistfights with classmates and received poor grades for conduct. The fights generally took place on the cement playground during recess or in the murky lunchroom where we were given subsidized lunches of evil-smelling vegetable soup and sandwiches of dry peanut butter on dry white bread.

The sun shone on our street only a few hours a day, and only one scraggly tree stood on the entire block; it probably was an ailanthus. Nor were there any nearby parks. My playground, when I could find someone to play with, was the sidewalk and street in front of the house, where the many children living on the block played marbles, pitched pennies, roller-skated, and traded baseball cards. I was still too young for the archetypal Bronx game of stickball, but we played punchball, stoopball, boxball, and various other games involving the red rubber Spalding (pronounced "Spaldeen") ball. By the time we reached this age, games were strictly segregated by gender. The girls skipped rope, played at jacks and hopscotch, and never, ever joined in the boys' games of cops and robbers, cowboys and Indians, or shooting down German and Japanese planes.

The attack on Pearl Harbor took place a few months after we moved. My cousin, Robby, and I and our families were visiting Abe and Minnie when the news came over the radio and the two of us ran outside to the lot across the street to look for enemy planes to shoot down. We were disappointed that none flew over.

For a small boy, the war was not a bad time. My father, thank goodness, was too old to be eligible for the draft. The war news was a constant source of excitement. I followed the battles on the maps in the newspapers brought home by my father and also on the radio broadcasts of the sonorous H.V. Kaltenborn and Raymond Gram Swing. I must have heard at least some of Edward R. Murrow's broadcasts from London during the Blitz, but I have no memory of them. My parents never missed a broadcast by Walter Winchell ("Good evening, Mr. and Mrs. North and South America and all the ships at sea—flash!") then still a Roosevelt progressive. With other children, I collected metal pots, pans, and tin foil for the war effort and saved my pennies to buy defense stamps at school.

For adults, however, it was an anxious and dangerous time. The Allies lost battle after battle to the seemingly omnipotent German and Japanese war machines. At home, rationing was imposed on many staples in short supply. My father, who was not able to afford his own automobile but drove and cherished a sleek black Buick with whitewall tires owned by Abe, had to give up the car because of a shortage of gasoline and tires. But my classmates and I had absolutely no doubt that the US Army and Navy would soon turn the tide. After all, America never loses wars. The nation was firmly united behind President Roosevelt, whose regular fireside chats made us certain that all would be well. My optimism was reinforced by propaganda-laden Hollywood movies such as *Guadalcanal Diary* and Humphrey Bogart's *Sahara*, which validated my faith in our moral and military superiority. It did not occur to me that someone I loved—my cousin Stanley—would die in the war.

Movies, which cost maybe fifty cents for adults, were a luxury. Our chief source of entertainment in those days before television was the radio, and wonderful, innocent entertainment it was. There was none of the nastiness and gratuitous smut that mars much of popular entertainment today. Whatever violence took place was nothing but sound effects; there was no gore and no sadism. On Sunday evenings, the whole family would sit in the living room listening to the Jack Benny, Fibber McGee and Molly, Edgar Bergen and Charlie McCarthy, and Fred Allen shows. The humor, built around the persona of the comedians, was real, and so was the laughter of the live audience. We hardly ever missed listening to the popular songs of the day on *Your Hit Parade*, which featured a rising young Frank Sinatra as vocalist, although I preferred Bing Crosby. *The Bell Telephone Hour* gave us weekly doses of classical and semi-classical music. On weekday evenings, I listened to serials such as *Captain Midnight* (with his secret code ring that could be had for a label from a can of Ovaltine plus twenty-five cents and for which I longed but never took the effort to obtain); *Jack Armstrong, The All-American Boy*; and, of course, *The Lone Ranger*. When I was sick with one of my frequent upper respiratory infections, I would lie in bed listening, often only half-awake, to daytime soap operas such as Oxadol's *Own Ma Perkins, Our Gal Sunday, Lorenzo Jones*, and *Backstage Wife*, all with their own lugubrious organ background music. Several hours of such stirring drama would drive me numb with boredom. One afternoon Minnie informed me that someday we would be able to see as well as hear our radio programs.

"You mean I'll be able to see Little Orphan Annie in there?" I asked, pointing at the tiny, fan-shaped illuminated dial face on our tabletop radio. What a thrilling prospect!

CHAPTER 3

THE HOME PLACE

The Grand Concourse, the Bronx

When I was eight years old, we moved again, this time about a mile north to an apartment on the west side of the Grand Concourse at 197th Street. I lived in that apartment until I was twenty-one years old and went away to graduate school in Chicago. I have dwelled in many places since then, including a much longer sojourn with my own wife and children in a comfortable house in the affluent, pleasant suburb of Chevy Chase, just outside the District of Columbia, and our much loved house in the Berkshires. When I think of "home," however, I somehow still have in my mind that cramped apartment on the Concourse I shared with my mother, father, and sister.

The apartment house was typical of the six-story buildings that lined the Concourse, though slightly more elegant and well cared for than the average. Like many of the buildings, it bore a somewhat grandiose name—McAlpin Court. And, in fact, it did have its own three-sided courtyard, with wide, raised beds of shrubs and flowers to the left and right. In front of the building was a privet hedge protected by a low, green-painted iron fence. Double wooden doors with frosted and etched glass windows graced the entrance. The spacious lobby had black-and-white marble floors and faux Tudor furnishings, including a massive oak table and chairs. Leaving our former dark, shabby apartment behind, I felt I was moving into luxurious quarters.

Our apartment was on the first floor. It was not luxurious.

Its door opened to a small windowless entrance foyer with three closets. One of them was designated the "junk closet" and was a repository for anything that could not fit elsewhere in the apartment. I dreaded having to retrieve anything from the closet because, inevitably, removal of one item would cause the remaining contents to come tumbling down around me, much like Fibber McGee's infamous closet of early radio comedy. This little foyer was given to me as a study, for which my parents bought a desk and chair where I could do my homework. A room of my own—a *place* that belonged to me—gave me a kind of identity in the world, more…selfhood.

A long narrow hall led to a door on the left, which opened to a large eat-in kitchen, and straight ahead to the living room, furnished with a rust-colored couch, three armchairs, some bookcases and side tables and a white pile rug, which my mother tried in vain to keep me from walking on while I was wearing shoes. There were various pieces of art deco bric-a-brac on the walls and tables, and on the bookcase sat a pair of porcelain horse heads, which, for some reason, were my mother's most cherished possessions. (I always thought they were ugly, but I could not bring myself to throw them away after my parents died. Now, over seventy years later, they sit on a shelf in the study of our apartment in Brookline, Massachusetts, where I am now at my desk.)

A small hall off those two rooms led to my parents' bedroom, a second bedroom I shared with my sister, and the single bathroom. Our bedroom had windows on two sides, one that looked out on the courtyard with its gardens and the other on the broad Concourse, which was lined with maple trees. After a summer rain, lower branches of the maple in front of my bedroom window, heavy with water on their leaves, would bow to brush the sidewalk. The apartment, though small, was light and airy, in contrast to the one we had just left. We heard a faint roar and felt a slight tremor in our rooms caused by the D train of the Independent subway system that ran beneath the Concourse. After a short while, however, we became used to it and did not even notice its frequent subterranean transit.

We did not have air conditioning; we did not even have an electric fan—such an expensive appliance was not in the family budget. On unbearably hot days, we walked to my Aunt Dodo's apartment and sat in a semicircle around a fan on the floor of her dining room. If there was a breeze, we might go up on the roof of Dodo's building and sit on lawn chairs while listening to baseball games on her portable radio—usually the Giants, for she had a deep crush on a brilliant young player named Willie Mays. When I was out walking, when the heat waves rose from the sidewalks like dancing snakes, I would pause in front of the movie houses to enjoy the cool blasts from their air-conditioned lobbies.

After we left the dark apartment and narrow street of our previous home, my world suddenly became more spacious. The side street next to our house was only one block long from the Concourse to "T" at Creston Avenue. The little street had virtually no traffic and served the neighborhood children as our quotidian playground and stickball and touch football field. None of the younger boys owned a football, so we made do with newspaper rolled into a tight cylinder and secured with a rubber band. For serious games of baseball and touch football, we went to the playing field next to Walton High School, a short walk away.

Two blocks away was Poe Park, named after Edgar Allan Poe, who moved to a house on the site in 1846 in vain hope that the country air of the Bronx would save his tubercular wife. The cottage, which still stands at the edge of the park, is preserved as Poe lived in it. The park was a small one with a few meager lawns enclosed by bench-lined asphalt paths. Its chief feature is a large, circular asphalt-covered area punctuated by a few large trees and an elevated bandstand in its center. The lawns all bore KEEP OFF THE GRASS signs and were battlefields for countless skirmishes between the children who wanted to play on the grass and the parkies who tried to keep us off. While I roamed the park with my cousin Robby or other playmates, my parents and their friends lounged on the benches talking for hours about the war news or affairs within the garment industry or gossiping about absent friends and relatives. The park was a communal gathering place, a kind of a country club for working families in the Bronx. It also seems to me that I spent more time with my parents in the park and at home than children do today. We had no organized soccer leagues, and few of us took music or ballet lessons. Most of our playtime was improvised and often involved our families.

Nearby, lying next to the Jerome Avenue El, was St. James Park, with its tennis courts, a lawn with a gentle slope for sledding in winter, a playground, and, crucial for my future happiness as a teenager, a basketball court. Like many city boys whose most accessible sports facility was a couple of basketball hoops on a concrete playground, I developed an unquenchable passion for the sport. I spent long hours at it, often playing after darkness settled over the court. Aside from the fact that I could not jump more than a few inches off the ground, was never able to dribble the ball well, and was an inaccurate shooter, I became pretty good at the game. The places we live in can dictate many things in our lives, including the sports we play. If we had remained in our former park-less neighborhood, my after school athletics would have been pretty much limited to stickball and touch football in our narrow street until I was old enough to walk to distant playing fields.

The great open space of these years was Van Cortlandt Park, another of the city's bigger parks, about a mile north on the border of Westchester County. It was just far enough away in those auto-less days to make a visit there an excursion. The park has a lake for boating in summer and skating in winter; a golf course, which none of my family ever used; a bridle path, also never used by any Shabecoff or relative; a stadium with a track, which my schools often used for field days; woods, meadows, streams, picnic grounds, scenic paths, and a six-mile cross-country track. Under a massive horse chestnut tree (I do not know if the tree still lives) stands the Van Cortlandt mansion, the oldest existing house in the Bronx, from which George Washington departed to claim New York City from the British at the end of the Revolutionary War. The park also contains an expansive meadow, the biggest open space I had until then seen, a flat, grassy field at least twenty or thirty acres in size. The field is lined by mature trees on two sides, by a low hill on the third, and by upper Broadway on the fourth. On fine days it was a Currier and Ives scene of happy activity—baseball and touch football games, soccer games (played then only by exotic foreigners; it was a game barely known to American boys of my generation), kite flying, model airplanes powered by tiny gasoline engines, and children running everywhere in the sheer exuberance of being free in such unlimited space. During warm months, our family, sometimes joined by friends, would picnic in the park, sitting under one of the trees at the edge of the big field and enjoying the spirited play that unfolded before us. While my parents napped in the shade or listened to a baseball game on a portable radio, we children tossed a ball around, went hunting for horse chestnuts or just wandered around the field. At that age, in that setting, time was an inexhaustible commodity.

As a teenager, I occasionally walked with my high school sweetheart to a small but dense copse inside the park. For a young man living in his family apartment and without a car, the little wood was one of the few places to find a bit of privacy. One day, however, we came to the park to find the trees gone and in their place a wide, ugly slash of raw earth. The chainsaws and bulldozers had come through to clear the way for a multilane highway linking the Sawmill River Parkway and the Major Deegan Expressway. The construction also destroyed a small, flat meadow that often served as a baseball field. Although I have since rung up a lot of miles driving on multilane highways, I have disliked them ever since I first saw what they did to my woods and my field. I am convinced that the chainsaw and the bulldozer, not the atomic bomb, were effectively the most destructive technologies of the twentieth century.

There was one other outdoor haunt not too far from my new neighborhood that greatly enriched my boyhood—the Bronx Zoo. For a number of years I went with my parents, always stopping at the children's zoo, where I could pet llamas, goats, sheep, and rabbits and take exciting rides on the backs of elephants and camels, for which my parents paid the princely sum of a dime. Later I would take the long walk from our neighborhood to the zoo with friends. We spent entire afternoons after school roaming the big park, stopping at the seal pool, the elephant house, and other favorite exhibits. Mine was the African Plain, where lions and other mammals from the East African savannah roamed in an open field, separated from spectators only by a wide ditch and low fence. For reasons I wouldn't begin to understand until much later, I found the sight of the animals moving in quasi freedom in the open field strangely hypnotic, stirring some unfathomable response within me.

To a young boy growing up in a cramped apartment in a densely populated urban setting, these public places, made affordable and accessible by the collective will and purse of the community—for that is what government is or should be— were absolutely essential to my happiness and physical wellbeing as a child and youth. For me, those simple places contributed mightily to my *mens sana in corpore sano.* They also helped germinate my lifelong love of green, open spaces and intense feelings that such places must be preserved, cherished and expanded.

My new school was P.S. 46, a short walk east of the Concourse from our apartment building. The old, three-story red-brick building had separate entrances for boys and girls, a concrete playground for recess games, an auditorium, and a gymnasium in which the boys took physical education courses once a week while the girls were marched away to their home economics class. The classrooms served about thirty students at a time—boys and girls who sat in precisely aligned rows of small wooden desks with attached chairs and tops that opened to receive our textbooks. Each desk had a hole containing a glass inkwell into which we would dip the replaceable steel tips of our wooden pens. Once every few days, some pupil was singled out for the honor of going around the room to fill the inkwells from a big bottle. And yes, once in a while some bad boy would dip the pigtail of a girl sitting in front of him into the inkwell. I honestly cannot remember if I was one of those boys.

The teachers in P.S. 46 were a mixed bag. Some of them should not have been entrusted with the minds of young children. Mr. O'Neill, my fourth grade teacher, was a shell-shocked veteran of World War I who held his job, someone told us, only because he was the principal's son-in-law. He was a disturbed man, who, when he became upset with one of his pupils, which was often, would throw a piece of chalk or an eraser or even a full waste paper basket at the offender. When a boy bearing a message from the principal's office was leaving the room, he would stare suspiciously at the boy's retreating back then say to one his own pupils, "Follow that boy and see where he goes."

To this day, I am shaky on fractions and decimals because we were supposed to learn those skills that year.

Several of my teachers, however, were truly dedicated and inspired educators. Mrs. Driscoll and Mrs. Reynolds, my fifth and sixth grade teachers, went out of their way to prod and encourage the brighter kids in their classes, giving them freedom to learn at a faster pace than the rest of the class and challenging them with more difficult assignments and responsibilities. I finished P.S. 46, by and large, well prepared for the competitive rigors of the rest of the New York City public school system, including Creston Junior High School and the Bronx High School of Science, and later Hunter College and even the steamy intellectual climate of graduate school at the University of Chicago in the 1950s. In retrospect I can attest that New York's public schools gave me a truly first-class education—and it did not cost my family one cent—except, of course, for our well spent taxes.

It seems to me that almost all of the public services in New York City were first rate in those years. The streets were swept and washed regularly, the garbage was collected daily, and mail was delivered twice a day. Parks were free of trash and well tended. Public libraries in every neighborhood were well staffed and stocked. Not only did the buses run frequently, but also their drivers made change from little dispensers at their waist. As hard as it may be for riders of today's malodorous, litter-strewn, graffiti-marred subways to believe, I actually enjoyed descending into the Kingsbridge Road station of the IND line because of its freshly scrubbed look and smell and the cool feel of the subterranean tunnel on a hot summer day. I usually had a penny to drop into one of the dispensers mounted on the steel columns that supported the subway tunnel and received in return a bite-size Hershey's chocolate bar or a tiny box containing two Chiclets.

While there undoubtedly was crime in the city—a young district attorney named Thomas E. Dewey made a political name for himself prosecuting leaders of an organization dubbed Murder, Inc.—we lived totally unafraid of violence or of our homes being violated. As a teenager, I walked down the streets in the darkest hours of the night without a twinge of fear, even when I heard footsteps behind me. Addictive substances—

except, of course, tobacco and alcohol—were unknown to all but a very few of my generation in the Bronx.

Only once during my childhood was I threatened with serious physical violence, and the threat came from a man who lived in my own building. The superintendent's assistant, John, an alcoholic, dirty, and foul-tempered man in his late middle years, would frequently emerge from the building, his face covered with greasy gray stubble and his speech slurred, and try to chase away the children playing in the street as he shook his fist and muttered threats. We would scatter and resume our game a few minutes later. Once, however, when I was by myself bouncing a ball against a wall of the building, John came out and started to chase me. He held an open straight razor in his hand. This time he did not go back into the building after a few threats; he continued to come after me, walking unsteadily but purposefully. He was mumbling, but I heard the word "kike." I ran halfway down the block, but he continued to follow. I sprinted off and easily left him blocks behind. Then I circled back to my house and told my mother what had happened. She immediately called the police. They arrived within ten minutes, and my mother and some neighbors and I followed them down to John's room in the basement. When he opened the door, we saw that the small room was crammed with items that building residents had missed from the laundry and storage rooms. That was the last we saw of John.

There was one threat of violence that did frighten children my age. We regularly had drills to prepare us for an atomic bomb attack. When the alarm bell sounded, we all dropped to the floor and crouched under our desks with our eyes closed. Young as we were, we knew that such preparation was futile and ridiculous. For years I was terrified every time air raid sirens were tested.

I don't want to romanticize the city of my childhood too much. There were serious social problems, including racism and poverty tolerated as the natural order of things. Race and class rigidly segregated the city, even more so than today. But today, at least, most New Yorkers regard racism as immoral and evil. When I was growing up, political corruption was swept under the rug. The community did little enough to provide for the poor elderly or the physically handicapped. Money ruled the city as much as it does today. But it does seem clear that although we were just emerging from the Great Depression and although the war effort had been an immense drain on public revenues, most public services were far more efficient and available to working class families in the Bronx than they are today. As a society we paid far more attention than we now do to our mutual needs as a community. Today we are so deeply into economic self-aggrandizement and individual fulfillment that we have shunted community needs and values to a much lower shelf on our stock of priorities. I never understood why middle-class and poorer citizens vote for politicians who impose lower taxes on the rich and give massive subsidies to giant corporations, when such policies rob them of essential and valuable public services that the rich provide for themselves.

I am completely mystified by the antigovernment rants of the so-called Tea Party activists and other right-wing extremists (which at this point in our history seems to include most members of the Republican Party). Government is what brings us together and makes us a society and a nation. It is what gives us our parks and subways and libraries and schools; cleans our streets; protects our health and our environment; provides our security; and, when functioning properly, helps create a just and compassionated community. The so-called conservatives who want no taxes or regulation—and who are in fact radicals undermining the social compact that binds us as a nation—are voices of greed and selfishness. What these people do not seem to understand is that, as Justice Oliver Wendell Holmes observed, taxes are the price we pay for civilized society. Regulations are necessary to protect ordinary people from the abuses of powerful corporations, abuses such as poisoning the environment and rigging the financial system. Government as such is not the problem; it is the glue that holds society together. If we have corrupt people in government—people who represent the corporations not the people—we put them there with our votes. It is not government that is harming the country. It is we who vote for the wrong people to govern us.

There are other reasons, of course, for the erosion of public services in the Bronx and other American cities in the latter half of the twentieth century. A major one was the flight of white, middle-class families to the suburbs and a concomitant decline in per capita tax revenues. Another was the terrible scourge of drugs and the violent crime that accompanied this cruel pandemic. Political leaders abdicated moral responsibility for the living conditions of the new African- and Hispanic-American population that flooded into the borough. Landlords burned their buildings for the insurance or simply abandoned them to decay. The erosion of communal values, however, is one of the chief reasons that a thriving, vibrant working-class culture is now a shadow of what it was in my boyhood and youth. The sense of community, of everyone being together in the face of adversity that emerged after the terrorist attacks on the city in 2001, was a commonplace attitude in the New York of the Depression and World War years. I had hoped the sense of solidarity among New Yorkers that followed the terrible events of September 11, 2001, would lead to a permanent restoration of the sense of community and the understanding that all citizens are responsible for the wellbeing of one another, but that sense of unity ebbed quickly.

I was crossing the Concourse a few days after I started at my new school, when three boys caught up with me, and one of them, a tall blond boy with a wide grin and easy manner, said, "Aren't you in our class?" When I said I was, they introduced themselves, and the tall one asked if I would like to walk to school with them. The tall boy was Arthur Pfeiffer; the other two were Lowell Fallick and Elliott Ratner. All three lived around the corner on Creston Avenue. The three, joined shortly thereafter by another new boy to the neighborhood, Leroy Aarons, became my "gang," close friends who played together, spent time in each other's houses, fought with each other, tried out ideas on each other, tried to figure out life together, and in a few years, tried to understand girls and sex together. After grammar school some of us went to junior high school and some of us didn't, and later we went to different high schools. For ten years, however, we were as close as brothers. Then we went to college, entered careers and marriages, and drifted apart. I lost track of Lowell and Elliott shortly after I got married in the late

1950s. I have no idea what kind of lives they have led. I last saw Artie Pfeiffer, whom I thought was my closest friend, at his home in Palo Alto about thirty years ago. Artie was married for the second time, this time to lovely, interesting woman; had two children; and had started his own company developing computer software long before Silicon Valley entered the national consciousness. When I last saw him in California, he was distraught because a big corporation was stealing his work. I spoke to him on the phone a few months later, and he sounded very bitter and very angry with me but would not say why. We have not spoken since.

Roy Aarons had a distinguished career as a newspaper reporter and editor. When last I talked to him about twenty years ago, he was head of the National Lesbian and Gay Journalists Association and had entered a firm, loving relationship with a young man some years his junior. Roy was in his late forties and executive editor of the *Oakland Tribune* in California before he told me he was gay. My wife and I were in San Francisco when Roy came to our hotel in his car to drive us to his home in Berkeley. As we were driving across the Bay Bridge, Roy, looking straight ahead, said, "Phil, I have to tell you something. I have entered into a homosexual relationship." To put him at ease I joked, "Roy, just tell me one thing. Is he Jewish?" Roy burst out laughing and said, "Not only is he Jewish, but he's from Israel, and we met in a synagogue."

I came across Roy's obituary in the *Times* a few years ago. I have not talked to or seen any of my close childhood friends since then.

Our new neighborhood on the Grand Concourse was a fairly homogeneous community. It was so white, in fact, that one could go snow blind looking at the faces of passersby in the street. About half the homes were occupied by Jewish families, the rest by Italian and Irish Catholics. Protestants were rare. We were mostly lower-middle-class families of workers and shopkeepers. Almost without exception the mothers stayed at home with their children while the fathers went off, usually to Manhattan, to earn a living for their families. There were no African- or Hispanic-American families around—not a single one. The only Asians were the Chinese family who owned and lived in the laundry on Creston Avenue.

As far as I could tell through all those years, there were no tensions among the three religious and ethnic groups in our community. World War II and the Nazis made anti-Semitism a recognizable evil, even among the old-fashioned Catholic priests who probably listened to the radio broadcasts of the infamous hatemonger Father Coughlin. National unity was the watchword. The Irish and Italian boys did not come into our homes, nor did we go into theirs, but we played ball and hung out on the streets or in the neighborhood candy store together. One of the bigger, stronger Irish boys took pleasure in beating me up periodically, and I used to walk home from school fearing that he would be waiting for me. I don't think there was anything of religious warfare in his bullying, just a streak of sadism. Then one summer I came home from Boy Scout camp bigger and stronger than he, fought once with him, bloodied his nose, and that was that—except, I am ashamed to admit, that with my newfound prowess in street fighting I became a bit of a bully myself for a short period.

We did our marketing not in big, impersonal superstores with parking lots, tended by bored clerks swiping bar codes over a scanner, but in small shops close to our front door, whose proprietors stood behind the counters and were our friends. Immediately adjoining our building was a dry cleaning and tailor shop owned by a young man named Dave, who always engaged me in conversation about books or baseball and was the first adult to talk to me as if I were his peer. Next to Dave's was the grocery store run by a couple named Mack and Bea. Mack looked a bit and sounded a lot like a red-haired version of the late Steve Allen, the comedian and television personality, with his dry-witted, red-haired wife usually happy to serve as the straight man for his jokes. At the end of our block stood Pete's Concord Pharmacy, where we had our prescriptions filled, bought Lucky Strike cigarettes for my father, and later, unfortunately, for me, purchased boxes of Whitman's chocolates and our first paperback books. At the outset of every winter, my mother sent me to Pete's for a dose of castor oil mixed with sarsaparilla syrup, served in a small paper cup. I assume she thought it had some beneficial medical effect. I certainly took no aesthetic pleasure from the experience. For comic books as well as ice cream cones, lime cokes, egg creams, newspapers for my parents, and just plain shooting the breeze with neighborhood children, I went around the corner to Leifer's candy store with its black-marble soda fountain, its red metal ice chest from which we fished out bottles of grape and orange pop from the pond of melting ice, its glass case filled with candy bars, and its racks of newspapers, magazines, and comic books.

These places were sort of neighborhood clubs where we exchanged small talk (the Yiddish word would be "schmooze") with the proprietors and other customers. We gave the stores our loyalty and received in return good service, reliable products, honest dealing, and friendship.

And now I have a confession to make about a shameful secret I have been harboring for nearly seventy years. When I was ten years old, I stole a comic book from Leifer's shelf. It was a crime that tormented my conscience so much that two years later I surreptitiously, with much dread of discovery, placed a dime on the soda fountain counter. (Comics cost ten cents in those days.)

Among the sharpest memories of my Bronx neighborhood are the smells: the clean smell of the streets cooled by a thunderstorm on a scorching summer day; the acrid smell of diesel fumes from passing buses; the dusty, chalky, inky smell of my classrooms; the pungent smell of pickles and sauerkraut in open wooden barrels and smoked fish at the appetizing store; the mouthwatering aroma of spiced meats at the kosher delicatessen (never "deli" in those days); the fresh outdoor smell of the greengrocer; and, best of all, the rich, promising smells of baking bread and cake that came from the oven of the neighborhood bakery. Whenever I have moved to or visited a new place since then—and there have been quite a few such moves and visits—I always have helped myself get a sense of place by testing the air around me.

Some of the Catholic children from the neighborhood went to Our Lady of Mercy parochial school, but most went to P.S. 46 with us. After school, many of the Jewish boys, including me, went to the Jacob H. Schiff Center for a few hours a week to learn Hebrew and prepare for our bar mitzvahs. We attended the center's synagogue on the High Holidays of Rosh Hashanah and Yom Kippur and precious few times otherwise. The center also offered the enticements of an indoor basketball court and swimming pool. Learning by rote what was then the dead Hebrew language, however, was unbearably tedious, and half the time I cut my classes and instead sat reading books in the old, red-brick public library around the corner. How were we small boys to know that the dead language soon would spring to vibrant life again with the creation of the State of Israel?

The public library, with its peeling green paint, scuffed wooden chairs and tables, and elderly librarians who scowled fiercely and hissed a peremptory "shh" at the slightest noise, was a favorite haunt and refuge until I left the Bronx for good. Every couple of weeks, I lugged home a stack of five or six books the half-mile from the library. One of the great pleasures of my childhood and youth was sitting in a deep armchair in our living room on a winter's night, with the radiator hissing and banging away as it heated up, a bowl of apples or a hunk of Uncle Morris's chocolate-covered pound cake and a glass of cold milk at my elbow, reading one of the novels I had brought home from the library. (In my teens I could put away an entire chocolate-covered cake along with a full quart of milk laced with chocolate syrup in an evening and not put on an ounce of fat. Where is the metabolism of yesterday?) I loved adventure stories and one that particularly enthralled me was *Wake of the Red Witch* by Garland Roark. So the next time I went to the library, I checked out a book called *Finnegan's Wake* by an author named James Joyce. It took me about ten pages to realize this was not going to be another book about derring-do aboard a tramp steamer in the Pacific and that, in fact, I didn't understand a word I was reading. Although I later read Joyce in my more educated years, I never have been able to bring myself to open *Finnegan's Wake* again.

I did a lot of reading in bed when I was a boy and young man because I was regularly bedridden with nasty respiratory infections. These included bouts of pneumonia that caused me to miss vital weeks of class in both junior high and high school. I was a frequent visitor to Dr. Fink's office, and my mother once took me to a specialist. No cause was ever found for my chronic health problem, and the doctors, my parents, and I attributed it to an inherent susceptibility to such illnesses. It never occurred to me, until many years later when my education was greatly expanded by covering the environmental beat for *The New York Times*, that the problem, in part at least, was not what was inside me but what was outside of me—the air of the city.

Although it did not seem so to me at the time, the air of New York City was often nastily fetid. On clear days I could stand in the middle of the Grand Concourse and see the Empire State Building a dozen or so miles away in midtown Manhattan, but such days were increasingly rare after the war ended. Coal-fired boilers heated most of the apartment houses, and there were no devices to remove sulfates and other polluting gases as the smoke emerged from chimneys. Many of the apartment buildings, including ours, boasted—yes, boasted— trash-burning incinerators. We dumped our garbage down a chute, and every day the superintendent's assistant set the accumulated pile in the basement on fire. Soon blackened scraps of paper and other debris spewed from our chimney and hundreds of other chimneys, darkening the city sky. The city buses that passed by my window on the Grand Concourse dozens of times each day could be counted on to eruct noxious clouds of black vapor every time I walked by. Although I could not know such vapors were poisonous, I instinctively held my breath. With postwar prosperity, the number of private autos in the city rose exponentially, and, in those pre–Clean Air Act days, poured overgenerous portions of pollutants into the miasma of smog that filled the city with increasing frequency.

Each year, at the end of summer, when the bus crossed over the George Washington Bridge, bringing me back into the city from Boy Scout camp in the foothills of the Catskill Mountains, I was embraced by a warm, moist envelope of yellowish air—the yellow coming, I now know, from sulfates created by the combustion of coal in thousands of furnaces and of gasoline in even more thousands of cars, buses, and trucks. Most of the gasoline then was leaded. I suppose it was only because traffic was relatively light in my formative years during the Depression and war that my cognitive powers were not lessened by the heavy metal in the air—or perhaps it did and only my ignorance prevents me from recognizing my ignorance. In my innocence, I actually welcomed the sight and feel and smell of the damp, dirty air, so different from the crisp mountain air I had left three hours before, because it meant I was home again. Within weeks I would be in bed, coughing spasmodically, baking in high fever, swallowing penicillin tablets, and inhaling medicated steam from a croup kettle.

In the latter third of the twentieth century, the rise of environmentalism spurred a surge of social and political activism that produced the Clean Air Act and many other landmark environmental statutes, as well as the Environmental Protection Agency and state and municipal environmental departments. Today the air of New York City, and many other cities, while far from pristine, is in much better condition than it was during my childhood. It is one of the few areas in which communal services are better now than a half-century ago. The high incidence of childhood asthma across the nation, however, strongly suggests that we are far from being able to claim victory over air pollution.

While New York City's air may have been unpleasant and unhealthy, the water that came out of our taps was not. Our drinking and bathing water was clear, cold, and delicious, with little of the chemical taste that characterizes most urban water supplies. Coming from collected rainfall in the Catskill Mountains to the north of the city, the water needed little treatment to meet public health requirements. When we visited friends on Long Island, we made faces when we drank their water and pointedly informed them about the taste and salubrity of our water in the Bronx. Again, it was not until I became an environmental reporter that I learned that municipal water supplies can be dangerously contaminated with lead, trihalomethanes, and other contaminants. But these days my family drinks filtered tap water, except when we draw from the cold, pure water of our own well at our home in the Berkshires.

For Americans, among the most abiding images of the end of World War II were the photographs and films of the celebration in Times Square, images vibrating with the joy of victory, with thousands of widely smiling faces, and with streams of confetti and the abandon of embraces between young women and men in uniform. In the Bronx the celebration was quieter if just as happy. There was no dancing in streets. Some of my friends ran off to Fordham Road to investigate the rumor that Fleer's Dubble Bubble gum was once again available at Walgreen's drugstore after being absent for the duration. For the adults in my family, still mourning the recent death in combat of my cousin Stanley, peace was a relief from fear and tension, but a relief mingled with sadness.

My eleven-year-old emotions also were somewhat mixed. I of course shared my parents' relief at the end of the fighting and with many Americans was exhilarated by the long-hoped-for victory, but the war had been an exciting time. With my friends I had collected scrap metal and aluminum foil to contribute to war production, and had spent most of my small allowance on war stamps, had built models of fighter planes (my favorite was the P-47 because it was the simplest for my inept hands to carve out of a rectangular block of balsa wood. Even so I needed help from Robby). We played games in the street involving the destruction of large numbers of "krauts" and "yellow-bellied Nips" as we called them in those days when such ethnic slurs were not only permitted but encouraged by official propaganda. I first heard about the atomic bomb and the destruction of Hiroshima when I was playing on a sparkling summer day at Ocean Beach in New London, Connecticut, where I was staying with the family of one of Sidney's many cousins. The announcement of the dropping of the bomb was made over a loudspeaker. It did not make much of an impression on me at the time.

Postwar life gradually seemed to fall into its old routine. Harold and his friends, two of them still limping from their wounds, came home from Burma, from Italy and Germany, and New Guinea and resumed their Friday evening gin rummy games at our kitchen table. In a short while, though, these men courted and married and had children and drifted away into their separate lives. The blackout curtains came down from the windows, and so did the little flags with blue stars from the windows of homes with husbands or sons in the armed forces. The little gold star flags for men or women who had died in combat usually were left in place. The WAVES departed from the Bronx Campus of Hunter College around the corner, which they had used as a training base during the war. My friends and I often stood at the chain-link fence that surrounded the campus to stare in fascination at the precise ranks of marching women looking smart and formidable in their dark-blue uniforms.

Soon thereafter, we stood again at that fence to watch a rare historic moment acted out in the normally prosaic work-aday Bronx. On March 21, 1946, as trains roared overhead on the Jerome Avenue El just across the street, long lines of lim-ousines and taxis drove through the gates to deposit delegates to the General Assembly of the United Nations at the door of the faux Gothic gymnasium building that was to serve briefly as the first UN headquarters in the United States. Such drama, however, was more than the Bronx could sustain. The UN soon moved to Lake Success on Long Island, which, for some reason, was considered a more conducive setting for the con-duct of international diplomacy.

Meanwhile, rationing ended, and we had access to unlim-ited supplies of bubble gum, not to mention rubber tires and gasoline, red meat, and most of the other consumer items that had been absent or in short supply during the war. The athletes returned from the war, and I was able to watch Joe DiMaggio lope gracefully across the outfield grass from my student-discounted thirty-cent bench seat in the bleachers behind center field in Yankee Stadium.

In at least one fundamental way, however, the war changed my world—or at least how I perceived it. Gradually, in the months and years after the war, the emerging details and imag-es of the Holocaust pierced deeply into my consciousness. At first the news about the systematic murder of millions of Jews; the pictures of skeletal men and women staring at the camera with hollow, haunted eyes; and the descriptions of cattle cars, gas chambers, and incinerators were so alien to my limited un-derstanding of life, so monstrous and bizarre that I could not integrate the information emotionally. In time, however, the full horror, the enormity of what had happened in Europe and what it demonstrated about evil in the world I lived in and the dark-ness in the human soul struck my still-unformed intelligence with hammer blows.

My response was to give up the practice of religion. Early in 1947 I celebrated my bar mitzvah, my entry into the adult world of Judaism. I was still a believer. Despite my boredom with the rituals, I donned a skullcap, phylacteries, and prayer shawl each day to recite the morning prayers, somewhat to the bemusement of my parents, who were believers and kept a more or less kosher house but were in no way serious about it. After a few months, however, I stopped. I no longer saw the point. Did God exist in a universe where such unbounded horror was possible? If he did, how could I worship a God that permitted such unspeakable atrocities to be visited upon his chosen people? I eventually heard the arguments about God giving humans free will to do good or evil. But what free will did the Jews herded into the death camps have? What free will did God give the infants who were carried into the gas chambers by camp guards because they were too small to walk over the threshold by themselves?

I am not an atheist. I never have been able to muster the intellectual arrogance to deny what countless millions of human beings, including many of history's great thinkers and teachers, have affirmed over the millennia—the existence of an all-powerful, beneficent God who created and still presides over the universe. But after Auschwitz and Dachau, Bergen-Belsen and Buchenwald and all the other unspeakable atrocities that I was learning about, I could not help question the omnipresence of a loving deity. Thinking of the tormented Jews of Europe who had prayed in vain for help and mercy to the God who had chosen them as His people, I realized I could not without hypocrisy continue to practice the rituals of worship.

Little that I have learned of religion since then has helped restore my previous unquestioning acceptance of the faith of my ancestors. German soldiers went into battle with the motto *"Gott Mit Uns"* ("God With Us") inscribed on their belt buckles to kill and be killed by the millions. Pogroms, inquisitions, stake burnings, *jihads*—young men sent by their religious leaders to commit mass murder and suicide with a promise of virgins in paradise—all in the name of God and his religions. Today deeply religious people commit murder and then contend they did it to defend a God-ordained right to life. People of different but similar religions are killing one another in the Middle East, in South Asia, in Indonesia, and, until recently, in Northern Ireland. I do not want to be part of that kind of faith. If there is a God, He/She/It must weep at the murder and atrocity committed in His/Her/Its name.

To be honest with myself, there were no doubt other reasons for my rejection of formal Judaism. Like my mother and father, I wanted to shed the trappings of the Old World so I would be thoroughly American. I felt irritation when on the subway I saw the ultra-orthodox Hasidic Jews with their long black coats, black hats, beards, and dangling sideburns, thinking, *Don't they know they're Americans now?* At a deeper level, I may have hoped that secularism would shield me from ever suffering the awful fate of the European Jews. At a more trivial level, I was made cynical by the slickness of our rabbi, a silver-haired, richly dressed man who drove an expensive car and was at his most eloquent when asking for donations. I found the rituals of prayer to be boring and the Hebrew liturgy to be essentially meaningless in its repetition.

Still, I consider myself to be a Jew and feel deeply that I cannot and must not break the line of my generations that stretches back to Abraham and Isaac. I cannot let happen by apostasy what Hitler and the pogroms and inquisitions tried with such cruelty to accomplish. One day when my daughter, Alexa, had arrived at marriageable age, we went for a long walk along a tree-arched country lane on Becket Mountain, during which I tried to persuade her that no matter whom she married, her children had to be raised as Jews. She argued and protested—and, as a lawyer-to-be, she was good at argument. But when she was about to marry a Catholic boy from Iowa a few years later, she first obtained his promise that their children would be raised in the Jewish faith. And sometimes when I am transfixed by the last vivid line of color in the western sky before the fall of night, when I listen to a Bach cantata, when I look at the lovely faces and perfect bodies of my grandchildren or some feared personal catastrophe does not happen, I begin to doubt my doubt.

Creston Junior High School, in the same building that had housed my grade school near our apartment on Morris Avenue, was a three-year blur of elementary algebra, music appreciation lessons with the stout teacher "Piano Legs" Murray, sheet metal shop, intramural basketball, handball, and fistfights in the schoolyard. There was, however, one great moment of revelation during those years—I discovered that I was destined to be a writer.

One afternoon a week at the end of the day, we were given the choice of clubs to join. Each club engaged in an activity that might develop skills or engage a young boy's interest. I had no particular interest, so I joined the woodshop club, where one practiced basic carpentry skills. I have no idea why I did it; I am absolutely useless in anything involving handwork. (We were required to take a class called Art Weaving. The first project for the class required weaving the word "Creston" in gold wool on a solid background of purple wool—gold and purple being the school colors. By the end of the semester, while other students were finishing their second or third projects, involving works such as maidens caressing unicorns in a forest, I was still manfully struggling to complete my "Creston.") After a few weeks, I complained to my friend Billy Applebaum (now Dr. William Appleton, a distinguished psychiatrist and author in Cambridge, Massachusetts) that all I was accomplishing in my woodworking club was nicking my fingers while destroying perfectly good wood. Billy suggested that, as I was always getting good marks on for my English compositions and book reports, I ought to join the press club, which devoted its time to writing and discussing articles and essays. I did, and Mr. Silver, the club's faculty adviser, lavishly praised my first effort there, a flowery piece about hearing President Roosevelt speak at the Easter egg rolling on the White House Lawn. He also published the piece in the Creston yearbook, and that same semester the club elected me as its president.

That sealed it. I decided irrevocably that I would be a writer when I grew up. Later, when I was in high school, my ambition became sharply focused. I would be a foreign correspondent for *The New York Times*. In fact, high school hardened my determination to be a writer because I learned there that I wouldn't be much good at anything else.

The Bronx High School of Science, as its name suggests, is a school that specializes in science and mathematics and that selects its students by means of a competitive examination. I took the examination not because I was particularly adept at or interested in math and science—I was most decidedly not—but because Bronx Science was reputed to be the best academic secondary school in New York City. The school was in an old, antiquated building and the facilities were not first rate, although it did have a swimming pool, called there, of course, a natatorium. The only outdoor space was a yard the size of a large room, completely covered with concrete and surround by a high chain-link fence. I never set foot in it. But in that place, place was not as important as the human material. That material, both students and faculty, was first rate.

Throughout elementary and junior high school, I had been at or near the top of my class, but I soon learned, to my dismay, that I was not going to be one of the top students at Bronx Science, not even close. I did well in my English and history and geography courses but bombed in chemistry, physics, trigonometry, and that unspeakable French language, often getting the equivalent of C and D grades. My inaptitude for science and mathematics was magnified by the fact that so many of my fellow students were brilliant at those subjects, and a handful probably approached genius levels. It was the most intensely competitive atmosphere in which I have ever been. The only place that came remotely close was the newsroom of *The New York Times*. I did manage to graduate in the top half of my class but just barely. I also did well in my journalism classes—thank goodness—after almost not being permitted to take part in those classes. Journalism was a popular elective course, and some of those who applied to take it, including me at first, were rejected, on what grounds I never found out. My mother, outraged by my rejection, visited Dr. Morris Meister, the autocratic principal, told him of my career ambitions—forcefully, I gathered—and I was reluctantly admitted.

There was one science course that I enjoyed and in which I did well. It was field biology, and as its name implies, it often took us out of the classroom on field trips to Pelham Bay and St. James parks and other outdoor locales. Mr. Rudin, our energetic, good-humored teacher, initiated us into the mysteries of Linnaean nomenclature, taught us to identify tree species in both summer and winter and how to preserve and mount insects, and introduced us to the rudiments of aquatic biology. The trips were an eagerly welcomed break from classroom routine and reinforced my already well-entrenched love of the outdoors. In it I also learned much that would help me a great deal in my later career as an environmental journalist.

Mr. Rudin also taught us basic laboratory techniques, such as drawing blood from our own fingers with a lancet, which was usually dull and painful, and pipetting urine samples from a jar we brought from home to a slide for examination under a microscope. One day he gathered the class around the bench of an African-American girl and in a loud voice said, "Valerie, this sample isn't your own urine, is it?" No, Valerie said, she had forgotten to bring her jar and had borrowed enough for her slide. "You borrowed it from a boy, didn't you?" Yes. "How did I know? Because there is a sperm cell on your slide."

Valerie's pretty, café au lait face turned a brilliant rose. The others students in the class roared with laughter. I doubt if one of us, however, thought for a second of any salacious explanation for that sperm cell. For one thing, Valerie was a shy, modest, plainly virginal young girl. For another, most high school boys and girls of that generation and social milieu did not engage in serious sexual relationships. A few of my classmates may have been bold enough to experiment with sexual intercourse, but they were the exception. In that pre-pill, illegal abortion era, premarital sex was a risky enterprise, and high school age girls and nice Jewish and Catholic girls from middle-class families in the Bronx, usually determined to keep themselves intact for marriage—a determination that lasted at least until they went away to college.

Sex, however, was not far from our minds—at least not from mine. Whatever unhappiness I felt because I was no longer one of the best students at school was more than compensated for by my great discovery in high school—girls. As I was entering puberty, I had attended an all-boys junior high school and spent my summers at Boy Scout camp, where the only visible female was the elderly nurse in the infirmary. Bronx Science, however, had introduced coeducation several years earlier, and nearly half of my class was female. O brave new world that has such creatures in it!

I found that I liked girls a lot. I liked looking at them, especially at the bodices of their low-cut peasant blouses that were then in fashion, and I liked bantering with them. I discovered, to my great surprise and infinite gratification that, despite my short stature and average looks, some of them liked me as much as I liked them. One young lady with a figure that I could not take my eyes off stopped in the stairwell as we were leaving a group bowling party together and looked at me with an expression that even to my total inexperience said, "Kiss me"—and I did. Shortly thereafter, on the balcony of the Loews Paradise movie theater on the Concourse, as pink clouds floated magically overhead on the blue-painted ceiling, she introduced me to the art of French kissing. Alas, she soon took up with an older boy. Soon, however, I started to see another girl, who, one evening while sitting on the couch of our apartment while my parents and sister were out, thrilled me to my very core by taking off her sweater and brassiere without my even asking.

In time I entered my first long-term relationship with a woman, "going steady" with a pretty, bright, and warm classmate for nearly two years. I had to work hard to earn the money necessary to support my romantic liaisons; boys always paid the girls' share of dates in those days. Before I graduated college, I held twenty-three different part-time and summer jobs, including working every Sunday behind the counter of my grandfather's bakery, and one Christmas season as Santa's helper at Macy's. (Girl helpers had to put on elf costumes but boy helpers only had to wear a suit with an artificial carnation in the lapel.)

A young couple, however, could do a lot with relatively little money in those days. My "steady" and I went to the movies and theater, often to the Windsor Theater on Kingsbridge Road near my home, which presented second-run but first-rate productions of Broadway shows such as *Finian's Rainbow*, *Arsenic and Old Lace*, and *A Streetcar Named Desire*. We were served our first drinks of hard alcohol at age sixteen at a night club with no questions asked, went to dances and bowling parties, and spent days at the beach or walking in the park. My favorite date, however, was spending Saturday night in her living room, watching *Your Show of Shows* with Sid Caesar and Imogene Coca, and indulging in a bit of what we then called "heavy necking." When we broke up toward the end of our senior year, I learned that male-female relationships could cause real, substantial pain.

I enjoyed no serious sexual adventures until I was a college freshman, but I did learn much in high school about the emotional demands of intimacy, a little about female anatomy, and the highly useful skill of unsnapping a bra with one hand. While I may be succumbing to the "things were better in my day" syndrome, it does seem to me that sexual relationships between young men and women were more meaningful and satisfying, deeper, and filled with more mystery than today's casual "let's hook up" approach. Intimacy involved far more emotional negotiation and required a closer friendship and higher level of commitment between partners than is often the case these days.

It was understood I would go to college. Most children of Jewish families in the Bronx did so, and practically everyone who graduated from Bronx Science proceeded directly into an institution of higher learning. Toward the middle of my last year in high school, I went to talk to Mr. Bloom, our class's guidance counselor, about where I might apply. At the time, public school teachers were agitating for pay raises, and because they could not legally strike, they were more or less boycotting chores involving extracurricular activities. Mr. Bloom grudgingly gave me five minutes of his time, convinced me that I had no chance of getting into an elite school, could hope for no scholarship money, and as my family had no financial resources to pay for a private school, suggested I apply to Hunter College in the Bronx, an all-girls school that was just about to admit men for the first time. Hunter, like all of New York's city colleges then, was open free of charge to all city residents who qualified with their grades and, at the time, a rigorous entrance examination. I could have gone to The City College of New York in Harlem, which had a fine faculty and outstanding academic tradition. Hunter, however, was also a highly reputed public school whose Bronx campus was only three blocks from our apartment, closer even than my elementary school.

The campus itself was one of its attractions. It was a large open space, about a half-mile long, with a grassy central quadrangle surrounded by four faux-Gothic style buildings, including two classroom buildings, a gymnasium building, and a student activities building. At both ends of the campus were wide playing fields with facilities for baseball, soccer, and tennis, and, of course, field hockey. Next to the campus was a small reservoir, guarded in those early Cold War days by a battery of Nike anti-aircraft missiles. Because of all the open space, the school had the feel of being in an almost rural setting—aside from the fact that the Jerome Avenue El thundered by across the street. It was, I thought, what a college campus should look like. Bronx students also could choose to take classes at the main Hunter facility, a high-rise building in midtown Manhattan. When I matriculated, the student body at Hunter numbered about six thousand women and two hundred men. It may not have been the Ivy League, but it was reasonably close to heaven.

The student activities building contained a cafeteria, the campus theater, the offices of the student government, and a small room that served as the Bronx office of the Hunter College *Arrow*, the school newspaper. I joined the staff of the *Arrow* early in my freshman year, and that little room, filled with talk and cigarette smoke and the clatter of superannuated Underwood typewriters, became my hangout and virtually a second home during my four years at the school. As a reporter and editor for the weekly newspaper, I learned the rudiments, responsibilities, and pleasures of real journalism as I worked as a cub reporter, columnist, and, in my junior year, editor-in-chief.

The top editor of the *Arrow* when I joined was a tall, very handsome woman named Ruth Myerson, the sister of Bess Myerson, the former Miss America who was then in charge of New York City's consumer affairs, who was herself a Hunter graduate. Each Wednesday evening the Bronx staff took the subway down to the *Arrow*'s office in Manhattan, where Ruthie, in her friendly but no-nonsense way, presided over laying out and editing the week's edition, followed by a discussion of what would be in next week's paper. Most of the other women in the upper classes who were the senior editors of the paper were bright, competent, and tough Irish and Italian girls. I entered a delightful but all too brief romantic relationship with one of them. She was a funny, sexy, black-haired, blue-eyed Celtic beauty who could—and occasionally did—drink me under the table. She once invited me to march with her as part of Hunter's Irish Society contingent in the St. Patrick's Day parade. I declined, thinking that every spectator lining Fifth Avenue would think, *Hey, what's that Jewish guy doing out there?* I was still thinking of myself as the "other," the outsider who did not belong. It was a mistake, and I have regretted not marching ever since. Even so, she seemed not to think any the worse of me. Because of her, I have had a special fondness for the Irish as a people. I have found so many of them so simpatico that maybe the Irish are indeed one of the lost tribes of Israel. Certainly the Irish have been persecuted and suffered enough to qualify as honorary Jews.

Hunter was filled with strong, bright, talented women, many of them with outstanding leadership skills. But at the time I did not think it odd that, although I was in the first class at the school to matriculate men, after two years I became editor-in-chief of the school newspaper and my friend, Billy Applebaum, became president of the student government. Only years later, when my wife raised the issue, did it occur to me that we two men were elected to those top student positions because it was still the pre-*Feminine Mystique* era and many or most women had not begun to acquire the self-confidence to challenge male authority.

I majored in journalism, and all our newspaper writing and editing courses in the Bronx were taught by a young, attractive teacher named Alice Venesky Griffin, a Eugene O'Neill scholar who probably had little more practical experience in newspaper reporting than did her students. She had the good sense, however, to simply give us writing assignments and then discuss the results with us. Her cheerful encouragement—and the good grades she gave me—helped give me the confidence that I would be able to accomplish my dream of reporting for *The New York Times*. Such confidence did not come easily, in part, I think, because of the place in which I had grown up. Spending my entire childhood and youth in the Bronx, surrounded by cookie-cutter apartment buildings and by hundreds of young people with as much or more intelligence and ambition as I, with virtually no economic resources, I could not help wonder if I would ever escape to a wider, more glamorous world of professional accomplishment. I loved the Bronx of my childhood, but sometimes it felt like a prison. This feeling was only slightly tempered by the fact that the Yankees won the World Series every year and I lived within their aura of invincibility.

My first encounter with major league journalism, however, nearly wrecked any shred of self-confidence I had acquired. One day in my junior year, the chairman of the journalism department called me into his office and said that the top editor of the school paper traditionally served as the Hunter correspondent to The *New York Times* if I would like to do it. Of course I would. Not only was it a plum job with prestige and the chance to start building a scrapbook for future job applications, but I also would receive fifty cents a column inch for all stories published by the paper. The next day I duly went the *Times* building on West 43rd Street and told the receptionist I was expected by the City Editor, Frank Adams. After waiting in an anteroom for a half hour I was escorted to the city desk at the front of the vast newsroom and waved to a chair by Adams, a short, bullnecked, bald-headed, red-faced man with an abrupt in-your-face manner. I innocently told him I was the Hunter's new campus correspondent to the *Times* and that the chairman of our journalism department had selected me for the job. I got no more words out. "*You* don't tell me who reports for the city staff," Adams said, almost shouting. "Your *professor* doesn't tell me. I am the only one who decides who writes for me." With that he turned away without another word.

I was crushed. I had no idea what to do next. I walked dejectedly away from the City Room and was almost out the door when a middle-aged clerk from the City Desk, a pleasant man named Gil Hagerty whom I would get to know years later when I joined the newspaper, came up to me, led me back to the desk, and showed me a box into which I should drop my stories. But Adams had shattered my morale. I never wrote more than a few short items for the *Times* as the Hunter correspondent and never talked to another soul on the paper during my tenure as campus correspondent. I never even submitted my string of articles published by the paper so that I could be paid for them. Later I found out that Adams was at heart a decent sort and most of his harsh behavior was bluster. But at the time I would never in my wildest dreams have guessed that I would spend a career as a *Times* reporter.

By the time I became editor of the *Arrow*, the McCarthy era was spreading fear across the country, nowhere more so than in academia. Joseph McCarthy, a Republican senator from Wisconsin, was a smarmy, alcoholic boor who abused his office by exploiting the widespread public fear of Soviet communism to aggrandize his own political power. Claiming he was rooting out the threat of subversion, McCarthy, abetted by a staff of amoral young right-wing zealots, launched a national witch-hunt against alleged communists or former communists in government, universities, and the arts. The threat of internal subversion by communist agents was miniscule, but McCarthy, with lies, innuendo, and distortion, created a national panic that seriously threatened to undermine the very foundations of the democracy he purported to protect. He also wrecked the lives of many decent people who served honorably in the nation's public institutions. McCarthyism was the most serious threat to American democracy until the second President Bush and his Attorneys General, John Ashcroft and Albert Gonzalez, launched a brutal assault on civil liberties and constitutional protections in the wake of the terrorist attacks of September 11, 2001.

One early morning, during my term as chief editor, I was awakened by my news editor, a competent journalist named Sue McMahon, who told me that three professors at Hunter had been forced to resign because they had been members of the Communist Party in their youth. Sue suggested we put out an extra edition of the *Arrow* with the news, and we did, cutting classes to get it to the printer by that afternoon. It was the only "extra" I have been involved with in a long career as a journalist. One of the three teachers had been my philosophy professor, a soft-spoken gray-haired man with a drooping mustache and rimless glasses, whom I had never heard discuss anything other than the concepts of Bishop Berkeley and Charles Peirce.

At my request, he came to the newspaper's office to be interviewed. I never had seen anyone look so sad and defeated. I wrote up the interview as well as an editorial for the edition, saying that while the firing may have been legal under New York State law, the law itself was the unfortunate result of the Red Scare hysteria fomented by McCarthy and his allies. It was one of several anti-McCarthy editorials I had written for the paper, an effort that was not without a bit of risk. The editors of the student newspapers of the three other city colleges, Queens, Brooklyn, and City, had been suspended for writing such editorials. In fact, I was summoned at one point to appear before Hunter's student-faculty council to defend my stewardship of the *Arrow*. They were disturbed, it turned out, not so much by my editorials but by the paper's running an advertisement for the Jefferson School, a private institution in Manhattan that taught Marxist concepts. I brought with me a friend who was a prelaw student and who collected a sheaf of precedents establishing that advertisements were protected under the First Amendment to the US Constitution. I argued that, as Hunter was a public institution, the school newspaper had no right to reject an advertisement on political grounds. After a few questions, the members of the council decided to take no action against me. But McCarthyism seriously eroded the principle of academic freedom in the '50s. It would not fully recover until the free speech movements and antiwar demonstrations that exploded on the nation's campuses a decade later. Personally, I have feared and despised the Torquemadas of the radical right in America ever since.

One of the reasons the poisonous seeds of McCarthyism were able to find fertile ground among the American people was that the communist war of aggression in Korea in the early 1950s had amplified the fear that the goal of communism was, as Nikita Khrushchev later expressed it, to "bury" us. The domino theory—that letting one country fall into the hands of the communists would cause all of Asia to topple one nation at a time— a theory later used to justify the tragic American misadventure in Vietnam, first gained prominence during the Korean War.

At the time, all fit American males eighteen and older were subject to the military draft, and several of my friends had to fight in that nasty, cold, and bloody conflict. It was my great good fortune that draft deferments were given to college students who kept their grades up and I managed to avoid being called until well after the armistice was signed and the fighting more or less ceased in Korea and well before it started in Vietnam. I did spend two years on active duty with the Army, but they were peaceful years. (I would later see some ugly confrontations between American and North Korean military police at Panmunjom in the neutral zone between North and South Korea as a correspondent for the *Times*. I also would have a carbine pointed at my chest in Vietnam, but that is a story for another chapter.)

As I write this, it occurs to me for the first time that, other than Uncle Harold and Cousin Stanley, I am the only member of my family of all the generations that I have known to serve in the military. Philip, my paternal grandfather, fled Russia to escape being drafted into the czar's army. My father was slightly too young to be called up during World War I and slightly too old for World War II. My son Peter came of age after the war in Vietnam was over and universal military training had ended. For a twentieth-century family, we were incredibly lucky to be spared the horror of direct participation in combat. I can only pray that my grandchildren and their posterity in the twenty-first century, and all who inhabit the future with them for that matter, will also be spared that horror.

I did well in my studies, particularly in journalism, and in my senior year, the chairman of the journalism department encouraged me to apply for a scholarship to study with the Committee on Communication at the University of Chicago. I had no real hope that someone from a branch of a city college in the Bronx could win against competition from the elite schools. I had more or less forgotten about it when, a few months later, I received a letter from Chicago congratulating me on winning a full-tuition scholarship. As I read the letter, I experienced one of those moments of pure happiness and satisfaction that come so rarely in life. I celebrated by going with a friend, a girl I had pursued unsuccessfully the year before, to the Flamingo Pizzeria under the Jerome Avenue El, where she treated me to a fifteen-cent draft beer.

Early in September, in a green Plymouth borrowed from my cousin, Robby, who was already married and working as a women's clothing buyer for Gimbels department store in Yonkers, my father drove me, with my mother and most of my worldly possessions to Chicago. It was the first time I was away from home and the Bronx for more than a month or two, and while I found graduate school stimulating and Chicago a lively, exciting city, I also suffered bouts of homesickness.

After finishing graduate school, I was drafted into the Army, got married, and when I was discharged, moved with my wife into a tiny apartment not far from her parents' house in Brooklyn. Except for a couple of months while I was completing my master's thesis and waiting to be called up, I never again lived in that place I had known for so many years as home.

That place was already beginning to change before I left. A tide of African- and Hispanic-Americans, following the path cut by the Irish, Italian, and Jewish families flowed from Harlem into the Bronx. Municipal services started to deteriorate, and landlords allowed their buildings to decay. The shrubs and flowers in our courtyard died off; the raised beds themselves were eventually removed and the privet hedge was moribund. The oak furniture in the lobby was stolen.

In 1960 the wool-reprocessing plant where my father had worked most of his life closed down—its product made redundant by new synthetic fabrics. At age sixty, Sidney was without a job, without a pension, and without any employable skills. He promptly suffered a heart attack. Shortly thereafter, when I had I joined the *Times* and was working as a news clerk in the Business and Financial News department, my father telephoned me at work. He was crying—the only time in my life I ever heard him cry. My mother had been diagnosed with breast cancer and would undergo a radical mastectomy that afternoon. She spent most of the next five years in and out of Montefiore Hospital, much of the time in severe pain and occasionally in terror. A woman who had complained and worried about minor ailments all her life, she bore the ordeal of cancer, including the indignities of surgery, radiation, and chemotherapy, with great courage and astonishing composure. My father then endured a second heart attack. By this time I was living in Germany as a *Times* correspondent, but Dodo and Minnie and my sister Lis, who was now on the staff of *The New Yorker*, were around to provide care. Amid so much physical and emotional distress, Sidney, who had previously displayed so little drive and initiative, took a training course sponsored by New York State and learned bookkeeping. He soon found a job in the South Bronx as a bookkeeper for a company that made hot dogs.

Things fall apart. In 1958, while I was in Germany with the Army, my grandfather, Abe, died; he was the first member of my close family other than Stanley to go. A decade later, when I was a correspondent in Germany, I received a telephone call from my sister. "Come home quickly," she said. "Mom only has a few days to live." I managed to get the first plane out of Frankfurt the next morning. They had not told Sylvia I was coming, and when I walked into the room, she gasped in fright. She knew what my abrupt appearance meant, but I told her I was in New York to talk to my editors about a pending transfer to Tokyo. I doubt if she believed me, but she was glad to accept the palliating story. I visited her hospital room every day, and she spoke to me calmly between spasms of pain. Then I had to return to work in Europe. On my last visit, I sat next to her on the bed, and she said in a wondering voice, "It's been like a dream." I knew she was talking about the passage of her life. Then she said, "The time has come for us to part." It was said with a trace of irony, as if she were reciting a quotation; she did not want to over dramatize our farewell. I held my cheek next to hers for a few moments and then got up and walked out of the room. Sylvia hung on for a few weeks and then died, shortly after turning sixty-one.

Three months later, my Aunt Dodo, my second mother, died. She had been suffering from leukemia for years, and the shock of her sister's death pushed her over the edge. Demanding and short-tempered with her own boys, she always had been patient and indulgent with me. Minnie, losing both her daughters one after the other, sank almost immediately into deep senility. She had remarried after Abe had died, but her new husband remained alive for less than a year. My grandmother lived for another ten years, but not in our world. Richie Gross, my neighborhood friend and younger protégé, had fallen heavily into debt supporting his demanding wife and their two children. One day he came home, shot his wife and children to death, and then put a bullet through his own head. His grieving father, Sol, died within months. My cousin, Barbara, my Uncle Harold's tiny, pretty, blonde daughter, married a gambling casino operator in the Bahamas and died with him in a suspicious plane crash. My cousin, Rob, now a grownup Bob, moved with his new family to new jobs in Cleveland and then Buffalo. Artie Pfeiffer was now in California and Roy Aarons in Washington, DC.

Sidney stayed on the Concourse. When I was reassigned from Tokyo to Washington in 1970, we urged him to come and join us there, but he could not bring himself to leave the home he had shared with Sylvia for nearly three decades. Then one week Pete's drugstore was held up, and Pete, tired of the repeated robberies that had plagued his and other stores in the neighborhood, pulled a newly purchased gun from under the counter. But one of the robbers was quicker and killed Pete instantly with a shot through his forehead. That same week, Sidney was driving to work along Bruckner Boulevard in the South Bronx when a sniper put a gratuitous bullet through his windshield, narrowly missing him. That was enough. Sidney reluctantly agreed to leave the Bronx. Shortly thereafter he moved into a small but comfortable apartment a few blocks away from our house in Chevy Chase. His leaving severed my last close connection to the Bronx. Sidney was with us for another fifteen years until he died at age eighty-seven, a wonderful friend and companion for us, especially for my children.

As far as I can tell, there is only one person whom I knew in the Bronx who is still there, a Hunter classmate who lives near the college. I don't know another soul in the borough. My big extended family—my friends, my neighbors, teachers, the shopkeepers—are all gone, dead, or dispersed into the American Diaspora.

The Windsor Theater, Alexander's department store, Sutter's Bakery, and the Brighton Cafeteria had all closed their doors long before. All the little stores—Dave's, Mac and Bea's, the bakery, the kosher butcher, the greengrocer, the delicatessen, the appetizing store—had vanished. The Loews Paradise, once a gilded, magical palace of dreams, was carved up into mini-theaters then shut down and boarded over but later miraculous-ly renovated and reopened. There is no S&B Bakery, no Jewish bakery of any kind in Pelham Bay. Hunter College in the Bronx is now Lehman College, and modern buildings have been added to my faux-Ivy campus. When I drove past our old apartment house a few years ago, the front door was scratched and scarred, its glass windows crisscrossed with tape; scrap paper blew around in the now barren courtyard. My sister, now Lis Harris, a distinguished author and teacher of writing at Columbia University and a longtime staff writer for *The New Yorker*, lives in Manhattan. So does my sister-in-law, Susan Edelmann, who used to run the liberal arts program at New York University's School of Continuing Education. They are my only family members still living in any part of New York City.

My Bronx, my childhood habitat, the home place, the world as I knew it as a child, has vanished utterly, never to be recovered.

But the place named the Bronx is still there and in some ways not all that changed. Elderly men and women still sit on Poe Park's row of benches along the Concourse on sunny days, although I would guess that few of them are Jewish. The Bronx Zoo is better than ever; so are the botanical gardens. Orchard Beach on Long Island Sound, the people's Riviera for Bronxites, unpleasant to visit for many years because of human waste and other detritus washing up on to the sand, is swimmable again, thanks to the Federal Clean Water Act. Kingsbridge and Ford-ham Roads are still bustling commercial thoroughfares, alt-hough the kosher delicatessens and appetizing stores have been replaced by bodegas and chicken takeouts—and of course the Golden Arches. The neighborhood seems to me more dirty and crowded than when I lived there, and the scourge of graffiti has marred it. It now looks more like the poverty-stricken southeast Bronx of my childhood. Yankee Stadium has been torn down and replaced by a new, more luxurious ballpark. The south Bronx remains a hard place, but there are fewer fires these days, and there are new houses and gardens. Bronx Science still at-tracts the brightest young men and women from all over the city, although now there are fewer Jewish kids and more Asians, Hispanics, and African-Americans.

So even if my Bronx has vanished, it is now some other young person's ecological niche, someone else's home place. Perhaps there is a short, average-looking Felipe or Tyrone or Takeshi or Krishna at Bronx Science, worrying about his grades, daydreaming about the girls in his class, wishing he had some money and a car, and wondering whether he will ever escape into a wider world of adventure and accomplishment.

CHAPTER 4

PLACES OF DISCOVERY
"The Country"

"Suburbia" was not a word in common usage in the Bronx of the 1930s and '40s. To most families living in the city, the suburbs were an alien country. My mother sometimes wistfully daydreamed aloud about some day living "up in Westchester." Of course, a big house with a lawn and garden in an affluent community was out of the question for a family of our very limited means. The suburbs were where rich, white, Protestants lived. We were a family, indeed an entire borough, of ethnic Jay Gatsbys gazing longingly at the green light on a distant shore. For us there was the city, which meant the Bronx and occasional forays into the magic kingdom of Manhattan. And then there was "the country."

The city and the country were two entirely different places, almost two different worlds as far as I was concerned. The country was not only an alternative landscape but also a different style of living, a different way of thinking and feeling. The enormous sense of release and freedom that I—and, I suppose, most other kids—felt on emerging from the last day of school each year was always accompanied by keen anticipation of wide spaces, warm sunshine, fresh air, cool water, green surroundings, and endless time filled with play that awaited me in the country.

As far as I knew, when I was a small boy, "the country" was a synonym for the Catskill Mountains of New York State, where we went every year we could afford it to escape the summertime heat of the un-air-conditioned Bronx. We traveled up narrow, crowded Route 17 on the Shortline bus or in a rented limousine we shared with another family, always stopping en route at the Red Apple Rest for a snack, usually a frankfurter and french fries, and to use the bathrooms. I knew we had reached the real country when I began to see blue cornflowers, clusters of tiny tourist cabins (there were no motels yet), and Burma Shave signs along the edge of the road. Children and adults alike enjoyed the little jingles about the shaving cream carried on the signs, each line inscribed on a separate small placard and spaced to be readable from a moving auto. I did not remember any of them, but I looked on the Web and to my surprise found several sites that reproduce the jingles. Here is one I took from the 1940 collection, one of the summers I spent in the Catskills.

> He's the boy,
> The gals forgot,
> His line was smooth,
> His chin was not
> *Burma Shave.*

The Catskills of our summers were not the mountains of the storied Grossingers and Concord hotels or their counterparts. We had no lavish sports facilities, no tummlers to keep us amused, no ballroom dances or stage shows, no sumptuous multicourse meals served to us in huge dining rooms, no maids to clean our rooms. Our summer resort was a much nicer place. We rented a two-room bungalow with a screened porch in the tiny hamlet of Spring Glen, New York. The little house, painted white with green trim, was part of a small colony of almost identical bungalows, a dozen of them strung out in two widely separated parallel rows. The recreational facilities were a big meadow filled with wildflowers; wild strawberry plants; butterflies and grasshoppers; a wide, swift, noisy creek just behind our row of buildings; and a deep wood beyond the colony that seemed to a small boy to be filled with infinite possibilities for adventure. Oh, yes. There was also a ping-pong table and a hammock.

It was in that field, that stream, those woods that I fell deeply, irrevocably in love with the natural world. My cousin, Robby, and his family usually stayed at the colony in one of the slightly bigger, slightly more expensive bungalows in the row opposite ours. Robby and I were part of a small tribe of young boys who played baseball and impromptu games of imagination that usually included killing Germans and Japanese, who were then launching aggressive wars into which our own country would soon be drawn. I also would spend hours by myself in the field and stream in states of pure, instinctive bliss. In the meadow I plucked violets, daisies, and buttercups and gorged on the small, sweet strawberries. The meadow was scythed a couple of times a summer, but otherwise it was left alone. No one doused it with pesticides or fertilizers, and to my young eye it was purely beautiful. I chased butterflies with a kitchen strainer for a net. Sometimes I just walked or ran around the meadow, feeling the sun on my bare back, breathing in the fragrant smell of hot vegetation. Even the grasshoppers seemed to have a pleasant scent—except when I deliberately crushed them underfoot in an act of small boy savagery, releasing a squish of acrid ichor. I was as wild and free as any young animal should be. After a thunderstorm the air would clear, the sky would be a vivid blue, and the meadow would be a sweet-smelling wonderland, covered with diamonds created by the sparkling drops of water dripping from the grass.

At the beginning of each summer, a group of the fathers/husbands went down to the creek to construct a dam of large stones across it, creating a small pool. The pool was no more than three feet in depth at its deepest, but for little children it was a perfect swimming, splashing, paddling and water-fighting hole. The fast-running water was always fresh and cool but not cold, the perfect place to while away a hot midsummer afternoon. I spent hour after hour crouching in the shallow water with the same strainer I used in the field to scoop up some of the abundant minnows in the stream, which I then placed in a big water-filled jar. I usually remembered to dump the delicate little fish back into the stream before the water became heated enough from the sun to kill them. There were bigger fish in the stream, rainbow trout and a kind of catfish we knew as suckers. They were too big and fast to catch in the strainer. One year someone, probably my older cousin, Stanley, or my uncle, Harold, made me a fish spear by embedding a nail into the end of a broomstick. I never did manage to spear a fish; the only flesh that nail ever punctured was Robby's hand.

It was along that creek that I first experienced the pleasure of solitude, although I did not yet know the word or understand why or even that I was happy. A couple of hundred yards downstream, the creek bed widened, leaving a bed of stones exposed by the receding spring flood. The waters also had left a deep pool a few paces away from the stream, populated by tadpoles, frogs, minnows, and a long slender fish with a jutting under jaw that seemed to stare at me with malevolent intent whenever I sat peering into the translucent water. I spent entire afternoons alone there in what I thought of as my private hideaway. I usually took a few matches from our kitchen and amused myself by building a fire of dried weeds and twigs on a flat stone that I named Fire Rock. Like many small boys, I was mesmerized by fire, a trait that would get me into fairly serious trouble several times during my childhood. I caught tadpoles and minnows in my invaluable strainer, tried unsuccessfully to grab frogs from the bank of the pond, and futilely lunged at suckers with my makeshift spear. Often, however, I simply sat on the warm stones, looking at, listening to, and smelling the exotic surroundings and feeling adventurous and intrepid (and just a little bit anxious) for wandering away from the safe, familiar world of parents and playmates.

I was a reasonably well-behaved and obedient little boy by the not-too-demanding standards of my parents. Yet I somehow found myself in frequent trouble, especially when left to myself in the freedom of summer vacation. For example, on the other side of the creek, near a cluster of small houses, was a large wooden bin filled with old car tires—discarded, I thought. One day I took one of the tires out of the bin to use as a float in our pool and left it on the bank when I went back to our bungalow. That evening, a gruff-looking man came to the cabin and, confronting my father, said I had stolen one of his tires. When my father asked me if it was true, I was terrified, but I faced up to the accusation like a man. I lied. I told him I knew nothing about the tire. My father chose to believe me and told the man to leave. Another time I was showing a smaller boy how to swing a baseball bat and, while demonstrating, accidentally hit him on the forehead with the bat, opening a nasty gash. The boy had to be rushed to the hospital in nearby Ellenville for stitches, and later, his father, furious in his belief that I had deliberately attacked his son, came storming to our house and threatened to call the police. I explained it was an accident, and my dad suggested we ask the little boy what happened. The father was only somewhat mollified when the boy confirmed my story. Of course, there was the spear fishing of Robby's hand and other inadvertent atrocities perpetrated against my cousin.

Our little bungalow provided cramped quarters. My sister and I shared a bedroom with our parents. My grandmother, Minnie, and often my grandfather, Abe, and their son, Harold, slept on cots in the kitchen/living area. But it did not seem uncomfortable to me. Except for a two-week vacation, Sidney was at the bungalow only on weekends, when he would sit at a bridge table in front of the house playing pinochle with other weekend fathers, or else playing softball with the men or taking Robby and me on long hikes into the woods.

Having all those familiar people in close proximity gave me a luxurious feeling of security. I usually went to bed while the sun still shone, listening to the sound of the creek rushing musically a few feet behind the house and to the reassuring murmur of conversation among the grownups sitting on the porch. We ate most of our meals on that porch, meals that relied heavily on fruits and vegetables, eggs, butter, milk, cheese, and sour cream from neighboring farms. Every year, Minnie took a large batch of small young cucumbers to make dill and garlic pickles in a big, green glass crock. The pungent smell of the pickles filled the little house, a smell that would remain one of my favorite perfumes for the rest of my life. (My wife now makes pickles from Minnie's recipe every summer with cucumbers we grow in our own garden.) We were friendly with one of the farmers whose daughter owned the bungalow colony at the time. He often brought us produce harvested that day from his fields. Once he came with a big watermelon, carved out a quarter of it, and handed it to me. I plunged my face into the sweet, warm flesh of the melon and thought I had never tasted anything so delicious.

For many, perhaps most Americans, such fresh, delicious, food is only a memory these days. Most of what we eat is grown across the continent or on other continents, not delivered from nearby farms. Our fruits and vegetables are usually grown with chemical fertilizers and "protected" by insecticides, fungicides, and herbicides, some of which have been shown to be toxic and carcinogenic. They are doused in additional chemicals to keep them edible and attractive during the long journey from farm to market. Our livestock and poultry are pumped with growth hormones and antibiotics, a practice many scientists believe has grave consequences for human development and health. Local farms near large cities largely have disappeared before the overwhelming tide of urban expansion, and our agricultural economy has been industrialized, not just to feed a swelling population but also to serve the technological needs and drive for profits of corporate agribusiness.

Some years ago, when my wife was director of the National Consumers League, she testified before a Senate subcommittee on the state of the nation's food supply. "Who told us," she asked, "that we can eat strawberries in every season but in no season would they taste good?" The only senator present at the hearing, Adlai Stevenson III of Illinois, did not reply. He had dozed off.

The growth of demand for organically and locally raised food in recent years reflects the dissatisfaction of many of us with the quality and safety not only of our strawberries but also all of our food. In the face of well-funded resistance by agribusiness and its paid allies in government, consumers have had only limited success in changing the foods they put on their tables. The emergence of genetically modified crops, meanwhile, raises serious new questions about the safety of our food supply. Do I dare to eat a watermelon? Perhaps the farmers' markets springing up in and around cities in recent years are a signal of better things to come with our food supply.

Downtown Spring Glen, adjacent to our colony, was a sleepy hamlet of three somewhat rickety buildings. One was a grocery-general store in an old frame house with worn wooden floors and dark shelves lined with canned goods. We bought most of our necessities there with occasional forays to the A&P in Ellenville, six miles away, for more serious marketing and to go to the movies and the barbershop, a nineteenth-century-looking place with high wooden chairs and spittoons strategically arrayed on the floor. Across the street from the grocery was the Spring Glen post office, which also served as a drugstore and soda fountain where we were allowed treats of Popsicles and Creamsicles and occasionally a bottle of a new brand of soda pop called 7UP. Next to the grocery store was the Tavern, a low, dark building belonging to the mysterious world of adults from which drifted the not unpleasant smell of beer and whisky, a smell I recognized from the occasional parties thrown by my parents in our Bronx apartment. I never set foot inside the Tavern, but Sylvia and Sidney and their friends made stops there throughout the summer. My mother and especially my father enjoyed their whisky highballs and Manhattan cocktails, but I never saw either one of them even slightly tipsy.

The bungalow colony was the closest I have ever come to living in a small rural community. The summer residents were a kind of clan; all of us were New Yorkers, all Jewish, all of modest means. Everyone was relaxed and happy to be away from work and school and the pressures of the city. Sunday evenings, before the husbands left to drive back to New York, they would build a big bonfire in the meadow, and the entire colony would gather round to toast marshmallows, sing songs, tell jokes, and look at the stars. The small boys shone flashlights into each other's eyes, waved sticks from the fire to make patterns with the sparks at their tips, and generally felt very grown up to be up so late under the endless stars. The shadow of war was growing darker, but we felt distant and safe in our mountains. It never entered my mind when we small boys were killing Nazis in our games that Stanley, my hero, would be dead on a battlefield in Belgium within three years.

When the nights started to turn cold, we knew we would soon bid goodbye to trees and grass and water and lazy afternoons. We left for the city after the first color appeared in the trees. I thought we would be coming back forever.

The first time I was actively conscious of being happy, I was fourteen years old, lying by myself on a bed of fragrant pine needles, smoking a cigarette and looking up at a vivid blue sky through the branches of the tree. The tall evergreen stood on a knoll overlooking a small, clear lake on which the sunlight created a treasury of flashing jewels. I had this whole splendid landscape to myself.

I had often been happy before, of course. For the most part, I had been a cheerful little boy. But this was the first time I self-awarely thought, *Hey, I am really happy right now, right here.* I was happy to be in the middle of such beauty, to feel the clean breeze on my skin, to breathe the tangy air; happy to be alone to enjoy my surroundings undisturbed; and happy to be smoking, a practice I had begun only a few weeks earlier and one that made me feel very mature and independent and, no doubt, a bit narcotized.

The knoll and lake were part of Camp Ranachqua, the Bronx unit of the Ten Mile River group of summer camps that served the Boy Scouts of New York City. The camp was divided into two units, one that served kosher foods for Jewish boys and the other that served Christian kids. I spent five summers there—in the kosher unit, of course—four as a camper and one as an orderly in the camp infirmary. It was there I picked up some of the basic skills of outdoor living: chopping firewood, building a fire and cooking a simple meal over it, putting up and ditching a tent, performing first aid, map and compass reading, and other means of finding my way around unfamiliar terrain. I learned to swim and to row a boat and paddle a canoe and was initiated into the cult of bird-watching. It was also here that I received my first lessons in conservation.

My initial exposure to the tenets of conservation was more than a little painful and embarrassing. It was my first year at the camp. I was twelve years old, and the youngest boy in my patrol. The older boys were a rather dopey lot, but they were my seniors and more experienced campers, and I tended to ape whatever they did. On our first overnight hike into the woods, we set up our tents and while waiting for the food to be distributed for cooking, some of the boys in my patrol started to hack at trees with their Boy Scout hatchets. They were not cutting firewood, just using their axes for the fun of it. Soon the entire patrol, including me, was doing the same thing. Seeing the damage we were inflicting, our young troop leader came by, told us to stop, and scolded us for injuring the living trees for no good purpose. The next day, my patrol was lined up in front of the entire camp at the evening flag-lowering assembly and required to recite some conservation code that included respect for life, including trees. I don't recall any specifics about the code, but the essential lesson sunk in deeply and was never forgotten.

The Boy Scouts are, or were in my time, a paramilitary organization with a hierarchy of rank and a structure similar to an army's. At Scout camp we were organized into troops and each troop into patrols. Each patrol had a patrol leader, and each troop had a troop leader, an assistant troop leader, and a senior patrol leader. We woke, assembled, went to meals, dispersed to activities, raised and lowered the flag, and went to sleep to the command of bugle calls. Our cabins were log huts with open sides and steep roofs, and we slept on double-decker cots with straw-filled ticks for mattresses. Some troops had tents. Our latrines were five-seater privies that emitted a pungent smell we came to ignore after a few days. Our cold-water showers tested our approaching manhood. We reported to our leaders with the three-fingered Boy Scout salute. We stood at attention and recited the Boy Scout Oath and Boy Scout Pledge.

I ate it up. Don't ask me why. Probably it was because I joined the Scouts immediately after World War II, and the men and women of our military were heroes and role models. Later, when I spent two years on active duty with the US Army, I came to loathe the simple mindedness of military discipline and protocol and found the routine of Army life in peacetime insufferably boring. At Scout camp, however, I felt comfortable in the orderliness of the routine and exhilarated by the camaraderie we felt as members of the same patrol and same troop. I was extremely gratified when my fellow scouts showed their approval of me by electing me first as patrol leader, then as senior patrol leader. I was pleased beyond measure when elected into the Order of the Arrow, also known as the "Brotherhood of Cheerful Service," a more or less secret fraternity supposedly based on ethics and rites of the Lenni Lenappe tribe of Delaware Indians. The induction routine included a day of hard labor with no food or drink, followed by a fire-lit initiation ceremony in the dark woods. It was silly, slightly sadistic, and absolutely thrilling to a boy in early adolescence.

Our cabins were spaced apart in small clearings surrounded by dense second-growth forest, mostly hardwoods. The woods stretched around the camp for hundreds of acres, but there was surprisingly little wildlife, save for the occasional skunk that came around to forage for leftover candy and salami sent to the campers by their parents. After a heavy rain, however, hundreds of red efts—tiny, bright-orange newts—emerged from wherever they had been sheltering to light up the forest floor with their electric color. They were pretty, harmless creatures, whose only sin was to urinate into the palm of your hand if you picked them up. One day, one of my cabin mates, a small, rather feckless boy, began to collect them and then coldly and methodically cut them in half with his Boy Scout hunting knife. When I saw what he was doing, I asked him to stop, and when he kept killing the little salamanders, I ordered him as his patrol leader to stop. He ignored me. So I went up to him, punched him in the face, and took the knife away from him. Afterward I realized I had acted shamefully by hitting a smaller boy, and the incident has bothered me whenever I've thought about it over the past fifty years or so. But when I recently had a telephone conversation with another of the Scouts who had shared our cabin and told him of my pained recollection of the incident, he said, "Aw, the little twit deserved it."

One of the great experiences of Scout camp was finding myself transformed into an amphibian. Neither my mother nor father could swim nor could I when I arrived at camp at age twelve. But the waterfront staff slowly and carefully turned me into an adequate swimmer. After that, I spent as much time as possible in or on the water. Lake Nianque was a little gem, about a mile-and-a-half long and a half-mile wide, with clear, sweet-tasting water and ringed with an intensely green fringe of trees. I was never a really good swimmer and always lost whatever races I entered. But I deeply enjoyed the cool, clean water supporting my body; the brief entry into a new and mysterious realm when I dived and swam underwater; and the intensely alive feeling when I climbed out of the water onto the wooden dock and stood in the warm sunshine toweling myself off. I also learned to row a boat and paddle a canoe, and most summers over the sixty-plus years since then, I have relished being out on the water, moving through the landscape by the peaceful, rhythmic exertion of my own muscle.

I don't care much for the Boy Scouts anymore. Its quasi-military organization is anachronistic at best. I am disgusted by the homophobia that seems to characterize the leadership of the Scouting community or at least did for some time. From a distance the organization gives off the faint odor of self-righteous, intolerant, religious fundamentalism. At the time, however, Scouting—and especially Scout camp—was just the right thing for an insecure, pale-skinned adolescent from the city. At camp I acquired a substantial degree of self-reliance and confidence, leadership training and outdoor skills, as well as physical strength and endurance, all of which would help me cope with and enjoy the adult world into which I would soon be entering. My summers there also determined that part of my life from then forward would have to be among trees and grass, water and boats, wood fires and wildlife.

About thirty years ago, my wife and I visited Ranachqua at the invitation of a former camp director, Joe Sonnenborn, who was then an executive of the Ten Mile River complex. I didn't recognize the place. The camp I had attended, the kosher unit, no longer existed. It had been obliterated. There were no longer enough Jewish kids in the Bronx, certainly not from families that demanded kosher foods, to support a separate camp. The clusters of cabins and tents, the big open-sided mess hall, the office and activities buildings, the latrines—all had been bulldozed away. The area had simply been abandoned. The three of us—Joe, my wife, and I—walked up to what had been the assembly ground where we had gathered for flag raising and lowering and for announcements each day. Now there was only a grassy meadow, in which a white-tailed deer was grazing until it saw us approach and then bounded away. The large open area, which had resounded with bugle calls, shouted orders, loud talk, singing, and laughter, was now a hushed, empty space. There was not another soul around. Tall grass undulating languidly in a light breeze was the only visible motion.

When I was very young I used to think that places were permanent. People changed. Events changed the world. But physical places always remained the same. I have long since been disabused of that notion. The Bronx of my childhood seemed, when I visited a few years ago, decrepit and dingy, with most traces of middle-class striving toward elegance long since removed—although its street life is more vibrant than ever. The quiet forest surrounding our Berkshire home is increasingly thinned, peopled, and suburbanized. The Catskills of Grossingers and the Concord hotels have long since vanished, although the last time I looked our bungalow colony was still there. Chevy Chase Village outside of Washington is now a leafy islet crumbling at the edges from intense urbanization and commercialization crowding in from all sides. Developers have appropriated much of the lovely, rolling farmland of the Maryland and Virginia countryside that surrounds the District of Columbia and encrusted it with mostly identical residential communities and with steel-and-glass boxes that house high-tech corporations and other business enterprises.

Some changes are good for places, of course. A real estate boom in Manhattan around the turn of the century, for example, rescued some decaying slum areas, such as the Lower East Side, transforming them into livable if yuppified neighborhoods. Industrial brownfields, reeking dead zones of pollution, are being reclaimed across the country. But when I see changes in places that, like Ranachqua, were important to me, I inevitably am submerged in a wave of melancholy, a feeling that part of my life has been negated, lost forever.

There is one more country place I would like to talk about, although I spent only two months there and that was more than a half century ago. In 1954, my friend Artie Pfeiffer and I answered an ad in the paper for jobs as counselors at a summer camp and were hired, I as nature counselor and Artie as tennis counselor. It was a summer that changed my life.

The place was the Ethical Culture Society School Camp, located on Lake Otsego in New York State, at the other end of the lake from Cooperstown, nine miles away. Otsego Lake, which James Fennimore Cooper called the "Glimmerglass" in his novel *The Pathfinder,* and its surroundings, is a place of gentle, pastoral beauty. The lake is, or was then, a sweet-tasting, limpid blue, encircled by rounded, heavily forested hills, and grassy fields speckled with dairy cows. Along with beauty, however, I found a model of what a society can and ought to be. And I found a woman to love.

The Ethical Culture Society, founded in 1876 in New York City, is a secular religion that aims for a more humane society based on ethical behavior. It emphasizes both the worth of the individual and the importance of community. At the summer camp, I saw firsthand a society in miniature that sought to live by those precepts and by and large succeeded. Unusual for those days, it was a multicultural society; kids and counselors were white, African- and Asian-American, Jewish and Christian. After a few days, I, and I supposed most others, did not even think about differences. The kids were almost all bright, lively, and interesting and the counselors friendly and mutually supportive. After the children went to bed, the counselors gathered in our own recreation room, which was quickly filled with talk, music, laughter, and in those pre–Surgeon General's report days, cigarette smoke. We were a fairly intellectual lot, and the talk, aside from the day's events at camp, often turned to books, art, politics, and the latest social theories. Competition and one-upmanship were at a minimum. There were no cliques—except that the two married couples among the counselors tended to hang out together while the rest of us went through the usual mating rituals. One day, when a bunch of us were walking down to the waterfront together, chatting, laughing, and enjoying one another's company, my friend Artie burst out with, "Why can't we be like this for the rest of our lives?" We were all still very young.

A few days after camp started—a sunny, clear, crystal-etched day—we were all down at the lake for a free-swimming period. After a few minutes in the water, I climbed onto one of the sailboats moored just outside the swimming area to rest and enjoy the sunshine. I had not been there long when two small hands appeared on the gunwale. They were followed by a mop of short, curly, dark hair; a pair of beautifully molded shoulders; a narrow face with deep dark-brown eyes; and the rest of a tanned, slender, but delightfully rounded young woman in a green bathing suit with a ruffled fringe at the bodice. As she climbed onto the boat, I took one look at the gentle white curves down that bodice and thought, *This is for me.*

I was not for her, however, at least not at first. Her name was Alice, and she was one of the swimming counselors. Her voice was already husky from shouting instructions to kids in the water. I had seen her once or twice during camp activities, and she did not look particularly friendly; she projected a keep-your-distance wariness. We talked and I learned she was from the distant and alien land of Brooklyn and had just completed her sophomore year at Oberlin College. She played the guitar and sang in a sweet, small voice that after a while would suddenly rise up unbidden inside my head. We found we shared a number of enthusiasms—the out of doors, classical music, children, the same books. However, while I was ready for a romantic attachment, she was not, or at least she was ambiguous about it. She invited me to go for a swim with her and sped far ahead of me out to the middle of the lake and then waited for me to catch up. As soon as I did, she raced away from me. That summed up our relationship for several weeks. It was very discouraging. I told my woes to one of my fellow counselors, with whom I had become friendly, a brilliant, sweet-natured young African-American named Hubie Jones who counseled me to be persistent. (More than fifty years later, Hubie remains one of my closest friends.) It was not until I started to hang out with another young woman, however, and Alice's competitive juices kicked in, that she finally agreed to spend time with me.

When not with the children, the two of us went on walks through the moist summer woods, sat and listened to old 78 rpm records of Dvorak quartets and Gilbert and Sullivan operettas in the recreation hall, and swam side by side in the lake. Our first real date was a trip in a rented motorboat to Cooperstown at the other end of the lake, where we had a meal at a restaurant and, sheltering in a barn during a sudden shower, talked about books. In the mysterious way such things happen, we bonded.

At the end of the summer, we had a few dates together in New York before we headed back to school. On the three-hour subway ride from her Brooklyn home to the north Bronx after a late date, I realized this was a serious relationship. Three years later we were married.

That summer on Lake Otsego marked the end of my child-hood. I completed my senior year at Hunter College and the next summer worked in a small public relations firm before heading off to graduate work at the University of Chicago. After that it was the Army for two years and then back to New York where I began to climb the ladder at *The New York Times*. Children came, first Alexa and then Peter, bright, lively, and utterly adorable. Alice and I agree that raising them was the best part of our lives.

Eventually we would have our own small piece of the country, our own place, on a small mountain in Becket, Massachusetts.

CHAPTER 5

A PLACE OF LIGHT AND LONGING
Manhattan

Manhattan always has been just out of reach. When I was a young man, I longed to be part of it, to live there, to work there, to walk casually along its streets, to implant myself in its noisy, exciting, expensive, glittering essence, instead of being merely a visitor. I daydreamed of someday being a *New Yorker* New Yorker. To be a Manhattanite meant being successful and affluent, to live in a large apartment on the West Side, to drink martinis and talk books and politics and banter with bright, articulate, accomplished people, to be able to walk into any shop that caught my eye, to have lunch at Longchamps and buy my suits at what was then the only Brooks Brothers store, to stand on line at Zabar's for my Sunday smoked salmon. Manhattan was everything the Bronx or Brooklyn or Queens or Staten Island was not—glamorous, lively, endlessly varied, filled with possibility and adventure. Unlike the prosaic work-aday Bronx, it was the real New York City, or so a poor but ambitious young boy thought.

In the 1940s and '50s, when I was a boy and young man, Manhattan was the heart of the triumphal world metropolis. The other great cities of Europe and Asia still were emerging from of the wreckage of war. My city was the center of art and literature, of commerce, finance, and billowing wealth. It seated the tallest buildings on the planet. It was still a great manufacturing center. The United Nations had chosen the city as their headquarters. It was what a great city should be, a place of creativity, social experimentation, and limitless opportunity. For some Manhattan was, and remains, a place to amass wealth, to achieve fame or to become an artist among other artists. It was the place every aspiring young person wanted to be. Why would anyone want to live anywhere else?

But the price of real estate and restaurants, theater tickets and concerts, the financial demands of daily life and family, and later my career path kept me away. Now, as I am nearing the end of life, it seems I will never make it.

I am not complaining. I have lived and worked in many interesting, beautiful places; witnessed many memorable events; and met many fascinating people. I would not change any of the choices that kept me away from Manhattan. Still, there is this place in my life that is unfilled.

My parents and other family members frequently took me to Manhattan—"downtown" was the word they used most often—when I was quite little. I dimly remember standing on a long line on the sidewalk to see the first opening of *Snow White* at Radio City Music Hall, a vast art deco cavern where an organ and organist rose magically from a pit before each performance to play lugubrious music and where the lounge outside the lavatories was the most luxurious room I had ever seen. Every Thanksgiving, Uncle Jack would take me to the Macy's parade, where I would perch on his shoulders to watch the bands, the floats, and the huge balloons floating high above; my favorite was the balloon of Dumbo after I had seen the movie. We went a few times to the zoo in Central Park, but even at a young age I patronizingly regarded it as much inferior to the Bronx Zoo, one of the few places my home borough could claim ascendancy. During the Christmas season, my mother took me with her to look at the lavishly decorated department store windows on Fifth Avenue and on 34th Street, always imaginative, brightly colored, and cheerful spectacles, often with Christmas music floating mysteriously in the air above them. We went occasionally to the American Museum of Natural History, where, like any young boy, I was mesmerized by the dinosaur skeletons and even more by the lifelike dioramas of plains Indians and big animals presented in their natural habitats. For some reason I was never taken by my parents to the Metropolitan Museum of Art, whose intense pleasures I did not discover until I was in college. When a teenager, however, I was required to take my sister by subway to her drawing lessons at the Museum of Modern Art and, while wandering around the building waiting for her, began to develop an untutored enthusiasm for painting and sculpture. Sending my memory back to that time, I see most clearly Picasso's *Guernica* and a graceful, wing-like piece of golden metal by, I think, Brancusi.

The most enticing place for a young boy, however, was Times Square, a whirling kaleidoscope of light and color, motion and sound and smell. All around was vibrant, noisy, milling life and a promise of endless fun. My first images of being there go back to when I was on a day's outing with my father. We went to one of the movie houses on Broadway, where we saw not only the usual film, newsreel, and short subject but also a live performance by one of the popular big bands of the day. I seem to recall that that band was Charley Barnet, whose orchestra played loud, highly syncopated swing with the brass and winds rising periodically to their feet to riff on the music. After the movie we went to my father's favorite restaurant, McGinnis of Sheepshead Bay on Broadway, where we ate roast beef sandwiches with the top of the rolls soaked in gravy and drank Coke filled with cracked ice, a novelty to me. Sidney saved the best for last; he took me into a big penny arcade near the restaurant, where I spent an hour feeding coins into pinball machines and shooting electric bullets at moving animals and airplanes. This was during World War II, and there was a concession where you could shoot live small-caliber bullets at metal enemy soldiers, but I had to be older before I was entrusted with those guns.

When we emerged from the arcade, it was already dark. The crowds were thicker than ever. I was hypnotized by the flashing, blinking, rainbow colors of the advertising signs that surrounded me. The most vivid and entertaining one was the largest, a Pepsi-Cola ad, which showed, animated in moving light, the then popular song "Three Little Fishes in an Itty Bitty Pond." I was upset for the little fishes when they swam "right over the dam." They reappeared safely in the pond a few moments later, however, quite ready to swim through another chorus of the song.

The subway ride home on the D train was part of the fun. I always asked to ride in the first car so I could stand at the front window as we sped through the dark tunnel watching the green, red, yellow, and blue lights that cast a faint glow on the tracks that ran endlessly before us. In later years, when I took the subway to school or work, I developed a love-hate relationship with the vast underground network of the New York City subway system. I loved the convenience of getting from one part of the city to the next and the speed at which the trains took me there. The subway offered the freedom of the city, for a nickel a ride at first, later a dime, and by the time I left for good, a quarter or maybe fifty cents. (What is the fare now? Two dollars? Two dollars and fifty cents? Still a bargain.) I liked sitting on the clean wicker benches and, on hot days in that pre-air conditioning era, feeling the breeze from the slowly turning fans on the ceiling of the car. What I hated was cramming myself during rush hour into a car so densely packed with other commuters that I could not even move my arms while trying to avoid eye contact with a fellow passenger whose face was inches from mine. At some point, I am not sure when or why, subways became dirty, malodorous, smeared with graffiti and dangerous.

Still, New York's subways are a wondrous thing. Think of what the surface traffic would be without them. Think of how much more air pollution there would be, how many more accidents and fatalities. Think of how poor urbanites without a car would have to get around. The subways are the people's transport and ought to be strongly supported and subsidized.

My Manhattan ambit widened and so did my cultural horizons as I grew older. My parents occasionally took me to the theater on and around Broadway. Their tastes were eclectic. I think the first Broadway show I saw was a revival of the Victor Herbert operetta *The Red Mill*. Or it might have been a slapstick comedy review called *Hellzapoppin'*. Later we went to see more serious dramas, including Arthur Miller's *Death of a Salesman*, with Lee J. Cobb and Tennessee Williams's *The Rose Tattoo*, with Eli Wallach and Maureen Stapleton. In those years, live theater was affordable even for families like mine with little money to spare. There were also many more theaters, with sepia photos of actors like the Lunts, Helen Hayes, Katherine Cornell, and Zero Mostel displayed below the marquee. They offered many more dramas and romantic comedies and fewer lavish musicals than today. Broadway, called "the Fabulous Invalid" because the legitimate theater seems always on the edge of extinction, continues to survive despite heavy blows inflicted over the course of the twentieth century, first from movies, then radio, television, DVDs, and the whole panoply of electronic entertainment, but its influence on our culture is sadly diminished.

During my later high school years, I discovered and began to haunt Greenwich Village, a practice that accelerated as I started at Hunter College and came frequently to its 68th Street building, a short subway ride away. The village has faded as the center of American Bohemia. E.E. Cummings, Maxwell Bodenheim, and most of the writers, artists, and actors who gave it its tangy flavor in the 1920s and '30s were gone; the Beats were around, but their self-conscious bohemianism had a false ring to my ear. Still, a lingering romantic and, to a hormonal adolescent and young man, vaguely erotic aura continued to infuse the narrow streets and inviting small shops and restaurants of the Village. Its narrow streets were lined with small shops that sold pastries and crusty breads, inviting displays of fruits and vegetables, salamis and hams, earthy-crunchy clothing, folk art, books, and phonograph records. Tiny, affordable restaurants, mostly Italian and French, wafted aromas redolent of garlic and herbs into the streets.

It was a relatively cheap place to take a date. The best pizza I have ever eaten anywhere, including Rome, was in a tiny storefront called La Maschera on MacDougal Street. The pie was not only a sublime, crusty, smoky slab slathered with dripping mozzarella and homemade sausage, but you could also order a cup of "Sicilian coffee" and get a cup filled with red wine. The waiters never asked for proof of age or said a word about an alcohol license. It was the beginning of the folk song boom, and on a number of sunny weekend days, my date and I would stand at the edge of the fountain in Washington Square listening to amateur but quite good guitar and banjo players play and sing. I could take my current girl to a café on Barrow Street and spend the entire evening at a small table next to a wood fire, with classical music playing softly in the background, for the price of a bottle of cheap Chilean Riesling. Or, for a modest admission, we could go to the Amato Opera, in a small storefront theater, and hear a semi-amateurish production of *La Boheme*, with a superannuated soprano essaying the role of the young Mimi.

Most of all, Manhattan promised adventure around the next corner, walking along the crowded sidewalks, down the subway steps, on a Central Park pathway. Something exciting was going to happen, some extraordinary opportunity, some totally new experience, some pretty girl. For me it was a promise that never seemed to be quite fulfilled, but the promise itself was always exhilarating.

Although I grew up in the Bronx, Manhattan was the place that probably most defined my life: what I aspired to be, what I became, what I regret not becoming. Manhattan remains my idea of "city," of the fullness of life that city should encompass. It is the place where people strive, work, seek pleasure, experience danger, and find fulfillment or disappointment. It is also a place of constant, perpetual change.

Manhattan is no longer the same Emerald City I yearned for when I was growing up. It is not the center of the world anymore. Today there are many financial, artistic, and cultural world centers. And while the population of those who work in the city is just as diverse and interesting, maybe more so, the endless variety and possibility that I saw there is diminished. A franchise and chain store sameness has taken over much of the city. The many department stores that offered a world of merchandise have been whittled down to a few. Gone are Gimbels, Bests, Bonwit Teller, Altmans, Wanamaker's, Stern's and Klein's. The city has become Gapped and Kmarted and Starbucked. Only the Strand remains of the many used bookstores that lined Fourth and Third Avenues. Amazon and Barnes and Noble dominate the retail book trade, and Germany and France have conquered the publishing industry, which is now anyway endangered by the rapid emergence of electronic books. The Polo Grounds on Coogan's Bluff is only a fond memory, and so is the old Madison Square Garden on Eighth Avenue. Even my beloved Yankee Stadium, just across the river, where I watched Joe DiMaggio lope gracefully across center field, has been torn down to make way for a stadium with luxury boxes. The Bowery and the Lower East Side have been largely yuppified, and Harlem is becoming so. The dining scene is more varied and elegant than ever; gone, however, are old favorites such as Longchamps, Lindy's and Luchow, Schraffts, McGinnis and Roth's, the Brass Rail, and the Paramount. The Horn and Hardardt Automats, where three nickels dropped into a slot opened a golden window containing a bologna on white bread sandwich or dozens of other delicacies, also have vanished. The price of apartments, always expensive, soared through the ceiling and seemed to remain there even after the housing market meltdown of 2008. It seems that only millionaires can afford to live below 96th Street anymore, and perhaps not even above it. And yet...

There still is no city on Earth that is as entrancing as Manhattan at night seen from the Brooklyn or Jersey shore, or from an airplane passing over, its millions of blazing lights creating a glowing, enchanted landscape. After the tragedy of September 11, 2001, the Empire State Building again presides over the city skyline like a stately art deco god. And is there a more beautiful skyscraper in the world than the Chrysler Building? Central Park is the same lovely island of tranquility it always has been, with even more enticements, music, and theater, and food, to amuse and soothe the public. Its zoo is better than ever (but still not nearly as good as the Bronx Zoo). Rockefeller Center Plaza at Christmastime, whether owned by the Japanese or anyone else, is still greeting-card perfect. Despite a hostile corporate takeover, Times Square and 42nd Street are as bright and kinetic as always, despite having lost much of their appealing seediness. The Metropolitan and Modern Art and the many other museums, Lincoln Center, Carnegie Hall, the Broadway and Off-Broadway theaters, the art galleries, and the libraries offer a rich cultural bounty second to no other city in the world. It is still a city of excitement and possibility. It would not be a bad place to live—if you are rich.

I nearly got to Manhattan. I was hired by the *Times* in my mid-twenties, shortly after my discharge from active duty in the Army. I worked in its 43rd Street newsroom for nearly five years, first in clerical jobs and then as a cub reporter. I had a foothold! I also had two new children, first my daughter, Alexa, and then my son, Peter. They turned out to be bright, lively, funny, beautiful little kids and a joy to raise. However, now that we were married and with two small children, with a modest salary even for journalism, a Manhattan apartment was impossibly expensive. So we lived for a while in a Brooklyn tenement and then in an affordable co-op in Irvington-on-Hudson in Westchester.

In the newsroom, I was a kid reporter on the periphery, watching the stars pound away at their clacking, bell-ringing typewriters, taking notes with the phones cradled to their ears, yelling for a copy boy (no girls yet), reading the paper, chatting, or sometimes playing cards in the smoky, fluorescent miasma. The immense space was stuffed with a phalanx of gray metal desks that stretched in unbroken, precisely aligned rows from 43rd to 44th Street. A loudspeaker summoned reporters to the City Desk for their assignments. To me it looked, sounded, and smelled just the way a big city newsroom should—and now I was part of it.

When the new *Times* building on Eighth Avenue opened in 2007, I visited the newsroom. It seemed like an alien place— nothing like the bright, noisy space I had worked in more than forty years earlier. The news department occupies two floors that surround an atrium open to the sky. The lighting is soft, the colors muted, and the place hushed. The computers that had replaced the typewriters make little sound, and because each reporter occupies his or her own square of space surrounded by shelves and cabinets, there is little conversation. No calls of "Copy!" were to be heard during my visit; reporters' stories are sent to the editors by the push of a computer button. There was no smoke, of course. Smoking was no longer allowed in public buildings. It was an attractive place, but standing in the strange surroundings, I felt a little distressed. I had quit the *Times* sixteen years earlier after working for the paper for thirty-two years, and now I only recognized one face in the entire newsroom, an editor who had been the Washington bureau chief for a while when I was a correspondent there. What really bothered me, however, was that the place was so different from the newsroom in which I had entered the world of journalism.

As I think about it, it seems to me that the change in the appearance of the *Times*'s newsroom reflects—or at least can be a metaphor for—what has happened to newspaper journalism since I was a young reporter. The front-page news then tended to be hard; the writing, although often elegant, was straightforward. The opening paragraph of news stories, or "lede" in journalese, answered the questions who, what, when, where, how, and why. A reader did not have to look halfway through the story to find out what it was about, what the "nut" of the report was. Now the news stories, often as not, are "soft," frequently beginning with an anecdote or description of the setting in which the stories take place and the news itself buried deep in the report. This is an observation, not a judgment. The change in the style of newspaper reporting has happened for necessary reasons. Americans now want their news reporting to be entertaining as well as informative. To stay competitive in attracting readers and advertising revenue in the age of the tweet, the *Times* and most other surviving newspapers have had to re-craft their approach to news to reflect the shorter attention span of Americans as well as their demand for amusement and diversion. The news pages of the *Times* have grown smaller, and it has added a number of sections such as science, sports, food, and arts to appeal to the interests of various segments of its readership. There are more feature stories as opposed to news reports. There are hardly any transcripts of speeches or important documents, a staple of the old *Times*. The *Times* is a far different paper than the one I joined in 1959 and has made some unfortunate choices in selecting its editors. But it still is, in my opinion, far and away the best and, for the most part, the most trustworthy source of news in the world. I am not sure, however, how long it will survive in its print and paper format.

I had a mostly successful and satisfying career at the *Times*. As with many things in life, the success, at least initially, involved pure dumb luck.

My first reporting job was in the business news department covering foreign trade stories among other things. It was a start and I was happy to be on my way, but I wondered if my way would ever take me beyond reporting on business and finance, subjects that had no particular appeal for me and for which I had no academic background. This was in the early 1960s when the civil rights movement was gaining momentum. Almost every day produced dramatic stories from Montgomery or Selma, Alabama, or about atrocities committed in Mississippi, and there I was writing pieces about why the dollar had weakened against the Deutschmark. I would have loved to have been a part of reporting from the South, but I was an untried novice, unworthy of an assignment to cover a story clearly history in the making.

Then one morning the business news editor, a decent, competent man named Tom Mullaney, stopped by and dropped a piece of graph paper on my desk. It had nothing written on it except a telephone number. "Some company called and said they had an interesting story," Mullaney said. "Do you have time to check it out?" I called the number, which turned out to be the public relations officer of a big grain trading company in lower Manhattan. He had a news story that the *Times* would be interested in, he said. Representatives of the Soviet Union had approached his and other American grain companies to ask about purchasing a large quantity of American wheat.

As inexperienced as I was, I recognized a dynamite story. This was in 1963, at the chilliest depth of the Cold War. The United States and Russia were barely on speaking terms and had no commercial relationships to speak of. A big Soviet purchase meant a significant jolt of money for American wheat farmers. More than that, it was a signal that Soviet agriculture was in trouble, that the communist regime was unable to feed its people. Moscow must have been in serious trouble or it would not have come to the US, pocketbook in hand.

I jumped on it, and the next day, the Russian wheat deal story was at the top of page one. It was the first time my byline was on the front page. Soon all the media were after the story, but with my inside sources, I stayed consistently ahead of the competition with exclusive reports. The national news editor at the time, Harrison Salisbury, suggested I write a series of articles following the wheat from farm to Russia, but that proved impractical because of the complex route and long delays in shipping. I did visit rural South Dakota over a couple of cold, snowy winter days to talk to farmers growing the durum wheat the Russians were buying. As I flew over the heartland, the geometrically formal checkerboard patterns that the European settlers had imposed on what had been a wild prairie amazed me. I also went to a port in Virginia to watch the wheat being loaded on freighters bound for Murmansk. I felt like a reporter.

My wheat deal stories won me one of the half-dozen or so Publisher's Prizes given out each month for outstanding reportage or writing. Then I was assigned to go to Geneva for a couple of weeks to cover a meeting of the United Nations Conference on Trade and Development. I was not the senior *Times* reporter at that event, but I sensed that I was being tested as a possible foreign correspondent. And, in fact, shortly after I returned to New York, the foreign news editor, a formal, shy man named Emmanuel Freedman, called me to his desk. I had learned some German while in the Army, he had noted from my resume. Would I be interested in going to Germany as the number-two man in the Bonn bureau?

Indeed I would. I had dreamed of being a foreign correspondent for the *Times* since I was a young boy. Now it was happening, much sooner than I could have hoped. Just short of thirty years old, I was, at the time at least, one of the younger reporters ever assigned to an overseas bureau in peacetime.

So I and my family spent four years in Germany for the *Times*, and then went to Japan for two years where my job evolved into being a kind of troubleshooter for all of East and Southeast Asia, taking me on frequent reporting trips to Korea, Taiwan, the Philippines, Indonesia, Hong Kong, Singapore, Malaysia, and Vietnam (but not China, which was not then open to American reporters). After that I spent twenty-one years in the Washington bureau. While there I declined an offer to become the editor of the paper's Sunday Business News section, a job that would have taken me back to Manhattan, because I was then covering the White House, an assignment I enjoyed greatly. When I quit the paper in 1991, I started and published a daily online environmental news report called *Greenwire* from an office in Northern Virginia, just across the Potomac from our home in Chevy Chase. When the *National Journal* bought out that publication, we moved to Boston to join our daughter and her family.

By then I was well into my sixties. Manhattan, it seems, will be a place never lived in, a goal never attained. I have no regrets. Well, maybe a few.

CHAPTER 6

A HAUNTED PLACE
Germany

After five days of heavy swells and seasick soldiers, the troop ship *Buckner* docked at the North German port of Bremerhaven. Debarking in the middle of a dank, foggy night at the end of October 1957, we walked from the harbor toward the railroad station through a small square surrounded by narrow, baroque buildings made indistinct by the murky air. The only sound other than the shuffling of our booted feet was the slow *plonk, plonk* of water from a marble fountain in the middle of the square. My immediate thought was that this would be a great setting for a Gothic novel.

My second thought was, here I am, a Jew in a country that hated Jews enough to slaughter them like cattle. Surrounded as I was by soldiers of an army that had defeated the Nazis a little more than a decade earlier, I did not in any way feel fearful, but I was uneasy. What was it going to be like to live for nearly two years in a place that I had learned to think of as the epicenter of all that is evil in the human soul? As it turned out, I spent nearly six years in Germany, returning as a correspondent for *The New York Times* a few years after my brief, undistinguished military career.

I had arrived with Headquarters Company and other units of the 4th Armored Division, which had departed en masse from Fort Hood, Texas, to replace another armored division, which was rotating back to the US. We were headed to a base outside of Göppingen, a small city in Swabia in the southern part of the country. A pleasantly pastoral backwater, Swabia was known chiefly for producing romantic poets and noodles and as the birthplace of Albert Einstein in the small city of Ulm.

I had been in the Army for nearly seven months, having been drafted for two years of active duty, serving first at Fort Dix, New Jersey, for basic training, and then at Fort Benjamin Harrison, outside of Indianapolis. While at the Adjutant General's school at Harrison, I learned stenography (a skill that would later help me get a foot in the door at *The New York Times*). I was sent to that school not because I had a master's degree but because I knew how to type).

When I finished the course, I received orders for Fort Hood but was told I would be leaving for Germany in two months. So I went to a phone booth, called Alice at her parents' home in Brooklyn, and asked her to marry me. We had been keeping company for three years, and it was more or less understood that we both wanted to spend the rest of our lives with each other. I thought we would wait until I finished my Army obligation and then found a job. But now I was going to Europe for the first time and wanted to share it with her.

"Yes," Alice said after a brief pause. "When?" "Next weekend," I replied. "I have a three-day pass before I have to go to Texas." I then explained about going to Germany and wanting her with me. There was a longer pause this time. "Can we do it so quickly?" she asked. "We'll need a license, and I have to have a blood test." We could. The next Saturday, we were married the living room of her parents' Brooklyn home in front of our immediate families. Our honeymoon was two days in the Roosevelt Hotel just off Times Square, and then I was off to Fort Hood and Alice went back to her parents' house and her work for a trade journal. We did not see each other for the next three months. By then I was already in Germany.

The base for Headquarters Company and other units, including Division Trains, a support company to which I was then assigned, was an old German military *kaserne* or encampment. If it had a name, I do not remember it. The barracks was a long, curved masonry building that smelled of disinfectant and generations of male bodies. It struck me as a bit bizarre that American soldiers would be sleeping in beds used by their enemies of a few years before. German civilians, glad for the work in an economy that still was struggling to recover from the devastation of war, staffed the mess hall. It was a luxury for specialists and us privates who were thus spared from loathed KP duties.

My new unit did not know what to do with a stenographer, so I was assigned to the motor pool that serviced trucks. I did not last there long. When I reported for duty at the pool, the sergeant in charge told me to lubricate one of the trucks. I said I did not know how, so he patiently showed me how to use a grease gun to squirt lubricant into the little nipples on the underside of the chassis. When I finished he told me to drive the truck to a nearby parking area. I told him I didn't know how to drive. "You don't know how to drive!" he exclaimed in genuine astonishment. "Aren't you American?" I explained that I had grown up in New York City, that my parents did not own a car, and that we had used public transportation. He shrugged and turned away. The next day I was assigned to the division's payroll office as secretary to the officer in charge. I spent the rest of my time as a warrior taking dictation and filling out payroll forms.

When Alice arrived, I left the barracks, and together we lived "on the economy," that is, in private housing off base. We did not have a car at first, so I had to find a place within walking distance. About two miles from the base entrance, a little town called Eislingen straddled the small river Fils, so I concentrated my search there. It was a charming, Old World–looking place, surrounded by farms, with narrow streets lined with half-timbered houses, and small shops with enticing displays of produce, breads, and meats. There was a *gasthaus*, a tavern that served platters of *wurst* and *schnitzel* and tankards of delicious, creamy beer, and also had a few rooms for travelers. As I walked along, self-conscious in my uniform, I became aware of an unfamiliar smell in the air, a mixture of cured meats, coal smoke, freshly turned earth, and night soil—composted human waste carried in horse-drawn "honey wagons" to fertilize the fields. It was a smell I came to recognize as characteristic of rural Germany. Farm fields, still green despite the late autumn, surrounded the town.

I found a place I thought acceptable on the outskirts of the village. It was in a newish stucco house occupied by an older couple named Koetzle, their plump and jolly daughter, Irmgard, and her husband, Joachim, a former Wehrmacht soldier who had lost one of his hands in combat—on the Russian front, he said. In all the time we lived in Germany, I never met anyone who admitted to fighting against Americans or its Western allies. In the late 1950s and early '60s, the German people were just beginning to come to terms with the horrors their nation had perpetrated in the years of the Third Reich. Many of the older generation were still in denial. They did not know what had been done to the Jews, they claimed; it was all kept secret from them. When I came back to Germany as a reporter, there was a news assistant in the *Times* bureau, a decent enough young man named Hans-Juergen, who had been a boy in the city of Weimar during the war years. On a hill just above that city stood the notorious Buchenwald concentration camp. The railroad cars that brought the prisoners to Buchenwald rolled right through the center of the city. The camp's atrocities were taking place right above his head, yet he claimed he never knew of its existence. Still, there was a troubled look in his eyes as we spoke, a look I came to recognize as familiar among the Germans I encountered whenever the subject of the Holocaust came up. That look told that they really did know what was going on or had consciously decided not to know.

When Alice arrived from New York, I took her to our "apartment" on the top floor of the Koetzle house, picked her up, and proudly carried her over the threshold of the first home we would share together. It consisted of a one-room garret with two beds, a kitchen table with two chairs, a two-burner hot plate, and a little coal-burning stove for heat. Our tiny bathroom had no bath or shower, just a toilet and a sink that put forth only cold water. I had thought it a rather nice place. It was clean, light, and airy, and from the small skylight in the bathroom, we had a view of a ruined castle on a distant mountaintop—and we could afford it on my Army pay. Alice, however, was dismayed. She had grown up in a big, comfortable house in a nice section of Brooklyn and was taken aback by the Spartan accommodation. After a while, though, she settled in, and our time as an Army family in Germany turned out to be enjoyable.

We had made it a point to let the Koetzle family know we were Jewish. We don't know how they absorbed this fact, but we soon became friendly, even intimate, exchanging daily gossip and occasionally sharing meals with them. Our intimacy was enhanced by the fact that we had to use their bathroom to take our baths. They allowed us one bath a week, and they charged us a mark, about twenty-five cents at the time, for the use of their hot water.

With money from Alice's savings, we soon bought a car, a brand-new Austin A35 Saloon. We paid nine hundred fifty dollars for it—it may have been the last new car in the world that cost under a thousand dollars. I then taught myself how to drive by inching the little car back and forth on a dirt road that traversed the field that adjoined our house. (I suppose I was an autodidact.) With the car, we first chugged all around our area of Germany, first to nearby towns and castles, then farther afield to Stuttgart, Heidelberg, Frankfurt, Munich, and the German Tyrol. On one furlough, we drove to Paris, and like many Americans, I fell in love with the city but disliked the Parisians—or, rather, reacted to them taking our tourist dollars with condescending hauteur. We went to Switzerland and beyond the Alps to Florence, Venice, and Rome. One Christmas we took a boat train to London, where we bought clothes and books, went to the theater, and ate roast beef and Yorkshire pudding. We usually traveled in modest fashion on my Army pay, staying in youth hostels and eating at the least expensive restaurants. To someone like me, however, who had wondered whether he ever would get to see Europe, it was, to borrow Hemingway's title, a moveable feast.

Europe in the 1950s was still pleasantly European. It had not yet been subdued by American culture. English was still not widely spoken, at least not in Germany. Many people still wore traditional clothing there—lederhosen for the men and dirndls for the women and feathered *jaeger* hats for both sexes. Little shops and taverns lined the streets of the small towns. Many of the houses and public buildings had been around for centuries. Walls surrounded farmhouses, and the farmers walked behind horses to plow their fields. A small city like Göppingen had its own symphony orchestra, which gave concerts in the town hall. This was the Europe I had imagined in the many years I had dreamed of visiting. In those years, the dollar was powerful and went a long way in Europe, even on a private's pay. A steak dinner with a beer at a *gasthaus* cost the equivalent of one dollar. It may not have been Hemingway in Paris after the first war, but I was a happy young American in Europe.

Change was taking place of course. The cities were still digging out from the destruction of war. Parts of Stuttgart were still punctuated by huge mounds of rubble left over from the bombing. What would replace the rubble in the cities would be modern American-style buildings, malls, and supermarkets; McDonald's; rock and roll; and many other artifacts of late-twentieth-century American culture.

Insulated by the Army and happily absorbed by my brand-new marriage, I did not get to know Germany or Germans very well during my military service. I did, however, pick up a smattering of German—"G.I. Deutsch," we called it—which, it turned out, was one of the reasons the *Times* decided to post me to Germany and fulfill my early ambition to be a foreign correspondent.

When the *Times* assigned me to Germany, it first sent me to study German at a Berlitz center in Manhattan. I spent three months, five days a week, three hours a day, one on one with an instructor. After the final lesson, she said, "Congratulations, Mr. Shabecoff. You have done very well. You will now be able to function as a reporter in Germany." As it turned out, unfortunately, when I got there I was barely able to order an egg in a restaurant and not much more. It would take me more than a year before I could do my job comfortably without an interpreter.

As Berlin was then a divided city in the middle of communist East Germany, the West German capital had been set up in Bonn, a small university city on the Rhine River. It was chosen chiefly because the first post-war West Germany chancellor, Konrad Adenauer, lived in the area. The Times bureau was in nearby Bad Godesberg, a well-kept resort town also on the Rhine, which also hosted the US Embassy to West Germany. Our housing was one of a number of garden apartment buildings that bordered the river. The apartments, spacious and well appointed, were mostly occupied by American embassy staff and other foreign diplomats as well as journalists from a number of countries. Local German residents called the complex "the golden ghetto." From one of our windows we saw the constant flow of rake-masted barges moving slowly back and forth along the Rhine. Directly across the river rose the Drachenfels, a small mountain on which the mythic hero Siegfried supposedly slew a dragon. ("*Drachen*" means "dragon" and "*fels*" means crag.) On the surface a prosperous but rather dull suburb, Bad Godesberg was in fact a bubbling caldron filled with politicians, diplomats, journalists, and spies; John Le Carre's novel *A Small Town in Germany* was set there.

On one of our first days in Godesberg, we took our children for a Sunday stroll on the promenade along the river, first dressing Alexa in a dirndl and Peter in lederhosen. Both of the kids were blond and blue-eyed and, if I do say so, quite beautiful. An older couple stopped in front of us and said, in German, "Ach, those are real German children!" I regret to this day that I did not have the wit or command of the language to respond, "Thank you, but we are American Jews."

Bonn, separated from Godesberg by a mile or so of farm fields, was not a bad little city. It housed the *Bundesrat*, or federal parliament, the presidential palace, the university, the house where Beethoven was born, a concert hall, and other cultural amenities. Still, it was a drowsy place, and as Europe's oldest established provisional capital, it was the butt of numerous jokes. It was called "the Klatsch on the Rhine," and described as "half as big as the Chicago cemetery and twice as dead." One morose aphorist pronounced the judgment "See Bonn and die—of boredom." But it was, as the Germans say, *gemütlich*—cozy and comfortable—and we enjoyed our domestic lives there. Our kids went to the American School on the Rhine just across the street from the golden ghetto. We mingled with and became friendly with American embassy personnel, German government bureaucrats, and journalists from different countries, often meeting at the American Club, which also stood at the edge of the Rhine. Alice zipped around in her secondhand Volkswagen Beetle (I had a company car, a German-built Ford) to the little shops in the center of Bad Godesberg and brought home freshly baked rolls and pastries, sausages and smoked goose breast, and produce, eggs, and milk from nearby farms. On weekends when I was not working (few and far between), we took the kids to picnics and explored old castles perched on crags above the river or to swim in a quarry near the Drachenfels. We went to concerts in the Godesberg *stadthalle* and attended diplomatic parties. Occasionally we drove to the nearby Eiffel Mountains to visit a favorite *weinstube* that served us a delicious, sweet sparkling red wine as we sat in its small, leafy courtyard. Germany seemed to us to be a congenial, civilized country. Like many others, we could not understand how such a place could have descended into such brutal, murderous barbarism only a few short years before. We never did figure it out, even after living there for nearly six years. Nor did we ever lose our sense of unease.

The West Germans were not much preoccupied with their past during our years there. That would change in time, but in the early 1960s, they seemed to be doing their best to forget it. The country's *wirtschaftstwunder*, its economic miracle, was just emerging in full flower, and people were enjoying their new prosperity. Getting and spending, not soul-searching, was the order of the day. The only burning political issue was the division of the country and the debate over how to relate to communist East Germany. Tensions rose when the East Germans blocked access to Berlin by cutting off rail and autobahn traffic, but those episodes usually lasted only a few days. (I was called back from a vacation in Italy to cover one of the blockades.) The Berlin wall had been erected only a few years before, in effect making East German citizens prisoners in their own country.

The Wall in Berlin was a strange manifestation of the tortuous, inflamed politics of the Cold War and how that strange conflict distorted places as well as people. Even more bizarre were the walls erected in dozens of towns and tiny villages along the border between East and West. I visited one village, called Moedlareuth, no more than a hamlet really, in upper Bavaria on its border with Thuringia. The area was filled with wide, quiet fields of wheat and alfalfa and dotted with pinewoods and huddles of half-timbered houses; no part of Germany appears more peaceful and bucolic. But here is what I wrote for a *Times* Sunday magazine article: "As the road curved into what used to be Moedlareuth's central green, appearances give way with shattering abruptness to harsh reality. There, slicing straight through the village out into the empty fields beyond, is a high, thick concrete wall—white, raw-looking, and ugly in the bright sunshine.... Set against the soft rural background, it is as eerie and surrealistic as a Magritte painting." The wall was punctuated by watchtowers manned by guards with orders to shoot anyone crossing either way across a wide strip along the border, and the strip was strewn with landmines. Several residents of the village had been killed or injured trying to leave their own community.

With the hindsight of nearly half a century since then, it seems obvious that a political system that imprisons its own entire citizenry could not be sustained. At the time, however, there was no indication that the existential standoff between East and West would not remain a permanent fixture of geopolitics. When the walls finally came down, it marked a signal triumph of the human spirit. It was also a result of the fundamental flaws and final failure of an authoritarian system that ruled not with the consent of the governed, but with walls, landmines, and armed guards.

Despite the Wall, West Berlin was a lively, thriving if truncated metropolis. The Kurfürstendamm, the boulevard that runs through what was then the heart of the city, had largely recovered from the ruin rained down by Allied bombs and Soviet artillery, although the wreckage of the Kaiser Wilhelm church had been left standing as a memorial. The broad street was lined with restaurants crowded with patrons drinking *café mit schlag*, or eating *blutwurst* or *leberwurst*, and with shops at which thick-bodied matrons clad in ankle-length woolen coats and Tyrolean hats paused to *tsk, tsk* at the miniskirts and bikinis in the display windows. The Ku'damm was the center of Berlin's rich avant-garde cultural scene and housed a number of theaters, cabarets, and art galleries. The cheerful residents did not act as though they lived in a city under siege by enemies that planned to take away their freedom and pleasures.

The intellectual center of West Berlin was the Freie Universitat, the Free University, so called because it was free of the ideologically driven curricula of the Soviet bloc schools. It also served as the center of the liberal and radical student movements that slowly emerged in Germany following the war.

I made several reporting trips to East Germany. The East Germans had not forgotten the Holocaust, at least not their government and its propaganda machine. Citizens of the demi-country were reminded regularly about what had happened during the war and why. Millions of Jews had been murdered, according to the official line, not because of virulent German anti-Semitism, or slavish subservience to the ravings of a lunatic dictator or passive indifference to the fate of their fellow humans, but because of…capitalism!

On one trip to the East, I visited the Buchenwald concentration camp. While it was not an extermination camp like Auschwitz or Treblinka, many thousands of Jews, gypsies, communists, and others had died there of malnutrition, disease, or simply being worked to death. Many were shot by guards. By the time I arrived, the government had turned the camp into a museum. The barracks for the prisoners had simply been leveled, but one building left standing showed photographs of the terrible conditions under which the prisoners lived and died. There were also many inscriptions declaring that this was all the fault of the capitalists and that East Germany and its leaders bore no responsibility for the atrocities.

Reporters from the West who visited East Germany were required to be accompanied by an "interpreter," who was really a *wachhund*, a government watchdog assigned to make sure reporters did not see anything or talk to anyone they shouldn't. We also had to travel in a government car driven by a government driver. During the trip that included the Buchenwald visit, on which I was accompanied by a British reporter friend, the driver was a middle-aged, barrel-chested, bald-headed man who reminded me of the actor Erich von Stroheim. During our weeklong travels around the country, he said not a word. But when he stopped at Checkpoint Charley, as we were about to return to West Berlin, he turned around to face us in the backseat and said in German, "Nothing has changed here. Only the color, from black to red."

In West Germany in the early '60s, however, there already were signs of change. In a nation with a mostly deserved reputation for subservience to authority, many young Germans began to challenge the conservative government's economic and policy decisions, particularly its support for the war in Vietnam. "Red" Rudi Dutschke led antiwar protest marches down the Kurfürstendamm, ignoring the catcalls of construction workers and the disapproving grimaces of the thick-bodied matrons in their ankle-length coats and Tyrolean hats. I met with Dutschke and his American wife several times. He was an intense but pleasant and reasonable young man. But he was shot in the head by a right-wing fanatic and, although he lived a few years longer, died all too soon of his injury.

One group of students formed an organization they called Action Atonement to begin to expiate with good works the atrocities committed by Germans against the Jews. I came to understand that we should not hold young Germans accountable for the unforgivable sins of their parents.

Why were Germans consumed by such virulent hatred of Jews? I still don't know. Of course they were not the first to kill or brutalize Jewish people, although they committed genocide with unmatched, meticulous efficiency. In his book *The Pity of It All,* a history of German Jews, the late Israeli author Amos Elon, a friend of ours in Germany, described how Jews had been major contributors to that nation's culture and economy and had desperately—but vainly—tried to integrate themselves into the mainstream of German society. Yet the Germans were led willingly by a lunatic to commit one of the greatest crimes in history against Europe's Jews.

Over the many years that have passed since then, as I watched the world pass through more wars, genocide, racial and religious strife, terrorism, and other forms of fanaticism, as well as our relentless destruction of the natural world, our only home, I have reluctantly concluded that there is a fatal darkness lurking in all of us and that homo sapiens, we violent primates, may be a failed evolutionary experiment.

And yet . . .Germany transformed itself in those years to a liberal democracy. It is now integrated into the European Union among other nations that were its traditional enemies and with which it warred for centuries. Western Europe has been at peace

PLACES

with itself for more than half a century. Perhaps there is hope. Perhaps there can be redemption.

CHAPTER 7

A CLOSED-IN PLACE

Japan

Our house in Tokyo had a wall around it. Everybody's house in Tokyo had a wall around it one way or another. We never went into our neighbors' homes. They never came into ours. After two years in Japan, I didn't have a Japanese friend, except for one man I considered a friend. But he committed ritual suicide that year.

I was assigned to the Tokyo bureau of the *Times* after my four-year stint in Germany. Unlike my preparation for that tour of duty, I had no language instruction and had learned only about a dozen words of Japanese from a tape. Alice and the children were not with me when I first arrived; they had gone to spend time with family in New York. I didn't know a soul in Japan or in the entire Asian continent for that matter. The reporter I was replacing left after a few days. My mother had died after a long siege of cancer just weeks before. I felt terribly alone.

And yet the place did not seem quite alien; it was almost familiar in fact.

The *Times* bureau was in the building of the *Asahi Shimbun*, one of the city's major newspapers. It was located in the heart of the Ginza, a commercial and cultural section of the city that was as close to being the center of Tokyo as any of that city's many distinct neighborhoods. There were tall office buildings and endless shops, restaurants and theaters, all surmounted by flashing, flickering, rainbow-colored electric advertising signs. Traffic was always thick, the sidewalks always crowded, and the noise level, measured by an electronic device mounted over a busy cross street, approached the level of a jet plane taking off. Pedestrians walked rapidly and purposefully with "don't get in my way" expressions on their faces. The streets pulsed with life. It was Times Square!

But not really. The signs—except for a few in romaji or Roman letters—were in a script I could not read, and the words of the passersby were in a language I did not understand. There were no signs identifying the streets I walked down. I never lost a sense of disorientation in Tokyo; after two years in the city, I still could not easily find my way around. Even today, more than forty years later, I still have dreams of being lost in Tokyo. The odors were also unfamiliar, composed of, among other things I could not identify, raw fish, frying noodles, and the acrid, oily smell of pollution from the thousands of vehicles that crammed the streets. Sometimes the air pollution was so intense that it covered the sun, turning daylight into murky night. On a clear day, it is possible to see Mt. Fuji from high points in the city, but I only saw the fabled mountain from that distance three or four times during my stay, although I saw the conical peak several times while passing by on Japan's bullet trains. The most characteristic sounds, aside from the traffic roar and the hubbub of human voices were the *ching, ching, ching, ching* of the pachinko machines, popular gambling devices that filled countless gaming parlors.

The *Times* put me up for a few days in the Imperial Hotel, a beautiful, odd-looking cross between a Zen temple and a Mayan pyramid, designed by Frank Lloyd Wright. In addition to its aesthetic value, the building was famous for having remained relatively intact during the Great Tokyo Earthquake of 1923, which killed more than a hundred thousand people in the city and surrounding areas. Those who sheltered in the building were unharmed. A few months after I arrived, however, the hotel, inexplicably to me, was torn down to make way for a modern steel-and-glass new Imperial Hotel, a replacement for what was irreplaceable. But postwar Japan, like the United States, placed relatively little value on the past or, at least, physical manifestations of the past. Indeed, much of humanity seems to place little value on places, tearing down buildings, remaking cities, destroying neighborhoods, and razing villages, all in the name of money and utility. But then, human societies treat places of the natural world with even less respect than the manmade environment. We rip the living forests from the soil, pave over pastures and meadows, foul the waters, block the rivers, pollute the air, and poison the land, for economic growth and profit and then define the destruction as progress. Of course, none of this occurred to me until much later in my life, after I had been writing about environmental issues for many years. At the time what I worried about was orienting myself in a strange new culture well enough to do my job as a newspaper correspondent.

Japan, then in the early stages of its remarkable post-World War II economic growth, was especially frenetic in tearing down the old and building the new. Skyscrapers built to withstand earthquakes sprung up like giant beanstalks. The city recently had hosted the Olympics and razed large swaths of the city that had been spared by the US bombing to build stadia and other public facilities. Even in the short time I spent in Tokyo, I experienced some of that impatient development firsthand. During my first few weeks in the city, I spent many hours looking for a place to live for when my family arrived. In my search I was accompanied and helped by the *Times*'s office manager, a tiny, dignified but sweet-natured man named Junuske Ofusa—always addressed as "Ofusa-san"—who had been with the paper since the 1930s. During the war he had carefully protected *Times* property and at the outbreak of hostilities had brought food and comforts to the *Times* correspondent at the time who was briefly detained before being exchanged. Throughout my stint in Japan, Ofusa-san served as my interpreter, guide, adviser and all-around fix-it, including making sure I paid as low a tax to the Japanese government as possible.

After looking at more than a dozen houses and apartments, all of which were too expensive, too small, or too far from the office, I was fortunate to be able to rent a house that had been home to several previous *Times* correspondents. It was in an unusual, for Tokyo, quiet green neighborhood of single-family homes in a hilly area that overlooked a broad stretch of the city. The house was a lovely dwelling with traditional Japanese amenities, including straw-mat floors, rice-screen-paper sliding doors, a black tile roof, wooden alcoves, and a low dining table over a sunken pit designed to hold a charcoal brazier for cold days. It also had some Western conveniences, including modern heating and plumbing and a well-appointed kitchen. And it had a delightful rear garden, an American-style lawn surrounded by Japanese plantings, including a flowering cherry tree, a small fishpond, and a stone lantern.

Shortly after we moved in, however, the single-family home next door was torn down and replaced with a multistory apartment building. After we left, our house was also replaced by another multifamily dwelling. Most of the wood, bamboo, tile, and straw homes that had been spared in the wartime bombing have been obliterated to make room for high-rise buildings. Such buildings are no doubt needed. Tokyo is a crowded city, and most of the residents live in cramped apartments with tiny rooms. It is a shame, nevertheless. Houses like ours were an expression of a fundamental Japanese aesthetic called *shibui*. The word connotes stark, formal, refined elegance. It is a minimalist philosophy of beauty: a single flower in a porcelain vase; a painted scroll hanging in a small alcove framed with polished wooden posts; a precise, ritualized pouring of tea into delicate cups; the slow, quiet notes of the lute-like *samisen*. Even back in the '60s, however, there was little public evidence of *shibui* in Tokyo. The city was a brash, rowdy, noisy, glittering somewhat vulgar but always exciting place that appeared to be the polar opposite of the old aesthetic.

My first full day in Japan could have been my last. I left the hotel in the morning just to walk around the Ginza and get a feel for the place, as I always like to do in a new city. I had walked a block or two when suddenly I felt an intense pain in my shoulder. I looked down, and there was a good-size rock at my feet. At the same time, I became aware of a lot of shouting. Across a wide street was a large group of young men, most of them wearing helmet liners, and some were throwing rocks. It was a student demonstration, the first of many I was to see and cover, that protested the pending resigning of the US-Japan mutual defense treaty. This was during the middle of the Vietnam War, and the United States was unpopular with many Japanese, particularly the young. Student protests against the war had started in the US but had spread around the world and evolved into generalized protests against the established order. In Paris a fiery redhead named Daniel Cohn-Bendit led a student movement. In Berlin, where I reported frequently on riots and was becoming something of a connoisseur of the various types of tear gas used by police, the students were led by Rudi Dutschke, whom I got to know and liked. As far as I could find out, there was no single leader of the Japanese students. As a general but not universal rule, charisma and leadership tend not to be highly regarded in Japan, where not standing out in the crowd and strict conformity to social norms are national characteristics, even to the norms of the radical student movement. At least that is what I saw while I was there.

I didn't know what the demonstration was about at the time, but I was angry. Why did they throw a rock at me? I hadn't been in town long enough to do any harm to anyone. If that rock had landed a couple of inches higher, it would have hit my head. If it had been thrown with enough force to do serious injury, it might have killed me. Welcome to Japan! I resisted a strong urge to pick up the rock and fling it back at the nearest rioter. There was no point in provoking an international incident on my first morning in Asia.

Alice and the kids arrived from the US in a couple of weeks. Our furniture still was en route from Germany, so we installed ourselves in a small, quiet hotel used primarily by Japanese, not by *gaijin*—foreigners—like us. Alexa and Peter, Alice said, had behaved like troupers on the eighteen-hour trip from New York to Tokyo. Indeed, the kids were unfailingly wonderful, cheerfully going with the program no matter where we dragged them on our peregrinations throughout my newspaper career. They were our friends and companions as well as our children. They were our anchors, as we were theirs. But Alice and the children were quickly tested. That night I received a telephone call from the foreign desk in New York telling me to go to Korea as soon as possible. There were reports that the crew of the *Pueblo*, a US Navy ship that had been seized by North Korea months before, ostensibly because it had ventured into that country's territorial waters, was to be released. So the next morning I flew to Seoul on my way to Panmunjom in the demilitarized zone of Korea, leaving my family behind on their first day in Asia. As Alice later described the experience, "There I was. I didn't know a soul in the whole country. I couldn't speak a word of Japanese. Nobody in the hotel spoke a word of English. The next day all three of us came down with the flu. We couldn't find a doctor. The next day there was an earthquake. I was terrified."

I, however, was having fun. After less than a month in Asia, I was already reporting from a second country. I checked in to the New Korea hotel in Seoul, got on the elevator to go to my room, and nearly choked on the smell. The other passengers in the elevator had been eating kimchi, a Korean sauerkraut made with large amounts of garlic and hot red pepper that gave off a strong—and, at first encounter, almost overpowering—odor. When I started eating the stuff, however, I stopped noticing the smell. We now frequently eat kimchi at home in the US.

South Korea in the 1960s was a repressive quasi-dictatorship under its then president, Park Chung-hee. It had not yet entered its period of rapid economic growth that brought its people a modicum of prosperity then unknown in Asia outside of Japan and Singapore. The *Times* office was in a dingy office building permeated by the scent of human waste. The office was presided over by Sam Kim, our Korean stringer, interpreter, and office manager. A cheerful and helpful guide, Sam, as I was later told, was also an operative for the KCIA, the Korean Central Intelligence Agency. His connection proved useful to me once when I was stopped at gunpoint by South Korean soldiers for taking photos of a defense installation near the demilitarized zone. After Sam explained who I was, the general to whom I had been taken cordially dismissed me. But my confiscated film was not returned.

The demilitarized zone is a two-mile-wide strip of uninhabited land along the 38th parallel between North and South Korea that was established as a buffer between the two countries by the armistice that suspended hostilities in the Korean War in 1953. That unresolved, uneasy peace has now lasted more than half a century and, as of this writing, seems as fragile as ever. In the middle of the zone stands Panmunjom, an installation set up for meetings between the North Koreans and United Nations forces to meet for resolving disputes. If the *Pueblo* crew were to be released, it would be here. After I spent a few hours staring through the windows of the squat building where the two sides met, it was clear that the crew was not going to be freed, at least not then. (They were, months later.) I did, however, get an idea of how hostile the two sides remained. A row of US soldiers stood almost face-to-face with their North Korean counterparts outside the building. Suddenly—why I do not know; perhaps someone said something—the two sides started to shove and punch one another. It continued for perhaps a half-minute until a North Korean officer emerged from the building and barked an order and the combatants reluctantly parted. I was later told that this was a fairly common occurrence and reflected the dangerously low flashpoint that could end the armistice. Both sides assigned the biggest, toughest men in their armies to guard duty in Panmunjom. It was the age of chivalry redux—hostilities between nations reduced to single combat between selected champions.

The demilitarized zone, interestingly, has become one of the most bountiful wildlife preservation areas in Asia because of the absence of human activity there.

As it turned out, my orders to go to Korea were a preview of my duties throughout the time I was based in Tokyo. I became, in effect, the *Times*'s troubleshooter for East and Southeast Asia (not, however, for China, which was closed to American journalists at that time). I would be lying asleep in my bed when, usually at four in the morning, the phone would ring. I would wake up with a start, bang my head against the bookshelf just over the low headboard, and hear an editor on the foreign desk in New York (where it was four in the afternoon) say something like "Rioters in Manila have just thrown bricks through the window of the US embassy. Get there right away and see what's going on." The New York editors seemed to think that getting from Tokyo to the Philippines was like taking the subway from Times Square to the Bronx instead of a twelve-hour flight with a changeover in Bangkok. Nevertheless the next day I would be on a plane to Manila. Or to Indonesia to write about the Suharto dictatorship, which had replaced the Sukarno dictatorship. Or to Singapore to write about the burgeoning economy there. Or to Taiwan or Thailand or Malaysia. Or Vietnam.

It was mostly wonderful—an all-expenses-paid tour of some of the most beautiful and exotic places in the world. Every place I went, a *Times* stringer—a contract reporter—smoothed my way by setting up interviews, guiding me around, and acting as an interpreter. I stayed at luxurious hotels and in dirty fleabags. I sampled and came to love the food of all the countries I visited. I could write whatever I wanted because there was no editor within ten thousand miles to tell me what to do. Once I was traveling by car with a driver from Jakarta, on the western part of Java to Surabaya on the far eastern tip of that island. It was a three-day trip. We started driving early to take advantage of the cooler part of what could be a brutally hot day. One day, just after sunrise, I got out of the car to relieve myself at the edge of a broad swath of rice paddies. I looked out across the lush green landscape where a group of women wearing big conical straw hats were bent over planting rice, and beyond them stood a line of palm trees and, in the distance, a smoking volcano, and thought, *I can't believe I am getting paid to do this.*

There was a downside, of course. I spent about two-thirds of my time in Asia away from Japan and Tokyo, meaning away from my wife and children. They coped very nicely, but I missed them. On two occasions the *Times* management, probably feeling a bit guilty about keeping me away from my family, paid for Alice to accompany me on one of my long reporting trips. I took sporadic lessons in Japanese, but being away from the country for so long, I never learned much more than enough to get me around in a taxi or order a meal in a restaurant. I saw little of Japan outside Tokyo but enough to know that it is a lovely country. Coming back from a trip to Indonesia, in July 1969, I joined my family at a cabin at a place called *Nojiri-ko* (Lake Nojiri) in the mountains about five hours by train from the big city. It was a pretty spot, a big clear lake surrounded by heavily wooded mountains. (Although a densely populated, industrial country, much of Japan is forested. The Japanese export their deforestation by importing most of their timber from places such as Indonesia, the Philippines, and Thailand, and from the US, Canada, and Russia. Japan's appetite for wood has left large swaths of these countries deforested.)

The cabin was a bare bones kind of place. The water supply came from a hand pump about a hundred yards away, and the icebox was a small cave dug into the mountain half-filled with snow from the previous winter. The beds were ropes strung over a wooden frame and covered with a thin rubber pad. We loved it.

After I had been there only a few days, however, a boy pedaled laboriously up the mountain bringing me a telegram. It was from the *Times* foreign desk. Nerve gas had escaped from a US Army facility on the island of Okinawa. Go check it out. It took two days to get to Okinawa from *Nojiri-ko*, and by the time I got there, the story was old. No one had been seriously injured, and the leak had been stopped. July 20 was a beautiful, sunny day on the island, but I was not interested in the outdoors that day. Sitting in my darkened motel room, I stared at a television screen of grainy, flickering gray-and-white images of the landing module *Eagle* descending to the moon and at astronaut Neil Armstrong stepping onto the moon's surface, leaving the first human footprint on an extraterrestrial body. I was riveted to the screen, but I gradually became aware of talking and laughing outside my room window. I parted the curtain and saw a group of people, all of them American I think, lounging around the pool seemingly oblivious to the fact that one of the most momentous and exciting events in all of history was being acted out at that moment.

Like millions of others, I was awed by the technological achievement and human bravery that had sent men to the moon and brought them back safely. But like others, I have sometimes wondered whether it was worth all the money and effort that otherwise could have been used to improve the human condition here on Earth. The moon is not my kind of place. It is dead and sterile and silent. Places should be filled with life and color and growing things; noise and music and the sound of human voices or the song of birds. I would not want to visit the moon. Or maybe I would if I could be there for only a few moments, just long enough to gaze at the blue Earth from space.

As I noted at the beginning of this chapter, I had little social contact with Japanese people while I lived in Tokyo, but I did get to know one man fairly well, or so I thought. His name was Yukio Mishima, and he was a writer. He was, in fact, one of Japan's greatest and most prolific writers of the twentieth century, producing a stream of extraordinary novels such as *The Temple of the Golden Pavilion, The Sound of Waves, Confessions of a Mask,* and his tetralogy, *Sea of Fertility*, as well as short stories, plays, poetry, and essays. Mishima was also something of an oddity, a man of many interests and activities. He studied karate, swordsmanship, and *kendo*, a kind of combat with wooden staves. He was an assiduous bodybuilder. He acted in Japanese gangster movies and posed for nude photographs. An activity that brought him some notoriety in Japan was creating his own small army, a group of young men he trained in military discipline and weaponry. Early in my stay in Japan, I wrote an article about right-wing extremists and institutions in Japan and included Mishima and his little army. The next day I received a phone call from him. He was upset that I had classified him as a right-winger and wanted to explain why I was mistaken. We agreed to meet for lunch the next day.

As soon as we sat down, Mishima, a short, compact, handsome man, launched into a monologue in fluent English that lasted much of the afternoon. I don't recall him actually eating anything. The reason he formed his army, he explained, was to do something to restore Japanese culture and values, much of which, he said, had been lost in the twentieth century. His army, he said, was an attempt to re-instill the tradition of *bushido*, the code of honor of the samurai warrior. In its rush to become a world power, Japan had westernized not only its weaponry but also its code of military conduct and in so doing had lost the samurai spirit. The military junta that had led Japan into World War II was the antithesis of the *bushido* tradition. But all of Japan had lost its way, Mishima insisted. He hoped to set an example to help lead it back to its traditional ways. (Here I might interject that, unlike the Germans, the Japanese I met seemed untroubled by their conduct during World War II and in fact seemed almost obsessively uninterested in that period of history. As far as I could tell, postwar Japan was single-mindedly concentrated on getting and spending.)

The *Times* asked me to write an article about Mishima for its Sunday magazine, so I spent a lot of time with him, following him around to his various activities and sitting down for frequent talks. I grew to like him and thought he might have liked me. He was the one person in Japan whom I found open and accessible, unlike all the others who were never quite comfortable with me as a *gaijin,* a foreigner. Japan, of course, is an island nation, and the people I encountered were truly insular; at least they were when I was there more than forty years ago. If I approached a man or woman on the street to ask directions, I would invariably confront a look of panic that said, *Oh, no. This foreigner is going to speak to me.* But not Mishima. He was interested in the world and seemed ready to engage it. He had an encyclopedic familiarity with Western literature and was always willing to talk books. Despite his desire to return to traditional Japanese culture, he lived a Western lifestyle. He once invited me to his home for dinner. I was surprised to find that he lived in an Italianate villa, with marble Venuses and other rococo bric-a-brac strewn around on tables and hung on walls. We had Scotch whisky, broiled steak and hearts of palm salad. The only thing traditional about the meal was that his wife, an educated, highly literate woman, cooked and served and otherwise kept out of sight.

After dinner Mishima poured cognac and lit a cigar (I turned one down; I had just quit smoking), and we talked about the differences between Japan and the West. In the West, he said, there is a method for everything. If Westerners want to get from the first floor to the second floor, they always build a staircase. But in Japan, people always look at a problem and then think of all possible solutions. To get from the first to the second floor, they might use a staircase. Or they might use a rope or a ladder or even jump to the second floor. There was no one method. He added, whimsically I think, that in India they have a third way. They sit on the first floor and imagine themselves on the second but never actually get there.

At one point I asked why he bothered to spend so much time lifting weights. He replied, "I intend to die young and want to have a good-looking corpse." Then he laughed. I laughed with him.

That evening was the last I saw of Mishima. I was unceremoniously transferred to the Washington bureau in the summer of 1970. A couple of months later, Mishima led his little army to the headquarters of the Japanese Defense Ministry and gave a speech demanding that the military return to the code of *bushi-do.* Then he plunged a short sword into his abdomen in the act of *seppuku,* ritual disembowelment. As he lay on the ground, his second-in-command beheaded him with another sword and then also committed suicide.

I never understood Japan or the Japanese. Nowhere in all the places of the world that I have lived in or visited did I feel so alien, not even among the Germans who had murdered millions of my co-religionists. It is probably my fault. Had I stayed there longer, I might have come to appreciate that interesting land. I certainly enjoyed its culture, its kabuki and noh dramas, its elegant old architecture, its beautiful gardens, its samisen music, and even its slow, ritualized sumo wrestling.

But it was one place that, in the end, eluded me.

Alice and I standing in front of the Barn looking down toward the
pond. October 2012.

My father's parents, Bessie and Philip. Both died before I was born.

My mother's parents, Minnie and Abe, an important presence in my life until I was a young adult.

(left) Me at six years old with my father Sidney posing fashionably in front of the much-loved Buick.
(right) My mother Sylvia at age 31 during a happy trip to Florida.

The Barn under construction, with the 150 year old beams and posts installed over a foundation made from stone walls on our land.

Granddaughter Sophie standing in the pond and grandson Adam on the bank, both hunting for tadpoles.

Daughter Alexa, six years old, standing in the court of our apartment complex in Bad Godesberg, Germany. Occupied by foreign diplomats and journalists, the complex was dubbed the "Golden Ghetto" by town residents.

Our house in Tokyo. Note the walls and fortress-like appearance of the exterior. The interior was traditionally Japanese, filled with light and charming.

Me on the black beach in Bali. The figure in the distance is a young mother who had approached us while singing a lullaby to her baby.

Children surrounding Alice in a remote village on Bali after a rain-storm. Although they seem solemn in the photograph, many of them ran up to us laughing and touching us when we entered the village unannounced.

Giraffes eyeing us warily over the top of an acacia tree in the Rift Valley in Kenya. These were the first big wild animals I had ever seen outside a zoo.

While on a reporting trip, I visited a Masai kraal, an enclosed settlement, in Kenya's Masai Mara wildlife preserve.

The rear of our house in Chevy Chase Village, Maryland, just over the border from the District of Columbia. We lived there for 27 years.

The New York Times team in Times headquarters trying to pry a coherent story out of the massive transcript of the Nixon tapes in 1974, a short while before President Nixon was forced to resign. I am at the typewriter in the center of the photo.

Shaking hands with President Ford during a visit to the Oval Office with some other members of The Times's Washington Bureau. The white-haired gentleman to my right is Clifton Daniel, then the Bureau chief, who was married to President Truman's daughter Margaret.

President Ford pointing to me (standing center with my arm raised) for a question at a White House press conference in the Rose Garden. Two places to my right, with a Prince Valiant haircut, is Tom Brokaw, then also a member of the White House press corps.

(left) Alice in the valley of Yosemite National Park. She accompanied me while I was gathering material for a series of articles on the state of the national park system.
(right) Me in Prudhoe Bay, Alaska, above the Arctic Circle, at Mile Zero of the Trans-Alaska Pipeline. The woman behind me is an oil company employee.

A row of traditional houses in England's Cotswold district near where Alice and I spent a summer month in a thatched cottage. The Cotswolds have somehow retained the flavor of 19th century pastoral simplicity.

CHAPTER 8

A MYSTERIOUS PLACE
Bali

We stood on the jet-black sand looking out over the cobalt-blue lagoon when a figure emerged from a tiny thatched hut a few hundred yards down the empty beach and started to walk toward us. As the figure approached, we saw it was a young woman with delicate features, wearing a sarong and carrying an infant in her arms. She swayed gently as she crossed the sand. When she was almost upon us, we heard her singing a strange, sweet melody in a low voice to the baby. She stood singing a few feet in front of us, as she stared at us curiously. Then, still singing, she turned away and walked slowly back to the hut. Her song quickly faded away in the wind that rushed past us from the sea. She vanished into her hut a few moments later. It seemed almost like a dream.

The three of us—Alice, I, and the young driver who had brought us to this beautiful and, to two Westerners, strange and alien but somehow perfect place—were alone again on the black sand. The only sounds were the keening wind, the slap of waves, and the rattling fronds of oil palms.

Although tourists were already coming to Bali in large numbers by 1969, the year of our visit, the black beach was difficult to reach, and visitors to it, our driver told us, were rare. He had taken us on a spine-wrenching drive down a dry riverbed to get there. The black sand, he explained, was pulverized lava that had originated in Bali's still active volcanoes. Throughout the island, streams sliced deeply into this soft volcanic soil, and the terraced paddies cut by the rice farmers descended layer after deep green layer as far as the eye could see. Although Bali is densely populated, away from the towns and tourist centers it is possible to imagine oneself in a remote time and place. Villages are tucked almost invisibly into the folds of the landscape, and the figures stooped over in the distant rice paddies could have inhabited the dawn of the agricultural epoch.

For a few minutes, we stood on the black sand without talking then walked off the beach and across the riverbed. On the other side, up a gentle slope, was a wide cave, the front of which had been elaborately carved with figures from Hindu mythology. It was a bat cave, our driver explained, and sacred to the people of the island. The Hindu rites of the Balinese people contain strong elements of animism. We walked a few feet into the cave, and when our eyes became accustomed to the dim light, we could see the bats, thousands of them, seemingly dripping from the high roof of the cavern. Again we stood in silence, half-stunned by the strangeness of the place, as well as by the intense, acrid smell of the guano that covered the cave floor.

This was my second trip to Bali. The first time I had come alone on a reporting trip and had been entranced by the beauty and mystery of the place. I unfortunately had booked a room at the Intercontinental Hotel, a modern high-rise, the first on the island, an antiseptic structure that seemed totally inappropriate in such a lush setting. But that evening my driver, the same young man who brought us to the black beach on my second trip, took me to see a dance performance at a nearby temple. I sat on the damp ground inside the ornately carved walls, feeling enveloped by the hot, humid darkness, the scent of clove-infused cigarettes, and smoke from the flickering torches that dimly illuminated the temple interior.

There were other Westerners around, but most of the spectators seemed to be locals. A group of musicians sitting along the far wall played unfamiliar but appealing music on native instruments—a kind of xylophone, gongs, drums, and wooden flutes. The music, I learned, was called *gamelan*. It was native to the Indonesian archipelago, and the Balinese version used a five-tone scale but had been influenced in the twentieth century by the rhythms and dynamics of Western music. It was like nothing I had heard before, but to me, at least, was much more accessible and pleasing than the dissonant twelve-tone music that was fashionable among Western composers for much of the twentieth century. The first dance was a solo by a lovely,

136

slim young woman in an elaborate, gold-encrusted costume. Her movements, particularly of her head and fingers, were precise and formal yet sinuous and elegant. She was followed by a group of lithe, bare-chested men performing an energetic "monkey dance" with much leaping and whirling accompanied by rhythmic chants and shouts. It was both amusing and riveting. The total experience of the temple dance was like an immersion into a warm, dark amalgam of primitive rites and sophisticated aesthetic.

There is gentleness to the Balinese character that seems to be shaped by both their landscape and their art (although there are darker shadows lying dormant in the hearts of the people of Bali). It is a place very much of the natural world and yet humanized as well. The island itself—its landscape and its texture—has been shaped for endless generations by the people, their economy, and their culture. I suppose that is true of virtually every place on Earth, but it seemed so apparent on the island.

From childhood on, almost every islander engages in some kind of artistic endeavor: music, dance, painting, sculpture, woodcarving, or *wayang* shadow puppetry. Entire families work together on artistic projects. One sunny afternoon, Alice and I were walking down a street in Ubud, a small town that attracts both Balinese and foreign artists, when we came upon a family of a husband, wife, and two boys carving a Garuda, a bird god of Hindu mythology and a leitmotif of Balinese art, out of stone. When we paused to look at their nearly completed work, the husband asked if we would like to buy it. The price he set was the equivalent of two dollars. We immediately agreed and said we would come back the next day when it was completed. When we returned, the Garuda was ready for us, neatly tied up in straw. There was, however, one difficulty we had not thought about—how to get the sculpture back to our home in Tokyo. It was about two feet tall and weighed at least forty pounds. We resolved the problem by upgrading the airline ticket for Alice, who was returning to Japan while I went on to Jakarta to do some more reporting, to first class. She flew home sharing her seat with the Garuda. It has ever since stood fierce guard in the front hall of every place we have lived.

While in Bali I learned several instructive lessons in cultural differentiation, one of them from my young driver, whose name, I am ashamed to say, I cannot remember. He approached me at the airport as soon as I passed through customs on my first visit to the island and persisted in offering me his car and services as a driver—at a substantial price of course. Although I was wary of such solicitations, he seemed like a clean-cut young man, and I accepted. I am glad I did; he was valuable not only as a driver but also as a guide, interpreter, and companion in a place where I knew absolutely no one. But the next morning, when he picked me up at the hotel, he turned around after a driving for few minutes and asked me politely, "Do Americans bathe themselves?" "Why, yes," I replied. "In fact I showered just before I left the hotel." He said not another word on the subject, but the next morning he showed up with a small vial of perfume, which he held frequently to his nose throughout the day and on subsequent trips. I realized with a shock that I must have a rank smell to these people, almost certainly because of the difference in our diets. As an American I eat a substantial amount of meat while the Balinese, and probably most other Asians at the time, lived on a diet that consisted chiefly of rice, vegetables, fruit, and some fish.

While on my second and, I think, last trip to Bali, my wife and I took a stroll through Denpasar, the island's principal town. Alice, who had and has superb legs—if I do say so myself—was wearing one of the very short miniskirts then in fashion and a short-sleeved blouse. We were walking along a shaded side street when we saw a Balinese couple of roughly our age walking toward us from the opposite direction. The attractive young woman was bare-chested, as was the custom on the island, but her legs were chastely covered by an ankle-length sarong. As we passed each other, I cast a surreptitious sidelong glance at the woman's bare breasts. As I did so, I observed the man casting a surreptitious sidelong glance at my wife's bare legs. We both looked hastily away. What we find erotic, I realized, naively late I suppose, has as much to do with social custom as with biology.

One afternoon, after a heavy rain shower, we got out of the car in a remote part of the island far from towns and tourist haunts to look around at the glistening emerald landscape and to breathe in the bracing air. As we stood, we heard the sound of laughter nearby. We followed a narrow but well-beaten path through a wood toward the sound of the laughter and soon came to a small village that consisted of two lines of elongated thatched huts. Between the huts was a wide grassy lane dotted with large puddles from the just ended rain. A dozen or more children were splashing in the puddles, laughing, and chattering as they played. When they spotted us, many of the children ran to our sides, touching us and giggling while several of their elders watched smilingly from the narrow platforms of their thatched longhouses. The sun suddenly blazed out, turning the droplets of water on the grass into a brilliant multitude of twinkling jewels. The air around us became radiant with the golden light that is characteristic of the island but that I have never seen elsewhere.

When India's Prime Minister Nehru was returning from the Bandung Conference of nonaligned nations in Jakarta in 1955 he stopped over on Bali on his way home. So entranced was he by the lush beauty of the island and its aura of freshness and innocence that he announced he had seen "the morning of the world." With its gentle, pastoral people, its verdant landscape, pure air then free of pollution, and blue surrounding ocean, Bali did seem to us to be a kind of paradise, a mirage of that far-distant Eden that we in the West can barely envision.

But a seed of evil lies under even this lovely garden. In the civil war that followed an attempted coup d'état by Indonesia's Communist Party in 1965, the island was drenched in blood. The people turned on the communists with unrestrained ferocity and also used the war as an excuse to settle old scores with neighbors. By the time the killing stopped, at least eighty thousand people had been beheaded, hacked to death, or burned with gasoline. I talked to an American missionary who had lived on the island for nearly twenty years who said, "I never suspected the Balinese had murder in them. I always knew them as the most peaceful, artistic, and gentle people in the world. But in December 1965, they were like butchers. It was almost as if they were in a trance."

I have not been back to Bali since 1969, but I know another kind of serpent has taken over the island, less murderous but ultimately more destructive of its beauty, its art, and its innocence. The insatiable appetite of market capitalism is increasingly engorging much of the island and its economy. Tourism entrepreneurs, real estate developers, and others, often from Java or elsewhere, are exploiting its landscape and people for profit. The day we flew out for the last time was the day the island's jetport opened for the first time, opening the way for direct flights from virtually any place in the world. The island already had its first prostitutes—imported from Java—and there was talk of gambling casinos being opened. Since then the island has been profoundly altered by commercialization and westernization, according to all I have heard. Bali's once pristine environment has been an early victim. There is now inadequate fresh water for Denpasar because supplies have been preempted for resorts. Dredging has resulted in erosion at several beaches. Limestone from offshore reefs was quarried to build hotels. The government is planning to divide the island into twenty-one "tourist zones." A development company from Java plans to build a resort and golf course virtually next to one of the island's holiest Hindu temples. A water park complete with slides has been built on Kuta, one of Bali's most handsome beaches. A geothermal station to supply electricity to resorts is being erected at the sacred mountain lake of Bedugul. And the traditional and high culture of the island is being eroded. A reporter for *Asiaweek* magazine noted, "Even well-heeled Balinese would rather hang out at Kuta's Hard Rock Café than watch a classical dance." There has been talk of building a forty-story-high Garuda as a tourist attraction. As in many other places in the world, beauty and culture are being obliterated in the name of development and money.

As a distant foreigner enjoying a comfortable material life, I am in no position to make any moral judgments about what is taking place on Bali. It is likely that development is providing a welcome economic windfall for the island and has helped improve the standard of living of many of its people. But I cannot help regret what is happening to a place I fell in love with at first sight. I probably will never go back.

Modern transportation and communication and the globalization of once local, then regional and national economies, for all of the benefits and blessings they have given us, have inflicted an irreparable loss on the human soul and spirit. They have taken from us the strange places, the mysterious places, the hidden places. When I was young, I had a board game called Cargoes. The object was to move your ship around a flat map of the world, stopping at as many ports of call as possible to pick up cargoes of goods, which would then be sold when your ship returned to its starting point. I would take on a cargo of cloves at Trincomalee, copper at Valparaiso, palm oil at Surabaya, and diamonds at Durban. I would daydream about these faraway places and wonder what they were like and whether I would ever see them or any distant and exotic places.

When I was grown, I was lucky enough to have a job that took me to some of these and many other places I had heard and dreamed about. But these places have become with each passing year less distant and mysterious. The world has been explored, colonized, and touristed. I no longer have to dream about faraway places. I can go to them anytime I have accumulated enough frequent flyer miles and dollars in our bank account. Once there I will be surrounded by other Americans and Europeans, and Japanese and Latin Americans with frequent flyer miles. I am glad to have this freedom of the world, but some things that were very important—adventure, astonishment, freshness, remoteness, mystery—are gone forever.

I have one more story to tell about Bali. It is a story that starts but does not end on the island. Alice and I were walking along the virtually empty Kuta Beach when we encountered another American, a tall, slender man, very handsome but boyish looking. He introduced himself as Sean Flynn and said he was a photojournalist. Only well into a conversation that lasted most of the afternoon did we realize that he was the son of Errol Flynn, the dashing, dissipate movie actor and that he himself had acted in a few movies including *Son of Captain Blood*, a sequel to one of his father's famous films. My wife and I both took to him right away. Unlike his father, he seemed wholesome and modest and said he did not like the Hollywood lifestyle. He obviously was well educated and sensitive and like us was entranced by Bali. In fact, he told us, he had taken a ninety-nine-year lease on a house right next to Kuta Beach and would return to live there and immerse himself in photographing the island and its people—but he had accepted one more reporting assignment to earn some more money. He had spent a lot of time covering the war in Vietnam and would make one last trip there.

As it turned out, I was in Vietnam at the same time, on assignment for the *Times*, but I didn't see Sean Flynn again. On April 6, 1970, he and another photographer named Dana Stone rode together from Saigon on rented Honda motorbikes toward the Cambodian border, looking to get pictures of the first incursions by US forces across that border. They never came back.

I heard later that they had both been killed when they rode their bikes across a mined section of the road and for many years that is what I believed. But I recently punched in Flynn's name on the Web and was surprised to find a detailed report about him on the POW Network. It turned out that Flynn and Stone had not died on that April day. Instead they had been captured by North Vietnamese or Viet Cong soldiers, who later turned them over to the brutal Khmer Rouge in Cambodia, where the two of them were executed early in 1971, allegedly because they were suspected of being CIA agents.

Every now and then, I think about our meeting with Flynn on Bali and I wonder who is living in that house on Kuta Beach.

CHAPTER 9

THE SADDEST PLACE
Vietnam, 1970

While on assignment in Vietnam during the war, I learned the value of my life, almost to the penny.

I had been sent there from Tokyo in the early spring of 1970 to reinforce the *Times*'s Saigon bureau after the United States began its military incursions into Cambodia. When I arrived, other members of the bureau were too busy and preoccupied to give me much direction or advice about what to cover or where to go, so I tried to come up with my own story ideas. One was to describe how the war was affecting the lives of ordinary Vietnamese people.

On a hot April morning a couple of weeks after I arrived, I drove in a jeep along with a Vietnamese interpreter into the dusty square of Phulol, a so-called "pacified village" about thirty miles southeast of Saigon. Almost all of the trees in fields around the village were bare of leaves, probably the result of the spraying of Agent Orange, a toxic defoliant widely used by the US military during the war. The square was empty except for an old woman sitting at a table with a few forlorn mangoes and bananas for sale, and a man wearing the uniform of a South Vietnamese popular forces militiaman—a "friendly." As we slowly drove up, the soldier, bleary-eyed and unsteady on his feet, raised his hand in a signal for us to stop. After staring at me for a moment, he raised his M16 carbine, pointed it at my chest, and began to bark in rapid Vietnamese, the weapon weaving erratically back and forth. My interpreter spoke back, and the dialogue continued for a minute or two before the soldier slowly lowered the carbine.

"What was that all about?" I asked.

"This man is drunk," my interpreter replied. "He said he would kill you if you did not buy him a case of beer. But I got him to settle for one bottle."

So now, through the infallible dynamics of market capitalism, I know the precise value of my life—the price of one bottle of beer.

I had arranged beforehand to meet with the village chief, Nguyen Van Hai, a forty-two-year-old wounded war veteran. I found him inside a sweltering wooden shack, which, until the war closed in on the village, had been a shop and restaurant owned by a Chinese merchant. The merchant, who sat in the back of the dark room, said he had to shut down his business because "people don't come here anymore."

Mr. Hai offered glasses of iced beer to his visitors and spoke quietly about the effect of the war on Phulol. The village had become much poorer and emptier, he said. Because of the fighting swirling around it, there was far less land available on which people could grow the fruit that had sustained their local economy. Most of the trees had been cut down to give less cover to Viet Cong soldiers. There also were few young men around now because most of them had been drafted into the South Vietnamese army. Other villagers had moved away, leaving only a fraction of the prewar population behind. Even the woman selling fruit in the square, he said, was a former resident who had moved away and had come back only to tend to her stand. The remaining villagers were growing steadily poorer, in larger part because of rampant inflation that was draining the buying power of their earnings and savings.

After sipping wearily at his beer, Mr. Hai looked up at me and said, "Why don't you send me to the moon on one of your *Apollo* spaceships and let me be a village chief on the moon? I am tired of being a chief here."

"Why do you want to go to the moon?" I asked him.

"Because there is no war there," he replied.

South Vietnam was the saddest place I have ever been. I was there for only a few weeks, but that was long enough to see how thoroughly years of fighting and military occupation had scarred and degraded both the land and the people. Short of being hit by a very large meteor, war is the worst thing that can happen to a place, especially modern, high-tech, pitiless war.

The sadness began to close in on me almost as soon as I arrived at Saigon's Tan Son Nhut airport. No one was there to meet me, so when a villainous-looking man missing an eye and most of his teeth came up and offered in halting English to get me a ride into the city, I agreed. He took me out of the terminal to the parking area, where an even tougher and more villainous-looking man stood next to a dented, rusted old wreck of a car. The two stood talking to each other in low tones, looking up at me several times. Although they may have been decent citizens, and their menacing appearance caused solely by the scars of war, I began to think I had made a serious mistake. Just then a little man came hurrying up and said, *New York Times*? The cavalry had arrived in the nick of time. He was the *Times* bureau driver and took me to the office car, in which sat the office secretary, a pretty young woman wearing the traditional Vietnamese dress, which featured a long slit dress over narrow black pants.

As we drove through Saigon, it was clear that it was once a beautiful city, with wide boulevards lined with trees and French colonial houses set in gardens that must have once been ablaze with tropical flowers. But now the air was foul with smog; most of the trees were dead or moribund because of the carbon, sulfates, and nitrates; and the gardens neglected and disheveled. The streets were clogged with every kind of vehicle, from US Army jeeps and trucks, to ancient Citroens and Renaults, motorcycles, mopeds, and bicycles, and a variety of handcarts. The sidewalks were crowded and noisy. Many of the men were missing limbs, and beggars stood at almost every corner. Swarms of children, many of them dirty and half naked, loitered on the streets. Some of them, hardly more than eight or ten years old, were smoking; I could not tell whether it was tobacco or marijuana. Through the open windows of the car, I smelled heavy exhaust fumes, the spices of Vietnamese cooking, and human excrement.

I was dropped off at my hotel, with instructions as to how to get to the *Times* office just a couple of blocks away. I would be staying at the Continental, an old colonial structure with a wide veranda and a bar with wicker furniture and slowly rotating fans on the ceiling. It could have been a setting for a Somerset Maugham or Graham Greene novel. In fact I think it was. My room was large, with a high ceiling and tall windows crisscrossed with tape to prevent them from shattering if shells exploded nearby. At the end of the long, dark corridor outside my room sat two Vietnamese men who would remain there through the night, supposedly for security.

The *Times* bureau was quiet when I arrived. The only other reporter there was James Sterba, who was throwing darts at a board on the wall. Sterba was often out in the field, and his reports described what it was like for the "grunts," the ordinary soldiers, to be caught in this surreal, sickening war. Sterba, whom I had known as a cheerful young man in New York, was back from the jungle for a few days, taking out his aggression on the dartboard. Terrence Smith, the bureau chief, was out of the office gathering information, and Ralph Blumenthal, another young reporter, was away on leave. That evening, I had dinner with another *Times* reporter, Gloria Emerson, a brilliant writer who had only a short time before escaped from captivity on what was then called the paper's "women's page." Emerson was a tall, elegant, tightly strung, funny woman, whose reporting had, I thought, captured the bizarre quality and futility of the war as well as any of the many *Times* reporters who had passed through the Saigon bureau. At dinner, however, she was most interested in my having my wife send her some attractive Japanese paper from Tokyo with which to line the drawers of the bureau's desks.

That night, as I waited for sleep to come, I suddenly heard the *whump, whump* of artillery shells or rockets exploding, sounding uncomfortably near. I wondered whether the city was being attacked. The next morning when I asked Sterba about the sounds, he smiled and said that those were "outgoing" rounds fired against suspected Viet Cong positions and that I shouldn't worry because the city was safe. But I never felt safe the entire time I was in Vietnam. Just before I left Tokyo, I had quit smoking. I had stopped a couple of times before and then resumed for one reason or another. As I was flying to Saigon I thought that if I could keep from smoking under the conditions I would be facing, I would have the cigarette habit beaten. As it turned out, it was easy. I was so frightened all the time I was in Vietnam that I had a big lump in my throat throughout my stay there. I did not realize the lump was caused by fright. I thought I was sick, perhaps even had a growth in my throat. I visited a doctor who found nothing. So I went about my business, went out into the field, and filed my stories. I had no desire to smoke. By the time I returned to Tokyo, the habit was broken.

One evening Sterba took me around to a few of the bars that lined the Saigon streets. They were jammed with American soldiers and young Vietnamese girls. Many of the girls were slender and pretty and could hardly have been out of their teens. Occasionally one would come up and say, "You wanna party?" or "You want some fun?" When we declined, they would turn away with a dismissive obscenity. If not for the war and its attendant social disintegration, I supposed, most of those young girls would have been with their families waiting for a traditional marriage. Marijuana and stronger drugs were openly for sale at many of the bars, and a fair number of the G.I.s were strung out or drunk, some of them loudly and aggressively.

As curfew time approached, the bars, restaurants, and streets began to empty. When I filed a late story, I had to take my copy through nearly deserted, ill-lit streets to the Reuters bureau a number of blocks away for transmission to New York. There usually were a few figures loitering silently in the shadows and rats occasionally scuttled across the street in front of me. It was not an enjoyable walk. I thought about the young soldiers spending their nights in the jungles surrounded by the very real possibility of sudden death and understood how lucky I was not to be out there, night after night, waiting for terror to explode out of the darkness. Of course it was not entirely or even chiefly luck. I had determined when given the Vietnam assignment to avoid combat situations if possible. I had no romantic ideas about war, no desire or need to test my manhood. I had left a young wife and two very young children back in Tokyo and was not going to risk their future—and mine—if I could help it. I also felt that after so many reporters had been to the war before me, there was little or nothing that I could see or write to add to the truth about the war and or the horrors of men killing one another. And there was the fear—fear of death, of mutilation, of simply witnessing the unspeakable. Years later I read Michael Herr's remarkable *Dispatches*, which brilliantly described the nature of combat in Vietnam in stomach-churning detail, and I inwardly congratulated myself for my long ago resolve to avoid the danger and terror of combat.

One of the more instructive stories I did cover during my stay was the court martial of a young Army lieutenant named James Duffy who had ordered the killing of an unarmed Vietnamese civilian. The trial was held at the big US Army base at Long Binh, about a half-hour drive north of Saigon. Like many military posts, Long Binh was an ugly, barren place. All trees had been removed or defoliated and the soil had been trampled into a hard, concrete-like surface. Not a bush or a blade of grass was to be seen. The trial was held in a bare wooden building next to a concrete bunker, a place to shelter if the base came under artillery attack.

The facts of the court martial were not in dispute. Lt. James B. Duffy, a slender, boyish-looking twenty-three-year-old infantry officer, had given permission to his sergeant, a career veteran, to shoot a Vietnamese farmer named Do Van Man, whom Duffy's patrol had found in a village hut. Duffy later said he thought the man to be a Viet Cong guerilla and admitted he told his company commander that the man had been trying to escape.

What made the case intriguing was that the defense attorney for Duffy, a New York lawyer named Henry Rothblatt, sought to exonerate his client by turning the court martial into a trial of the American conduct of the war in Vietnam. Rothblatt argued that Duffy had not committed murder because he had only been carrying out what he believed to be Army policy of producing the highest possible body count as a measure of military success. The defense also produced as witnesses four young lieutenants, who testified that it was their understanding of Army policy to take no prisoners in combat operations in Vietnam.

One of the Army prosecutors, Captain Robert Bogan, vehemently rebutted the defense. "What the hell are we fighting for here anyway?" he said. "Are we fighting to be murderers? No. We are fighting so that the people here can have the same rights as we do—so that a man cannot be tried and sentenced

and executed by one other man. If we didn't believe these prin-
ciples, we wouldn't be here."

The military judge disallowed the defense argument, and
the court found Duffy guilty of premeditated murder. However,
when the judge informed the court that the verdict carried an
automatic sentence of life imprisonment, the officers sitting as a
jury asked to reconsider. The next day they changed their verdict to involuntary manslaughter, and Duffy was sentenced to
six months of confinement.

What *were* we fighting for in Vietnam? With this distance of
time, it is hard to remember. War is a strange activity, and this
one was odder than most. President Eisenhower had warned
that if Vietnam fell it would cause a domino effect, turning most
of Asia communist and drastically tipping the world balance of
power against the United States. Well, Vietnam did fall, and
eventually the world balance of power did turn drastically. It
turned completely in favor of the United States when the Soviet
Union and Soviet communism collapsed because of the internal
ineffectiveness of its communist system, while its satellites again
became free, independent nations. No countries in Asia or elsewhere have adopted communism since the United States was
defeated in Indochina. As this is being written, my local public
radio station is carrying offers of a "citizens of the world" trip to
Vietnam, including a visit to "one of the most romantic cities in
the world," Hanoi.

Would the world have been different if the United States
had not fought a war in Vietnam? Well, there would be many
thousands of Americans and Vietnamese still alive, un-maimed,
and leading productive lives if we had not intervened there.
With the hindsight of more than thirty years, it would seem
that the war was a foolish, tragic, ultimately meaningless epi-
sode. The upheaval it caused within American society rever-
berates to this day. But who can truly say? Relations among the
nations of the world are a complex business, and seeking to un-
ravel the tangled strands of geopolitics can be an exercise in ex-
treme futility.

There is no doubt, however, that the war was fought in the
spirit of the capitalist ethic. It was, for example, perhaps the
first conflict in which the Army collected the detritus of war

from the battlefield as it fought and then sold the scrap to America's allies in South Vietnam, South Korea, and Taiwan and to commercial bidders. I visited one of the scrap depots, and here, as I reported, is what I found.

> There are huge piles of jeep and truck chassis;
> here the fuselage of an airplane sticks out, and
> there bomb casings are stacked. There are
> mounds of boots, heaps of rubber and of
> canvas, bin after bin of heavy and light
> metals. There are wooden barrels and metal
> oil drums, broken bathtubs and refrigerators,
> long rows of useless typewriters and worn-
> out telex machines. There are twenty-foot
> high piles of helmet liners, endless rows of
> old tires, cans of photographic fluid with
> leaks in them, great heaps of rags that once
> were uniforms, odd electronic parts, and even
> a bin full of battered French horns.

Maybe that was what Vietnam was about—not just making war to save capitalism but integrating war more fully into the capitalist system.

Vietnam was a beautiful country before the war and presumably is again. Even during the conflict there were untouched, quietly pastoral places. Nhon Trach was only a few miles from sad, ravaged Phulol, but it might as well have been on another planet. The village had been settled by Roman Catholic refugees who left North Vietnam after the French withdrew from the country in 1954. When I visited Nhon Trach in the spring of 1970, the villagers were a tough, energetic, and tightly knit community who wanted no part of the Viet Cong, who gave the place a wide berth. The villagers also made it clear that they would resent being shot up by friendly Americans. The village had been spared the brutal ordeal of battle and despoliation. Neat cottages lined clean-swept lanes glowing with bright flowers and fruit-laden trees. It looked to me, as I wrote at the time, "like a nineteenth-century illustration for a book of Mother

Goose rhymes." A cottage noodle-making industry had kept the village prosperous, and its people seemingly were content. When I visited, the chief plucked a mango from a tree, peeled it, and offered to me as we settled under the tree to talk.

The loveliness of the spared village only served to underscore the desolation of the countryside that had been swept by combat, mined, defoliated, and turned into junk heaps. Human activity has been increasingly destructive of the environment and the life it supports in recent centuries, and no human activity has been as destructive as warfare, especially to human life. The inventive genius of our species has now created weapons that could more or less wipe out all life on Earth. But we proceed heedlessly on from one war to the next.

Perhaps human genes have a kind of primate hardwiring that makes warfare and killing an innate need. Our only hope, then, is that at some point in the not too distant future we will be able to genetically engineer our species out of that need.

In one of the letters I wrote to Alice back in Tokyo, I said that most of what I had seen of Vietnam "looked like a blasted landscape out of hell." But then I added, "I am sustained here by thoughts of the cool hills of Massachusetts."

CHAPTER 10

A PECULIAR PLACE
Washington, District of Columbia

I lived in Washington longer than in my native New York City, where I spent my childhood, youth, and part of my young adulthood. Strictly speaking, we did not live in Washington at all but half a block across the District of Columbia line in Chevy Chase Village, Maryland. Even so, downtown was only twelve minutes away by Metro, and a five-minute stroll brought us to shopping, restaurants, and our favorite movie house inside the district. So we considered ourselves to be Washingtonians, even though we were spared many of the indignities heaped upon city residents by its incompetent or corrupt city governments. We lived there, in the same old, comfortable frame-and-stucco house on a pleasant tree-lined street, for more than a quarter of a century. My children grew up there, and we had many friends and neighbors whom we cherish.

Nevertheless, I never felt quite at home in Washington. Despite the many years we lived in that one place, I was never *rooted* there.

Part of the problem, I think, was the manner in which we first came. We had been living in Tokyo and were in the US on home leave, expecting to go back to Japan for at least another year. Three days before our scheduled return, however, the senior editors of *The New York Times* decided they needed me in the Washington bureau immediately. It was halfway through the first Nixon Administration, and they wanted me to help beef up the bureau's coverage of the national economy. I protested that school for my two young children was starting on Monday and that I still had many stories I wanted to do in Asia, but it was to no avail. I grudgingly was given ten days to go back to Japan and pack our household.

"Don't look at me that way. I'm not a monster," said the executive editor, Abe Rosenthal, my boss at the *Times,* as he gave me my marching orders. "Yes, you are," I replied. Of course he was not really a monster, at least not compared to several other editors under whom I had the misfortune to work.

Leaving our children with my mother- and father-in-law (my own mother had died of cancer two years earlier), Alice and I flew to Washington and, in four days, found an apartment hotel to stay in while we waited for our furniture, bought a car, and found what we were told by friends was the best public primary school in the Washington area. After looking at every available home in the school district, we bought the house in which we lived for nearly three decades. It was the smallest house on the block of mostly big, expensive homes, and we could just about afford it. Making those important decisions and allocating all that money in so precipitate a fashion may have been foolhardy. But I had been told that the Washington assignment would last only two years, and then I would be given another foreign posting, so we assumed we were only making temporary arrangements.

We never could shake the feeling that one day the telephone would ring and Rosenthal would tell us to move to a new post within ten days. The two years, however, became four and then six and ten. I was moved to the White House beat as the Watergate scandal was approaching its endgame and obviously did not want to leave that fascinating story or its aftermath during the Ford administration. Our children moved from primary to secondary to high school. Watching them grow mentally and physically was the best part of my life. We brought a puppy home from the local shelter, a sweet, funny mixture of golden retriever and border collie named Tagalong, who was our friend and companion for seventeen years. Along the way we also acquired two kittens, named Nabi and Juba-Juba, from our children and had their company for nearly seventeen years. When we had a chance to go back overseas, my then teenage daughter begged not to be taken from her high school and her friends. Finally I was assigned to cover environmental issues and gradually became so intellectually engaged with them that it was clear that was what I wanted to do with the rest of my life.

So there we were, twenty-seven years later. My little children grew up, went away to college and law schools, got married, and moved permanently away from the Washington area—one to Kentucky and then to St. Louis and Boston, one to Paris and then to New York and Greenwich, Connecticut—and now have almost grown-up children of their own. I left the *Times* to found and publish *Greenwire,* a daily, online digest of environmental news from around the country and the world. Officially I retired from the *Times,* but actually I quit because a couple senior editors, for reasons that displayed appalling ignorance about the nature of the issues, took me off the environmental beat and assigned me to cover the Internal Revenue Service.

By the time we moved away from Chevy Chase, our house was appraised at about ten times what we had paid for it in 1970; we could not afford it if we were moving there today. We—or rather Alice—had remodeled it and furnished it, so it fit us like a glove. We built a small deck protected by an awning that overlooked our backyard, which we cultivated enthusiastically if inexpertly. We grew roses and hydrangeas, tomatoes, greens, and herbs. We tried some other stuff, but those were eaten by bugs or wilted in the hot, humid climate. The yard had a beautiful flowering cherry and a Japanese chestnut tree when we moved in. We planted a willow oak and a white pine and watched them grow to substantial height and girth over nearly three decades. We had friends we loved and neighbors we could count on. I got to know the area so well I could almost drive around it blindfolded. Yet for me it was never truly home.

Probably the chief reason I was never fully at ease there is that Washington is such a peculiar place. It is a company town; the only real business is the Federal government. Almost everyone we knew there either worked for the government, lived on grants and contracts from it, wrote about it, lobbied it, practiced law because of it, or provided the services to keep it going. It has been said that there only two topics of conversation in the city, politics and real estate. Some have suggested sex as a third topic, but in Washington even sex invariably has a political subtext—the effects of presidential and congressional peccadilloes on the nation's governance being only one dramatic example. Sex was, for example, a major theme in the careers of President

Clinton, Gary Hart, Gary Condit, Newt Gingrich, the sanctimonious Congressman Henry Hyde, and the Kennedy boys, not to mention the low comedy provided by the once powerful Congressman Wilbur Mills and his stripper friend Fanny Foxe cavorting in the Tidal Basin or Senator Larry Craig in the airport toilet stall.

By its nature, Washington is a society of impermanence, even more so than the norm in our peripatetic society. Friends, acquaintances, colleagues come and go like the seasons with each new administration, each new Congress, and even with each change of assignment. When I covered labor, much of my social life revolved around labor leaders, administration officials, and members of Congress and their staff aides involved with labor issues. When I dropped labor and covered only the environment, much of my social circle changed as well. And when I stopped being a Washington correspondent for *The New York Times*, a position that carries with it, perforce, a modest degree of political power and ability to help or harm people, I found that some men and women I had thought of as real friends no longer were inviting us to dinner.

The business downtown of Washington also was a physically transient place while we lived there, a LEGO kind of city. Buildings that I watched being constructed already have been torn down and replaced, usually by equally dull and faceless structures. Bethesda, the next town over from Chevy Chase, was a sleepy little suburban village when we arrived and when my children went to high school there. Today it is a high-rise commercial and financial center.

Yet Washington, and its extension into Montgomery County, Maryland, is one of the more beautiful urban areas in the world. Or, at least, much of the Northwest quadrant of the city that we lived and worked in is beautiful. When we first arrived in Washington, Arthur Olsen, who had been my bureau chief when I first joined the *Times* bureau in Bonn, Germany, and who later became a career diplomat, and his wife, Chela, took us one evening on a tour of the city. They drove us around the downtown section, pointed out the White House, and whisked us through Georgetown with its charming homes, pricey shops, and lively street life. Then they parked near the Lincoln Memorial and walked with us up the steps to stand at the feet of the brooding statue of Lincoln. "Look," Arthur said, pointing down the long, wide mall. Looking out we saw the Washington Monument towering in front of us and, directly in line another couple of miles away, the great white dome of the United States Capitol. The Mall, monument, and Capitol were bathed in the glowing light of a full moon. It was a breathtaking moment.

Like many American cities north and south, Washington remains a more or less rigidly segregated community. African-Americans and a smaller numbers of Latin Americans and Asians inhabit most of the city. Whites live chiefly in the northwestern part and its near suburbs in Maryland and Northern Virginia.

Chevy Chase Village, just over the district line, is a lovely place, one of the first planned communities in the country, with streets lined by old trees that arch into a tunnel and old, big, but for the most part unostentatious, houses set deeply on well-kept lawns and surrounded by carefully tended gardens. In the spring the village is ablaze with forsythia, jonquils, tulips, hyacinth, and the blossoms of azalea, rhododendron, dogwood and cherry. Washington is inside the mid-Atlantic flyway of migrating birds, and our yards and trees and bushes were alive with song and color for much of the year. I think Chevy Chase may be the epicenter of the American gray squirrel population; there were always a half-dozen or so frisking around our lawns or performing acrobatics in our trees. Increasingly, however, the village became a green island, with urban and commercial development lapping at its boundaries.

Some neighborhoods in other parts of the city inhabited by middle-class or wealthy African-Americans are just as pretty and green. But neighborhoods inhabited by poor workers and people on welfare are treeless, arid, and often neglected by the city, even after its administration fell largely into the hands of African-American politicians. I have found this pattern to hold not only all over America but also all over the world. It is the poor and marginalized in almost every urban area that are denied the consolation of natural beauty.

I have long believed that trees, gardens, and lawns are a cause as well as a result of affluence in a community. I also think the contrary is true; their absence is a cause as well as a result of poverty or, at least, of neglect of a neighborhood by its inhabitants and a factor in the descending spiral of communal decay. It is well established that tree-lined streets raise the value of real estate by a substantial amount in most neighborhoods. It is also a fact that they lower energy costs to homeowners substantially, help clear the air of pollution, and have a calming effect on edgy urban nervous systems. Treeless inner city areas enjoy none of these benefits.

Of course, even affluent neighborhoods cannot buy immunity from the devastating effects of urban pollution on the landscape. When we bought our Chevy Chase house, two big pin oak trees stood between our house and the street, both easily more than one hundred years old. The trees were one of the reasons we had been attracted to the house, but they both died within two years of our arrival. Weakened by air pollution, they were unable to survive an attack by a voracious swarm of seventeen-year locusts. From our back porch, the view of the village was dominated by huge old, luxuriantly spreading elms that were the giants of our urban forest. One by one, however, the elms died off, unable to resist the disease and pollution that has tragically decimated the American elm over the last half-century or more. We had a big old elm in our side yard with long branches that curved in a motherly embrace over our roof. We were able to save it, at least as long as we lived there. Every couple of years, we paid several hundred dollars to have the tree injected with a disease-resistant serum. We were skeptical, but we thought it worth a try—and it seems to have worked. When we sold our house, the only request we made of the buyers was that they continue to try to preserve our elm.

Chevy Chase Village is no longer legally reserved for white Christians as it had been until fairly shortly before we arrived. The deed we signed for our house had a restrictive covenant at the bottom of the page warning that "Persons of Hebrew or African extraction may not live on these premises except as domestic servants." But each letter of the sentence had been neatly lined through with a typed slash mark. The covenant had fallen victim, I suppose, to the federal Fair Housing Act of 1964. When we first moved in, however, the old-line white, Protestant establishment had ruled the politics and culture of the town. It was said the village's business began at the font of All Saints Episcopal Church and ended at the bar of the Chevy Chase Country Club, which filled the middle of the village and was closed to all but Christian whites except one or two token Jews. There were no Africans, Latinos, or Asians in the village except for a tiny handful of diplomatic families.

I was undisturbed by the knowledge that we were moving into a neighborhood where Jews might still be unwelcome. On the contrary, I felt a rather warm glow of schadenfreude that our breaching of a WASP stronghold might be causing discomfort to whatever bigots remained in the area. In fact we were made to feel welcome and accepted almost immediately by our neighbors. The day we moved in we found a loaf of home-baked bread left at our door by Ellen McKee, who with her husband, Bill, and daughters, Anne and Katie, lived directly across the street from us. The McKees, and their next-door neighbors, John and Peggy Thomson and their children David and Hillary, became our dear friends and everything one could hope for in neighbors. I want to talk about them a bit because people make places as much as or more than places make people.

Bill McKee and John Thomson both worked for the Central Intelligence Agency. Bill, a tall, bespectacled, scholarly looking man with a gentle manner, was an agent in covert operations. We had known him for years, and he already had retired before he let it drop that he had worked for the CIA. Of course his daughter Katie, who babysat for our children, told us about her father's job almost as soon as we moved in. Bill was the son of a Protestant minister but discovered late in life that he also had Jewish ancestors and spent time in retirement doing research on his Jewish roots in Germany. His wife, Ellen, is a slender, pretty, bright, soft-spoken woman with a ready smile and a multitude of talents, including printing beautiful documents using antique typefaces. John Thomson, a rugged, hearty outdoorsman with a thick mustache and a sly sense of humor, immediately told us he had worked for agency, probably while introducing himself. John grew up in China in a missionary family and had worked in overt operations as a Chinese expert and translator. He and a friend who also had worked at the CIA canoed across the Potomac to Langley nearly every day. John started the Potomac Canoe Cruisers Association, which promoted canoeing on the river and produced a number of Olympic team members for the country. John died a few years ago, and although we were never intimates, his departure has left a hole in our lives. His wife Peggy, a warm, vivacious, fun-loving woman and prolific author of books, chiefly for children, made us feel like old friends from the moment we met. Peggy's mother, who came here from Switzerland, lived in a house next to ours before she died and was also our friend. The McKee and Thomson homes had happy vibes.

The other house next to ours seemed to be just the opposite. When we first arrived, it was occupied by a young couple who seemed happy enough, but when Alice went to their house on some errand a few months after our arrival, the wife opened the door with her face wet with tears. Her husband's job required them to move, she said, but she did not want to leave. Another young couple, Frank and Connie, then moved in. Frank was a tall, handsome, athletic, and charming man who wrote several thriller novels and then worked as a lobbyist for the pharmaceutical industry. Connie—small, attractive, and lively—harbored aspirations toward a career in acting and singing. They had three young sons and seemed like an ideal family. Then one day their family dog came onto our front lawn and started to dig at a dogwood sapling I had just planted. I shooed it away, and Connie came out of her house to take the dog in. She apologized profusely then burst into great sobs. "It's only a tree, Connie," I said. But the dog and tree were not the cause of her misery. Her marriage to Frank was falling apart. After their divorce, Frank brought a new wife to the house, remodeled it, and built a swimming pool in the back yard. Within a few years, that marriage, too, failed and Frank moved in with and then married a handsome divorcée living in a big house just across the street. A couple of years later, Frank died of lung cancer in his fifties. The house was next occupied by the family of a dour building contractor who could barely bring himself to say "good morning" to us and who surrounded his house with floodlights that dimmed the stars in the sky above us.

In time we got to know most of the people living on our long block, and many became our friends. One who did not become a friend was George Will, the pet columnist of the conservative political establishment in Washington, who apparently felt he was of too elevated a social status to consort with his neighbors. He and I had appeared on the same panel on the *Meet the Press* television program, but he never gave the slightest hint of recognition when we passed on the street. I always thought of Will as a kind of journalistic lap dog for the Republican establishment. Another neighbor down the block with whom we had nothing to do was Richard Perle, the neoconservative "Prince of Darkness."

I was, finally, never fully comfortable in Washington. It just didn't feel right, it didn't smell right, it didn't talk or act right, as far as we transplanted New Yorkers were concerned. John F. Kennedy was on target when he described Washington as "a city of Southern efficiency and Northern charm." The climate was wrong for people like us who had grown up in the North. The winters were usually not cold and snowy enough, and the summers were much too hot and humid. Much of DC is built over a swamp, and the air often seemed palpably damp. The sky was rarely a deep blue; a milky haze of moisture almost always dulled it. Sometimes we felt as if we were living at the bottom of a dirty fishpond. In nearly thirty years, I never found a pastrami sandwich or loaf of rye bread that was up to New York City's standards.

Except for Georgetown, Washington's downtown seemed dull and dreary at night compared to the light and liveliness of Manhattan—or, for that matter, of Tokyo or London or Berlin or Hong Kong. Although there were plenty of bright, even brilliant people in and around the government and the media, the intellectual and cultural climate seemed a bit stultifying to us. It is a city where artists and writers other than journalists visit, not live—although Larry McMurtry did run a bookstore there for a while. The Kennedy Center and Arena Stage were oases of music and drama in what was a performing arts desert for much of the time we lived there. We talked about books and music with some of our friends, but most of the dinner party conversation was about politics or politicians—or about real estate. My kids, both budding intellectuals, were miserable in high school—Alexa because clothes and makeup determined the social standing of girls and my son Peter because he did not fit into the jock culture even though he was a well-formed and athletic young man. Even the surrounding countryside of Maryland and Northern Virginia, lovely, rolling farm and horse country bisected by the majestic Potomac River, was not the mountain, lake, and woodland landscape we had cherished in our formative summers. The fault was not Washington's; it was mine. I never fully adapted to an alien habitat. When we moved away, my only regret was leaving our friends behind.

While living in Washington did not feel like being home, working as a reporter there certainly felt like being at the heart of what was important and exciting in the world. (Vietnam during the war also felt like the heart of things, but it was more like the heart of darkness.) Washington is the seat of government of a nation that plays a preeminent role in world affairs as well in the affairs of its own people. When we moved there, the Cold War with the Soviet Union was still in deep chill. Disputes over the economy, the environment, social policy, justice, civil rights, and just about every other issue affecting the lives of the American people—and much of the rest of the world—were argued out, resolved, or exploded into political conflict within the District of Columbia. Richard Nixon was in the middle of the first term of what was one of the most volatile, disruptive and interesting presidencies in the nation's history. Almost every story that came out of Washington was by definition important news. Stories from the Washington bureau usually dominated the front page of the *Times*. Covering Washington is a dream assignment for reporters, and to be in Washington's *Times* bureau is the pinnacle of the newspapering profession—at least it seemed so to me.

The bureau was located in the center of the business district, first on L Street and then on K Street, also known as "Gucci Gulch," because many of the buildings were stuffed with tassel-loafered lobbyists for business, industry, agriculture, and state and local governments. In my last years there, the bureau occupied two floors of the Army-Navy Club building, which overlooked Farragut Square, a small patch of green surrounded by gray structures. There are no skyscrapers in the District of Columbia because of an ordinance that forbids the building of any structure that exceeds the height of the Capitol dome.

The inside of the *Times* bureau looked and sounded like the newsroom of a medium-size city newspaper. There were thirty-five or more reporters and columnists, a half-dozen editors, three or four librarians, news clerks, and, when I first joined the bureau, a team of teletype operators who were gradually discarded after we switched from typewriters to computers that linked directly to the home office in New York. Metal desks piled with papers and books crowded the space, and editors sat at a long desk at the front of the room, with the bureau chief off to the side in a private office. There was a permanent fog of cigarette smoke and a constant background music of ringing telephones, the hum of conversation, and, before we shifted to computers, clacking typewriters and shouts of "Copy!" summoning clerks to collect our stories as they rolled off our machines on multipage "books" of typing paper separated by carbon paper. (Does anybody use carbon paper anymore?) I had given up smoking earlier in 1970 before I joined the bureau, but there was no way I could escape the secondhand smoke of my colleagues' cigarettes. Many years later, when I had left the *Times* and wrote in my own private offices, I found the absence of noise and smoke distracting.

In those years, the bureau was filled with storied journalists. James Reston, one of the great reporters of the twentieth century, had just returned from a stint as executive editor of the *Times*, a job he filled for a time as a favor to the owners of the paper, the Sulzberger family, to resume work as a full-time Washington columnist. Another legendary columnist in the bureau was Arthur Krock, a favorite of President Franklin Roosevelt. He was always to be addressed as "Mr. Krock," unlike Reston, who was "Scotty" to all. Tom Wicker recently had been succeeded as bureau chief by Max Frankel—about whom, more later—who went on to become executive editor of the paper. Russell Baker was another columnist who soon moved his wit and erudition to the New York office.

The reporters were an all-star cast, many of whom I had been reading long before I joined the *Times* and who had helped burnish its reputation as the world's greatest newspaper. They included E.W. Kenworthy, Neil Sheehan, Nan Robertson, Tad Szulc, Edwin Dale, Eileen Shanahan, John Herbers, John Finney, R.W. Apple Jr., Dana Adams Schmidt, Juan de Onis, Robert Semple, and many more. I felt privileged and a bit overawed to be admitted to this high temple of American journalism. The feeling soon passed away, however, amid backbreaking work and the discovery that my colleagues were, like me, ordinary and sometimes flawed mortals.

One of the veteran reporters, who had been a daring foreign correspondent, spending months in the Iraqi and Turkish deserts with Kurdish rebels, had become hopelessly burdened with personal problems, which he sought to drown in alcohol. Inevitably his work declined, and he was gently invited to resign from the paper. At the farewell party the bureau traditionally holds for departing reporters, he said, "The *Times* has been like a mother to me, but sometimes a mother stops loving her child." Then he began to sob. I vowed then and there that when my time came to leave the *Times* there would be no party.

When I arrived in Washington, I let it be known that I would like to write about the environment. I really did not know much about the issues, but my boyhood experiences in the mountains of New York State and my travels through the industrialized wastelands of Europe and the ravaged landscapes of Asia had led me to believe strongly that this was a subject worth writing about. Moreover, the first Earth Day had been celebrated just a few months earlier, dramatically raising the visibility of environmental issues and changing forever the way many Americans looked at the relationship between themselves and the habitat in which they lived, worked, and played. Environmental issues seemed to be creating a lot of news. The Environmental Protection Agency had just been created by the executive order of President Nixon. Congress was then launching what would be one of the great creative legislative spurts in American history with a torrent of landmark laws to protect the land, the air, the water and human and non-human life from the assaults of industry, agriculture, and other human activity.

It would be some years, however, before I started to cover the environment. I was told that the *Times* already had a reporter assigned to write stories about the environment. Gladwin Hill, a veteran reporter then in the paper's Los Angeles bureau, was writing regularly about the issues and, all things considered, was doing a good job. But Washington was the center of environmental policymaking and activism, and the paper was neglecting a lot of significant developments. Nevertheless, Max Frankel told me that environmental stories were not important enough to occupy the time of a *Times* Washington correspondent. I was assigned instead to cover several other beats, including labor, the national economy, and energy policy. As it turned out, there was plenty for me to do.

Frankel was not only my bureau chief but also a neighbor, and our families occasionally exchanged dinners. But I found him to be a cold, judgmental, and autocratic figure, and we were never friends. As far as I am concerned, he was a poor fit both as head of the bureau and later as the top editor of the *Times*. Frankel, who had come from Germany to the US as a boy, had joined the paper as a *wunderkind* out of Columbia and rose rapidly on the news staff, covering the White House during the Johnson Administration. He won a Pulitzer Prize for his coverage of Nixon's visit to China. It always seemed to me, however, that he was excessively deferential to the authority figures, such as the president.

Early in 1971, when I had been at the bureau a few months, I began to notice items in the paper that suggested that the Nixon administration was playing fast and loose with civil liberties such as the right to privacy and due process. It engaged in activities including illegal wiretaps of people such as Daniel Ellsworth, whom it suspected of leaking sensitive information, or otherwise trying to suppress activities the White House considered to be hostile. When I collected a folder of such stories, I went to Frankel and suggested that we start a civil liberties beat in the bureau. He replied that the *Times* could not do anything like that because it would put the paper in the position of *a priori* judgment that the administration was eroding civil liberties. I have since believed that Frankel's unwillingness to see evil in the White House was one of the factors that caused the *Times* to lose the Watergate story, which was blown open and controlled by the *Washington Post*. In fairness, I must also recall that the bureau under his leadership did defy the White House by reporting on the Pentagon Papers.

Many of my stories in the first few months at the bureau had to do with labor strikes—strikes by the railroad unions and by the Teamsters that brought much of America to a grinding halt. Strikes by steelworkers; by Cesar Chavez's fledgling Farm Workers Union; by telephone workers, clothing workers and many more made work stoppages almost a daily occurrence. The strikes had many causes, but together they demonstrated fault lines cracking into the once granite-like United States economy. Inflation was creeping up, and so was unemployment amid deepening economic stagnation. Jobs were being sent overseas as employers sought low-wage workers in a competitive economy that already was beginning to globalize. The industrial Midwest, the engine that drove the American economy and supported American power in the world, was starting to erode into the rust belt—a wasteland of deserted factories and contaminated brownfields.

Among the labor leaders I met was the former Teamsters' president, Jimmy Hoffa, with whom I had lunch shortly after he was released from prison and shortly before he disappeared under circumstances that have still not been unraveled. We talked about his plans for the future and about the state of the Teamsters. Hoffa was jovial at our meeting, but he struck me as the kind of man you would not want as an enemy.

The unions, then still near the zenith of their membership and power, were able to flex their economic and political muscles and win substantial contract improvements for their members. The American Federation of Labor and Congress of Industrial Organizations, then led by George Meany, the gruff, redoubtable former plumber from the Bronx, was then a major player in the nation's economic and political affairs and spoke with authority for American workers—a paid workforce in which women were still a fairly small minority. Meany's decision to withhold federation support for Democrat George McGovern in the 1972 presidential election was a deathblow to McGovern's already ineffectual campaign. But unions have not since been able to demonstrate anything approaching that strength. The labor movement began to lose ground even before Meany died in 1980 at the age of eighty-six as employers became increasingly aggressive and sophisticated in their concerted drives to weaken and decertify unions. The movement's membership, power, and prestige went into steep decline when Meany was succeeded by Lane Kirkland, the federation's articulate secretary-treasurer, who always struck me as a dilettante more interested in having a voice in foreign policymaking and in fighting communism in Poland than in organizing American workers and building the strength of the trade union moment.

Covering the labor beat for the *Times* gave me privileged access to the world of work in the United States. I visited and wrote about a clothing loft in Manhattan, the entry point into the American workforce for generations of immigrants, and watched as elderly Jewish and Italian women and young Hispanic girls bent over their sewing machines. I climbed beneath the surface of Sixth Avenue (it will always be "Sixth Avenue" to New Yorkers of my generation, never "Avenue of the Americas") with utility workers to crawl among the maze of pipes and cables beneath the city's streets. I visited a turbine manufacturing plant in upstate New York and a tire factory in Akron, talked to striking grape pickers in the Coachella Valley of California, striking clothing workers in El Paso, and Jamaican sugarcane cutters forced to live in shameful third world conditions at a camp in Florida. I talked to happy workers at a dog food factory in Topeka, Kansas, who were proud of the creativity of their work. When I was given a highly interesting assignment to find out how a recession was affecting institutions such as school systems, city governments, symphony orchestras, churches, and others, I traveled to many places in the American heartland— Cleveland, Pittsburgh, St. Louis, the campus of Notre Dame University—places until then more unknown to me than Osaka, East Berlin, Surabaya, or Helsinki.

During twenty-one years of working out of the Washington bureau, I continued to travel around the country at frequent intervals and thus had the great good fortune to see more and learn more about the United States than is granted to most of its citizens. I was able to see for myself much of its great natural beauty and sordid manufactured ugliness, the astonishing diversity of its landscape and people and Banana Republic uniformity of its popular culture, its unprecedented wealth, and the unconscionable poverty inflicted on far too many of its citizens amid so much affluence. Having witnessed the xenophobia and unabashed racism of many of the countries I had lived in or visited as a correspondent, I grew proudly conscious of America as a nation where people of many nationalities, races, and religions lived together in relative peace. But I was also dismayed that even after the great civil rights revolution touched off by *Brown v. Board of Education* had swept the country, people of color often were treated as second-class citizens or worse and that religious fundamentalism and political fanaticism were again rearing their intolerant, ugly and dangerous hydra heads.

Covering labor, the economy and the environment often took me to Capitol Hill and into contact with congressmen, senators, and their staff members. Despite its vast size and white marble neoclassical facade, its dominating position on top of the Hill with its sweeping view of the Mall and the city, the Capitol always struck me as majestic rather than grandiose—an edifice that reflected rather than trumped the spirit of democracy. Walking around the building and through its long halls and soaring rotunda, I was sometimes struck almost physically by a sense of the nation's history and tradition. George Washington laid the cornerstone of the Capitol in 1793. The British torched the building during the War of 1812. Great issues such as slavery, the nature of the Union, America's role in the world, and the balance between liberty and equity have been debated in its chambers, sometimes eloquently.

Not all of the building's history is glorious. In his book *The Debt*, Randall Robinson notes that much of the Capitol was built by African-American slaves but the existence and contributions of African-Americans to our country are virtually unrecorded in its paintings and sculpture and that for many years the institution it houses, Congress, perpetuated the underclass role of black Americans.

When I arrived in Washington, there were giants to be found in both houses of Congress and in both political parties, able, ethical, intelligent men, and back then only a few women, who combined a fierce dedication to the public weal with rock-like personal integrity. Among the best were Phil Hart, Mike Mansfield, Ed Muskie, Hubert Humphrey, Walter Mondale, Frank Church, Sam Irvin, Margaret Chase Smith, Robert Stafford, Jacob Javits, Charles Mathias, John Chafee, John Heinz, Morris Udall, Philip Burton, Shirley Chisholm, and a good number of other talented and effective public servants from both political parties. Paul Douglas, the great Senator from Illinois, had been dealt a hard blow by a stroke and retired shortly before I arrived. I used, perhaps abused, my status as a *New York Times* reporter to set up an interview with him, for no other reason than I wanted a chance to meet him. I cannot even recall what I talked to him about. When I visited his home near the city's Rock Creek Park, he was unable to lift his head to look at me, but it was clear that his devotion to his country was undimmed and his passionate eloquence undiminished.

I was also astonished and gratified to find that members of Congress were fully accessible to reporters. One day shortly after I arrived in Washington, I was following some piece of labor legislation and wanted information from the then Senate majority leader, Mike Mansfield. Sitting in the Senate press gallery, I asked my colleague Ned Kenworthy how to approach Mansfield. I was stunned when he told me that any senator would come right off the Senate floor to talk to me. Ned led me down to a lobby off the chamber where I handed a note for Mansfield to an usher. Within minutes Mansfield emerged, led me to his nearby office, offered me candy from a bowl on his table, and spent fifteen minutes answering my questions. I was to find throughout my reporting career in Washington that members of Congress and—usually although not always—administration officials were ready to speak to me as a journalist, although not always happily. Of course, as I was a reporter for the *Times*, the closest American facsimile of an official publication, public officials felt they pretty much had to talk to me, either to reach the public with their agenda or to make sure the paper reflected their views accurately—or to find out if I spelled trouble ahead for them. I also believe that their readiness to speak to reporters showed they understood the importance of the media in a democratic society.

Despite the hundreds of times I did it, I never lost the thrill of watching the democratic process in action as I sat in the press gallery of the House or Senate, scribbling notes as I watched the people's representatives debate and vote on the laws that governed our country.

The conscientious men and women of Congress set the agenda and the tone for much of the nation's substantial progress on issues that ranged from the environment and civil rights to improvements in the status of American workers in the 1960s and '70s. Their tenure provided one of the brighter periods of American democracy. Democracy was also well served by the rising number of women and of African-, Hispanic-, and Asian-Americans elected to represent the American people in recent decades.

The thrill of observing the democratic process was frequently marred, however, by waves of disgust as the people's representatives engaged in petty partisan squabbles or voted against the people's interest to accommodate the corporate lobbyists who underwrote their electoral campaign.

Sadly, the quality of the United States Congress has been badly degraded in recent years by the power of corporate money and right-wing ideology, which are at least as great a danger to American democracy as internal communism ever was and terrorism continues to be. These days the American people often send intellectual and moral pigmies to represent them in those history-filled chambers.

Throughout my time in Washington, however, I continued to come into contact with extremely able and highly moral men and women in all branches of government, including the bureaucracy, totally dedicated to the public weal. One of those I respected most was David Bazelon, a senior judge on the United States Court of Appeals for the District of Columbia, and one of the most brilliant, accomplished members of the bench never to have been named to the Supreme Court. We met at a party, and for some reason, he took an interest in me and we became friends, lunching together at regular intervals. Occasionally he took me to lunch at Milton Kronheim's wine and liquor warehouse in a remote area of the city, which a number of distinguished Washingtonians frequented as a place to have a quiet, private meal.

One day I arrived at Bazelon's chambers and as we were getting into his chauffeur-driven car, he said, "I have a surprise for you today." The car stopped at the Supreme Court building a few blocks away, and Justice William Brennan, one of the great jurists of the twentieth century, in my view, got in. As we drove off toward Kronheim's, Bazelon and Brennan started to discuss a case then before the high court. The case had to do with cotton mill workers exposed to cotton dust, which caused brown lung disease. I was somewhat startled by their conversation. Bazelon had written the opinion in the case for the lower court, and I assumed that the two judges were not supposed to discuss it. So I broke into the conversation saying, "Excuse me, Mr. Justice, but I should tell you I am a reporter and, in fact, have been covering the cotton dust case." Brennan's only response was to draw me into the conversation and ask about my views. When we got to Kronheim's the conversation turned to lesser matters, mostly the Washington Redskins football team, in which both men seemed to take a high interest.

When we got back to Bazelon's chambers, I said, "David, I do understand that conversation about the cotton dust case was privileged."

"Privileged?" Bazelon said. "It was sacred!"

I feel I can tell this story now because both of those great jurists are dead.

I spent one more evening with Justice Brennan at a small dinner party given by our friends Joe Perpich and Cathy Sulzberger. All of us sat spellbound through dinner as Brennan told stories about the court and its justices. Most vivid was his account of what he called Arthur Goldberg's foolish resignation from the court. Yielding to the arm-grabbing blandishments of President Lyndon Johnson, Goldberg had resigned to take the post of US ambassador to the United Nations, allegedly being told he would be the next vice presidential candidate of the Democratic Party. Goldberg hoped he would be the first Jewish vice president, which, of course, did not happen. But his resignation, Brennan maintained, had opened the door to a series of events that produced the conservative court of Rehnquist, Scalia, and Thomas, and their allies on the bench.

David Bazelon died of Alzheimer's disease at a tragically early age. But we continued to be friendly with his wife, Mickey, who remarried and who was one of the liveliest and most fun-loving humans we knew until she died in her mid-nineties.

Richard Nixon was one of the most complex, loathsome, astute, and interesting men ever elected as president of the United States and surely the strangest. Much has been written about his aberrant mental behavior, but his policies and approach to his office are themselves sufficient indications of his oddness. He rose to power pandering to the right-wing crusade against communism, but his social and environmental policies, if not liberal, were not ultraconservative either. An avowed lifelong conservative committed to a free market economy with a minimum of governmental interference, he launched in the early 1970s one of the most radical policies of federal intervention in the economy in the nation's peacetime history. Faced with rapidly rising inflation and a weakening economy, he first froze wages and prices nationwide and then established an elaborate federal bureaucracy to control both wages and prices and set overall economic policy. I was assigned to report on this Rube Goldberg structure, which included a Cost of Living Council, a Price Commission, and a Wage Board. These ad hoc groups reached into nearly every corner of the economy and into the homes of every family. So much for conservative economics.

The whole complicated mess created by the Nixon administration had little lasting effect on the economy, but I had a lot of fun covering it. My stories ran almost every day, many on the front page and in the Sunday "News of the Week in Review." One day during a Price Commission news briefing to explain its procedures, the briefer, an economist named Arnold Weber, explained that prices would be controlled at the wholesale rather than the retail level. When one reporter asked why, since people bought their products at the retail rather than the wholesale level, Weber replied with a grin, "You are obviously not from New York City."

Covering the Nixon program was for me an advanced seminar on macroeconomics. Because I had started out on the *Times* as a reporter in the Business and Financial News department, I was typecast throughout my career with the paper as an expert on economics. In fact my only background in the subject had been an introductory undergraduate course through which I more or less dozed during a hot spring semester. Over the years I gradually learned quite a lot about fiscal and monetary policy, international trade, the structure of the industrial and agricultural sectors, the relationship between economics and politics, and many other aspects of the discipline, but it was trial-and-error, on-the-job training.

I also got to know the business executive who led the Cost of Living Council, a pleasant, smiling young man named Don Rumsfeld and another pleasant but serious young official on his staff named Dick Cheney.

On June 17, 1972, five men were arrested while breaking into the headquarters of the Democratic National Committee offices at the Watergate, a cluster of buildings along the Potomac River that housed upscale residential and commercial space. Dismissed as "a second-rate burglary" by the White House, the break-in, or rather the investigation that followed, unleashed a series of startling, ugly revelations about widespread illegal and unconstitutional activities by the Nixon administration. These revelations in turn led to the dismissal and imprisonment of many of the nation's highest officials, including the Attorney General, John Mitchell, and after a long, increasingly desperate rearguard defense by the White House and a confrontation with Congress that threatened to disrupt the country, the resignation of President Nixon himself—the first time in the nation's history that a president had resigned from his high office.

The cynical disregard for the law of the land at the highest level of government created a time of agonizing crisis for the nation and a real threat to its democratic and constitutional traditions. But it also was a time of high political drama—and, of course, red meat for Washington reporters. I was still writing about labor and economics, but as the Watergate story continued to unfold, I grew desperately unhappy about not having a part of what was clearly one of the great stories of our time.

One morning Bill Kovach, the bureau news editor and probably the most competent and courageous editor I worked for in my long career with the *Times*, asked me if I was free to cover a hearing by a subcommittee of the House of Representatives' Government Operations Committee. The subcommittee was inquiring into public spending on President Nixon's vacation homes, one in Key Biscayne, Florida, and one in San Clemente, California. Money was being spent by the Secret Service on the grounds and houses of the two retreats, ostensibly to make them secure from potential intruders. It seemed, however, that much of the money was being used for luxuries such as redwood and stucco cabanas, a terrazzo tile shuffleboard court, elaborate wrought iron fences, and other expensive items that had little or nothing to do with the physical security of the President. It was a relatively minor sidelight to the intensifying congressional investigations of possible illegal activity by the White House and the administration, but I was eager for any part of the Watergate action and leapt at the opportunity.

What I heard in the committee room convinced me there was a lot more to be said on the subject. In the following days and weeks, I dug as deeply as I could into the issue, cultivating sources within Congress, the Secret Service, and the General Services Administration who were unhappy that taxpayer money was being spent to satisfy Mr. Nixon's increasingly luxurious tastes and regal demands. I came up with several exclusive front-page stories that showed that many millions of dollars more than the White House was acknowledging were being used to support a lavish presidential lifestyle.

Early in 1974, I was asked on several occasions to fill in for one of the White House correspondents, John Herbers or R.W. "Johnny" Apple. I was first sent to be the *Times*'s reporter at a presidential press conference. It was the first time I ever had entered the White House, although as a four-year-old child I had been on the White House lawn for an Easter egg rolling festivity presided over by President Franklin Roosevelt. The press conference was held in the glittering East Room of the mansion, and as the *Times*'s representative, I had a seat in the front row of the crowded room. At recent such news conferences, Nixon had not been calling on *Times* reporters because he regarded the paper as hostile. But I was the first reporter he called on after taking the traditional first questions from the Associated Press and United Press reporters. He obviously did not recognize me as a *Times* reporter. The president smiled when he pointed to me, but the smile vanished when I asked him if he was planning to hire a personal lawyer to defend himself against charges that he was part of a conspiracy to cover up involvement in the Watergate burglary. He answered shortly that he had not thought about it. (He did retain private legal counsel a few days later.) I did not actually write up the story; that was done by one of the White House correspondents watching on television in the bureau in order to make the first edition deadline. Nixon, and Ronald Reagan after him, often held their press conferences just when morning newspapers should have been going to press. They were timed for maximum exposure on prime time television, but I always suspected there was also a bit of spite against papers such as the *Times* and the *Washington Post*.

Several days later, I was asked on short notice to get to Andrews Air Force base and board the press plane accompanying Air Force One on a presidential speaking trip to—if I remember correctly—Atlanta. To me, the trip was memorable chiefly for the novelty of being on the press plane, for the lavish first-class food and drink provided to reporters, and for meeting members of the White House press corps. Dan Rather was then the CBS White House correspondent and a young man named Tom Brokaw who sported long Prince Valiant–style hair, occupied the NBC slot there. Helen Thomas was a UPI White House correspondent as she had been since, I think, the administration of George Washington.

I gradually became more and more involved with the unfolding Watergate saga. At one point, Clifton Daniel, who had succeeded Frankel as bureau chief, asked me to coordinate our Watergate coverage. Later, when Nixon reluctantly released the first of the infamous White House tapes, I flew to New York with the transcripts, all 1,308 pages of them, including all the blacked out "expletive deleted"s, on my lap, accompanied by two other bureau reporters, Anthony Ripley and Walter Rugaber. Initially we were assigned to edit down the transcripts to fit a few pages of the next day's paper. The three of us divided the manuscript and then feverishly tried to winnow out the most telling passages. It was a Herculean task, not unlike, in fact, cleaning out the Augean stables. But after a couple of hours, Abe Rosenthal and other top editors decided they would run every page of the transcripts.

The next day, Ripley and Rugaber and I, now back in Washington, sat at our typewriters to begin writing a long news story that gave the gist and significance of the tapes. The article started on the front page of the paper and ran for nearly five columns inside. It began with this sentence: "Washington, May 5—The erosion of power—of men who control events gradually overcome by those events—leaps out from the huge transcript of White House conversations that President Nixon made public last week."

A few days later, Bill Kovach, who would soon become bureau chief, came to my desk and asked an unusual question. Had it occurred to me that I was being "used"? It had not. But apparently my occasional White House assignments had been used to put pressure on Johnny Apple, perhaps the paper's most versatile and talented reporter, who probably was getting tired of being confined to the executive mansion and who, the editors seemed to think, was not giving the story his best. Then Kovach asked me if I would like to succeed Apple as White House correspondent.

Yes, I would. Although it is a confining beat, with little opportunity for in-depth investigative reporting, too often dependent on scraps of information and "spin" fed to the media by the press secretary and other members of the staff, the White House is for many reporters the most coveted of all assignments. Nearly every story involving the president or his aides receives prominent display in the paper, usually on page one. Being given the White House beat indicates that the management of the paper regards you as one of the more capable reporters on the staff. Working as a White House reporter for *The New York Times*, with its reputation as the newspaper of record, is one of the most visible jobs in American journalism. To be given the job as one of the most dramatic crises in the history of the presidency was approaching its climax was particularly gratifying. I was psyched.

It seemed possible, however, that my new job would not last very long. On my first day on the White House beat, May 10, 1974, I started to keep a journal. The initial entry noted, "This could be an awfully short assignment. Rumors that the president is about to resign are flying all over the city. The rumor mill is generated by intensely negative public and congressional reaction to the transcript of White House conversations released by the president last week." As it turned out, however, I was at the White House for nearly three years. Nixon would be gone in just three months, but I stayed on to cover the presidency of Gerald Ford.

For the next three years, I went to work at the White House five or six days a week. I shared the beat first with John Herbers, a fine, thoughtful veteran reporter, and a Southerner who had distinguished himself with his objective, sensitive coverage of the civil rights battles in the South. Later, James Naughton succeeded Herbers. The tiny cubby assigned to the *Times* in the West Wing press room that contained a narrow table with a well-used typewriter was my office. There were soda and sandwich machines for members of the press corps, but the White House mess hall was open only to the staff.

One of the great pleasures of working at the White House was the stately aesthetic of the place itself. It conveyed a sense of confident but restrained authority, a trait that should be one definition of the American presidency but certainly was not while the Nixon administration thrashed about in its death throes. A white-painted classical building in the Palladian style surrounded by nearly twenty acres of lawns, ancient trees, and gardens, the White House is, I think, one of the most beautiful buildings in the world. Each day I passed through the North Gate and, after the Secret Service officer in the guardhouse looked through my briefcase, walked through the perfectly tended, park-like grounds along the curving driveway to the West Wing. Cameras and other security devices were artfully concealed. The press room then was not marred by the parallel rows of institutional seats that were later installed during the Reagan administration. During the daily press briefings, reporters sat at the few chairs and tables scattered around the room or made themselves comfortable on the carpeted floor. Occasionally I went into the executive offices to talk to the press secretary, Ron Ziegler or his deputies, Gerald Warren and Diane Sawyer, or to others on the staff, including the speechwriter, William Safire, who later joined the *Times* as a columnist.

Unlike its portrayal on the television program *The West Wing*, the executive office is rarely a scene of frenetic activity; it is usually a quiet place and its halls are mostly empty of people, at least while I worked there. The atmosphere in the Nixon White House suggested a state of siege. Virtually the only subjects reporters talked to the staff about were related to Watergate, the pending impeachment proceedings, and the possibility that the president would resign. I never saw the inside of the Oval Office until Nixon left Washington and, indeed, rarely caught a glimpse of the president in the flesh. Nixon himself was away from the White House and Washington almost as much as he was in it. He spent a lot of time at Camp David, at his home in San Clemente, and in Key Biscayne, where he spent days on end on the yacht of his friend Bebe Rebozo. He also took a couple of trips abroad in the short time I covered his presidency. He had been doing this not just after the Watergate scandal broke but throughout the time he had been president. At one point I asked in my journal, "Why is it that Mr. Nixon, who has spent most of his life seeking offices that would keep him in Washington, flees the city at every opportunity?"

I—and I suspect most members of the press corps—enjoyed the presidential trips. The press plane was a kind of clubhouse, with good food and drink, some serious discussion with colleagues of events and issues, and a lot of camaraderie and horseplay. Biscayne Bay and the Southern California coast are both pleasant places, and as the president tended to do little official business at his retreats, or if he did, he would announce it in the evening, there was occasionally time during the day for tennis and swimming and for a meal at a good restaurant after our stories were filed. I particularly enjoyed a trip to San Clemente in July 1974. We were able to take our families along on the press plane for a nominal fare and the *Times* paid for our accommodations at a comfortable hotel right on Laguna Beach, just up the coast from the president's house. It was our first view of the Pacific from the North American side of the ocean, but for my teenage son and daughter, the highlight of the trip was a visit to Disneyland. I found its virtual reality kind of depressing, but the kids loved it.

Reporters didn't usually get to see the president on these trips, but one morning we were summoned to San Clemente to watch him present a Medal of Freedom to a public health doctor. The event was intended chiefly as a photo op, but more than fifty reporters gathered around Nixon in a semicircle outside his cabana as he gave the award. When he finished his brief remarks, the journalists started to inch toward the president, firing questions about the ongoing impeachment proceedings and what he felt about so many of his closest aides being sent to prison. As the semicircle drew tighter and tighter around him, Nixon backed toward his cabana, his eyes darting from side to side, like a cornered animal seeking some way to escape. I had disliked Nixon ever since his days spent witch-hunting communists as a congressman, but now I could not help feeling sorry for him. He finally escaped only after someone, Ziegler, or General Alexander Haig, then his chief of staff said, "That's enough. Thank you, Mr. President."

Nixon's escape was only temporary, however. The next day the Supreme Court handed down a decision that the president must turn over more of the documents subpoenaed by congressional investigating committees and the special prosecutor. The White House had claimed that the court had no jurisdiction over the president because of the constitutional separation of powers. But my story at the top of the next day's front page said that "President Nixon, abandoning his challenge to Supreme Court's jurisdiction over him, said today that he would comply with this morning's court decision on subpoenaed data 'in all respects.' " James D. St. Clair, the president's lawyer, made the announcement about Nixon's submission just as the *Times* was to go to press, and the space was being held open for my story. I had no time to write but instead dictated directly over the phone to an editor on the national news desk in New York, furiously thumbing through my scrawled notes of St. Clair's news conference as I talked.

As it turned out, the smoking gun, the document that proved Nixon's complicity in the Watergate scandal and forced him to resign, was contained in those documents.

The week following the president's—and my—return to Washington, the House Judiciary Committee completed drawing up articles of impeachment and forwarded them to the Rules Committee to prepare for a debate and vote on the floor of the House. Thinking it would take at least a week to draw up the rules of the coming debate, I felt I could sneak in a few days of vacation and lit out for the Berkshires. It was a lovely mid-summer on our mountain, but I was not to stay long. Almost as soon as I arrived, the radio news crackled with rumors that the president had decided to resign. The smoking gun had been discovered, a transcript of a conversation with H.R. Haldeman which demonstrated beyond doubt that Nixon had known and approved of the attempt to cover up guilt in the Watergate break-in. I flew back to Washington on the first available plane. My journal entry for that day notes, "In an astonishing admission of culpability, [Nixon] says he was wrong to withhold information from his own legal staff as well as the Judiciary Committee." Then Nixon called a cabinet meeting that he opened by saying he was "about to discuss something everybody in the country is concerned about—the economy."

August 8, 1974 was a steamy, heavy day in the nation's capital. Dirty gray clouds hung low over the city, splattering occasional showers too brief to break the humidity. It was typical summer weather in Washington, but it seemed to suit the mood of the day. Crowds began to gather at the White House fence along Pennsylvania Avenue—waiting. Shortly after noon, Ron Ziegler announced that the president would be addressing the nation on television that evening. My story the next day observed, "Ziegler did not say what the speech would be about. He did not have to. He choked on his words several times and was struggling visibly to keep himself under control as he left the rostrum of the packed but hushed briefing room at the White House."

The press room was so crammed with journalists that there was scarcely enough oxygen to breathe. The lack of adequate air, combined with the tension of covering the most historic event of my reporting career, gave me a thudding headache that stayed with me the rest of the day. The climaxing Watergate drama, however, was so exhilarating that I was able to enjoy the day anyway.

My story in the next day's paper reported that on the penultimate day of his presidency and his long political career, with his staff and family in anguish, Richard M. Nixon went composedly about his duties. I learned somewhat later that my story was untrue. Far from being serene, as members of his staff had told me in telephone interviews, Nixon was close to physical and mental collapse on that day. In its final full day, the Nixon White House had misled me, as it had so many times to the press and the American people. In a way that final deception was a fitting coda to Nixon's tortured, devious political career.

When Vice President Gerald Ford assumed the presidency by saying, "My fellow Americans, our long national nightmare is over," the nation seemed to breathe a collective sigh of relief. Ford did not bring the most stellar credentials to his new job. He was a vice president who had reached that office without benefit of a popular vote. Serving as Republican leader of the House, he was selected by fellow members of Congress to replace Vice President Spiro Agnew, who had resigned in disgrace after being investigated on charges of bribery, extortion, and conspiracy, and sentenced to three years probation after pleading guilty to a charge of tax evasion. Many in Washington regarded Ford as an unimaginative conservative and a political hack. His public persona was as a physical bumbler, prone to banging his head on the edge of swimming pools. Lyndon Johnson allegedly but famously once said of Ford, "He can't walk and chew gum at the same time."

My perception of Ford, while reporting from his White House for nearly three years, was not that at all. An unelected president taking office at a time of intense national crisis and wounded public morale, and with the economy in fragile condition, he was in a difficult situation to say the least. But he proved up to the task. His combination of blandness and solidity was reassuring to a nation shaken by the Watergate affair. While he may not have been one of the great presidents of US history, he by no means disgraced himself in office. He raised a storm of indignation when he gave Nixon a blanket pardon for any crimes that he may have committed while in office, and some charged that the pardon was the result of a deal that enabled Ford to become president, a charge Ford repeatedly denied. My own view is that even if there had been a deal, pardoning the disgraced ex-president was the right thing to do. The country had been through such a trying emotional wringer during the Watergate investigations that a prolonged public trial of the former president would have been devastating. Ford was right in seeking to put the scandal behind us. By and large, Ford displayed a steady hand as he piloted the ship of state into calmer waters. Like Harry Truman, who was also viewed as an unqualified political hack, Ford rose to the occasion. Moreover, he was not the clownish pratfall artist his enemies sought to portray and the media loved to describe. He was, unlike several of his recent predecessors in the White House, a physically and mentally healthy man and an accomplished athlete to boot.

That is not to say Ford didn't have occasional Three Stooges moments. Once, the press was standing in a light rain at the airport in Salzburg, Austria, where Ford was to meet with Egyptian President Anwar Sadat, waiting for Air Force One to arrive. When it did, the president walked out onto the top of the steps and waved to the crowd with a broad smile. Then as he started down the steps, his legs slipped from under him and he bumped down the rest of the way on his presidential bottom. Fortunately he was unhurt, but a cameraman for ABC News captured the embarrassing scene on tape. That evening, a group of reporters sat in the lounge of our hotel drinking good Austrian beer while Anne Compton, the ABC White House reporter, played the tape over and over. With each replaying—and each beer—the scene seemed funnier and funnier until we were howling and holding our sides in pain.

The next day, Ford and Sadat met in a Baroque palace to discuss political and security issues involving the Middle East. When the meeting was scheduled to end, the international press corps, more than a hundred reporters from every continent, rode in buses to the palace, where we stood in the courtyard waiting for the two leaders to appear and give their accounts of the meeting. It soon began to rain, which steadily got harder and harder. The reporters tried to get back on the buses, but the Austrian police would not let us out of the courtyard. It grew colder, and the rain became steadily heavier as we waited. Then a voice in the crowd of journalists started to sing "We Shall Overcome." In moments every member of the international press corps—reporters from North America, Europe, Africa, the Middle East, and Asia—were standing in the pouring rain in the courtyard of a eighteenth-century palace in Austria, singing the anthem of the American civil rights movement. The incongruity of place, occasion, and song provoked numerous giggles among the singers.

Ford was friendly, open, and liked reporters, totally unlike his predecessor in these respects. He set a tone for his staff, which was accessible and usually, although not always, quite forthcoming. I got to know several members of the staff fairly well, including Ron Nessen, the press secretary, and Dick Cheney, Ford's chief of staff, who was invariably patient and pleasant when I pestered him with questions. I also had a good relationship with the chairman of Ford's Council of Economic Advisors, a saturnine, middle-aged economist named Alan Greenspan. Greenspan gave me a number of good stories as well as valuable economic lessons. He was using me, of course, to get his views on the economy directly to the public. As I was getting informative, exclusive stories, that was fine with me.

Reporters were occasionally invited to social events in the White House, including its annual Christmas party when the White House rooms were aglow with color and light and filled with the fragrance of evergreens. Our most enjoyable evening at the mansion, however, came when Alice and I were invited to a state dinner. These dinners are formal, of course, and Alice went out and bought herself a new gown at Loehmann's while I tried on my twelve-year-old tuxedo, which, *mirabile dictu*, still fit, albeit a bit snugly. We drove to the dinner in our old Volkswagen station wagon, which had a rusted roof rack and which my teenage daughter, Alexa, had recently banged up by sideswiping a gas pump. The driver's door was bashed in and only opened with difficulty and a piercing, grating screech. We drove through the White House gate between two long, black Lincoln limousines, and the Secret Service officer who examined our invitation was clearly trying not to grin. But then we parked across the street from the East Wing entrance, the street then still open to public traffic, and when I squeakily forced the door open and got out, the small crowd gathered on the sidewalk to gaze at the entering guests gave us a warm round of applause for the junkyard jalopy among the limousines.

Inside the White House, it was pure magic. In the long hall where we entered, a scarlet-jacketed Marine string quartet was playing, and another formally dressed Marine came up and, offering his arm to Alice, escorted us up to the brightly lit East Room. In front of us were Gregory Peck and his wife, and behind us was Henry Kissinger. The Marine handed our invitation to the major domo, who announced over the loudspeaker, "Mr. and Mrs. Philip Shabecoff." A little later the president and Mrs. Ford entered to the strains the University of Michigan fight song, accompanied by the evening's guest of honor, the Prime Minister of Australia. We then formed a reception line where Shirley Temple Black, then the president's chief of protocol, was whispering into the president's ear the name of each guest as he or she came up to shake hands. But when Alice and I reached the president, he said without prompting, "Hello, Phil, how are you?" and turning to his guest added, "Mr. Prime Minister, this is Philip Shabecoff, one of our finest journalists." It was a gratifying moment, until a moment later I heard Ford behind me saying, "Mr. Prime Minister, this is Fred Barnes, one of our finest journalists."

After the reception we were escorted, again by uniformed men and women, down the steps to the South Lawn, its luxuriant sweep brightly lit by the moon and by floodlights, with the nearby Washington monument soaring into the night sky. We walked through another line of Marines, interspersed with tall flaming sconces, into a huge air-conditioned tent held up by pillars twined with fresh greenery. Each table for eight had a bowl of wildflowers in its center and more pieces of cutlery per place setting than we would use for three meals at home. The food was elegant—duck with asparagus and rice as the main course—and the speeches and toasts mercifully short. Then we went back up stairs and into the ballroom where the president and prime minister opened the dancing with each other's wives. Alice and I danced a while then went out to the balcony for fresh air and to look out over the Tidal Basin to the glowing Jefferson Memorial. We were there a few minutes when we were joined by Shirley Temple Black, who chatted with us for the next twenty minutes or so, telling us about her childhood as a movie star and how hard she had to work and how she had missed out on much of her childhood. She was friendly and unaffected, and later we wondered how her early fame and fortune had left her so unspoiled. It was a memorable evening.

Compared to the Nixon White House, there was little drama during the Ford administration. There were moments, however. One came during a trip with the president to San Francisco. At the end of the trip, the White House press corps was in a conference room in the St. Francis Hotel filing its stories while the president and his staff departed for the airport. Suddenly a television reporter ran into the room and shouted, "Somebody has shot at the president!" We rushed outside, but the president's car and entourage already had departed, leaving only a confused crowd behind. Back upstairs again we could get no word on what had happened. Rumors were flying, but no one came to brief us. So I sprinted through the hotel to the room occupied by the White House press office during the trip. I found an assistant press secretary there, but all he did was look at me vacantly—he may have been drunk—and said I could use the phone link to Air Force One. A secretary put me through to the plane, and I spoke briefly to Ron Nessen, who told me that the president was unharmed but could provide no facts about the shooting. I went back to the briefing room, reported to the rest of the press corps what I had learned, and tried my best to find out the details of the assassination attempt. In the hotel conference room, however, we were left in an information vacuum. The lead *Times* story the next day reported that a disturbed woman named Sarah Jane Moore had shot at the president, but that her arm had been knocked away by a man standing next to her, thus saving the president's life. The article carried my byline, but most of the information had been obtained by Wally Turner, the *Times*'s San Francisco bureau chief, from his local police contacts and local radio news.

Covering the Ford White House, I came into occasional contact with his vice president, former New York Governor Nelson Rockefeller. I thought Rockefeller to be a bright, energetic, and broad-thinking politician with a rare talent for connecting to people at every level of society. He probably would have made a good president, a post he sought for much of his adult life. But he was too moderate a figure for the virulent right-wing ideologues who increasingly came to dominate the Republican Party, and he was never able to win his party's nomination for the nation's highest office.

During the 1976 campaign, I followed the vice president on a stump speaking tour to various cities around the country. While in Portland, Oregon, a tall, blonde, attractive, and talkative young local radio reporter named Megan Marschalk appeared among the White House reporters covering Rockefeller's speech and news conference. When we departed from the city, I was assigned as one of two "pool" reporters on Air Force Two, the vice president's jet. I thought it curious that the other pool reporter was Megan Marschalk, who had somehow wangled her way aboard. As was the custom during such flights, the pool reporters were summoned to Rockefeller's cabin to ask questions. When we got there, I introduced Marschalk to Rockefeller, and we spent about twenty minutes asking questions while the vice president munched on shrimp and responded. After we landed at Andrews Air Force Base, I said goodbye to Marshalk and never saw her again. I was astonished to learn when I read accounts of Rockefeller's death from a heart attack a few years later that she was in the room with him when he died.

I always will be grateful that Gerald Ford became president if for no other reason than because of him my family and I became skiers. Skiing was not the sport of choice for most kids from working families in the Bronx. Belly whopping on Flexible Flyers down a rocky slope of a nearby lot was the highlight of our local Winter Olympics. I was well into my forties without having any great urge to tie long planks on to the bottom of my feet. But Ford was an enthusiastic skier and spent his Christmas and New Year holiday at the resort town of Vail, Colorado. My family, all non-skiers, came with me again on the press plane to Colorado and the *Times* picked up the tab for renting a two-

bedroom apartment near the base of Vail Mountain. Ford generally spent all day on the slopes, so there was little for reporters
to do, except ski. So our family all rented skis and signed up for
a lesson. Alice and the kids took to the sport right away. But
when I got to the top of the gentle bunny slope where the instructor took our class, I stared down what looked to me like a
suicidal precipice and grabbed the nearby plastic safety netting
in terror. I managed to get down the slope, and after a few runs
thought I might actually be able to do this.

For the next few days of lessons, I was on my face or back
on the snow as often as I stood on my skis. It was the aesthetics
of the experience that kept me at it. Our instructor took us to a
beginner's slope on top of the mountain—I think it was called
Boomer—that offered a wide gentle run among scattered lodge
pole pine trees. At the top of the slope was a view of the Rockies
that seemed to stretch into a blue, white, and green infinity. The
sky was as deep and clear as I have seen from Earth; the air was
crisp, fragrant, and bracing; and all was silent except for the
pleasant, rasping whisper of our skis traversing the powder. I
was hooked. Having started late in life, I never became a good
skier, never able to handle more than intermediate slopes or easy
black slopes in the East. We have skied at other areas in the
Rockies and in the Alps, but I was most comfortable at Butternut
Basin, a modest little mountain near our Berkshire home. I skied,
however, with the blissful fervor of the late convert. Yes, I know
ski areas consume great gulps of otherwise unspoiled terrain, use
up substantial water in the water-scarce West, and displace a lot
of wildlife. I also know that skiing is a very expensive pleasure,
out of reach to many in our society, especially to people living in
poor inner-city neighborhoods who could use more pleasure in
their lives. I really shouldn't have given corporations that run the
ski areas my money. But in this case I cannot be politically cor-
rect. I liked skiing too much.

Alas, a few years ago, the effect of aging on my legs and
stamina forced me to give up skiing in my mid-seventies.

On our second trip to Vail, the president invited Alice and
me to a New Year's Eve party at his borrowed chalet. It was a
small gathering—about twenty people—and, as I recall, I was
the only journalist there; most of the guests were Ford's friends

and family and members of his staff. Everyone was cordial and the food was excellent; it was the only time in my life I have eaten as much caviar as I wanted. At one point Alice and I stood chatting with the president. It was not a serious discussion—mostly about the slopes we had skied that day—but I was feeling very good about the occasion. *Wow*, I more or less thought. *Here I am, the kid from the Bronx, having a nice, social conversation with the President of the United States. Not bad.* I felt a warm glow of wellbeing spreading through my body. Just then, Alice leaned over and whispered in my ear, "Your fly is open." I sidled casually into an adjoining room to make the necessary adjustment, the warmth instantly giving way to the chill of embarrassment.

As far as I am concerned, Gerald Ford served his country well during his brief tenure in the White House. He tried ineffectually to "jawbone" the economy back into health with his "Whip Inflation Now" program and other ineffective but harmless initiatives. His record on environmental issues was dismal. He was not a great orator and had little of the charisma that is considered to be essential for aspiring politicians. Although he was a sitting president, he nearly lost the Republican nomination to a former movie actor named Ronald Reagan, a hard-line conservative who, many experts thought, would never have a chance. During a whistle-stop railroad tour of his home territory in Michigan, Ford drew friendly crowds who gave him affectionate applause. But the crowds only grew excited when Walter Cronkite, the longtime CBS News anchor, got off the train and walked along behind the president. Nevertheless he was a calm, moderating presence for the country and made a number of intelligent moves, perhaps the best of which was to appoint John Paul Stevens to the Supreme Court. He gave the job all he had to give. Along with Jimmy Carter, the peanut farmer from Georgia who defeated him in the general election, Ford was one of our better ex-presidents. He left Washington believing history would be kind to him. At his death, the respectful and affectionate national reaction indicated that he was right.

White House reporters for the *Times* generally have the assignment for only one administration. At the end of the 1976 Republican Convention, during a party for the numerous *Times* contingents in Kansas City for the event, Hedrick Smith, then the Washington bureau chief, asked me what I would like to do next. Smith, perhaps fortified by good drink and Kansas City barbecue, was in an expansive mood, so I told him I wanted to cover the environment. Not wanting to press my luck too far, I said I also would cover other domestic issues, including labor and consumer affairs. He immediately agreed. I would soon embark on the richest part of my career.

First, however, I would remain in the White House until the end of what turned out to be the lame duck portion of Ford's presidency. I had decided I would write a book about his presidency, preparing a proposal and retaining the services of an agent. The agent, excited by what she thought was the book's potential, put the book up for auction, a step taken when it is thought there would be wide interest by publishers. But when Ford lost the presidency to Jimmy Carter a week or so later, interest more or less evaporated, and the auction drew only a couple of tepid bids. So I abandoned the book project and determined to just enjoy my final weeks at the White House, which included trips to Palm Springs and Vail. In those final weeks, Ford did little that was memorable. During the Palm Springs trip, Ron Nessen bet me a dollar that I would not be able to find a single story to write while the president was vacationing. I won the bet with an exclusive front-page story about Alan Greenspan's projections for the economy.

On the day before President Ford turned over the presidency to Jimmy Carter, Sheila Rabb Weidenfeld, Mrs. Ford's press secretary and a social friend at the time, invited me and my family to the White House, gave us a tour of the East Wing, followed by lunch at the White House mess hall. After lunch, Alice and the kids went home, and I went back to the West Wing to file my story on Ford's last day. I finished by mid-afternoon and left to go back to the bureau, walking slowly to the gate, savoring the finale of my White House tour.

Out on Pennsylvania Avenue, I encountered Dick Cheney, looking relaxed and also in no hurry. We chatted as we walked through Lafayette Park, and I said to him that now that the political bug had bitten him he would probably remain in Washington as so many other political appointees had done over the years. But Cheney said that no, he had had enough of politics and was going back to Wyoming to spend the rest of his life in academia. A couple of years later, however, he was back, first as a hard-line conservative congressman, and then as President Bush senior's secretary of defense and Bush Jr.'s vice president. Washington and political power are strongly addictive. Too bad he didn't spend the rest of his life in academia.

CHAPTER 11

EVERY PLACE

The Environment

Mainstream American journalism has not done well with the environmental story. I still do not fully understand why. The environment is a subject of transcendent importance. It is crucial to the health of the physical world and all of its inhabitants, most particularly its human inhabitants. It is a subject that embraces nearly all of the other things journalism follows, including politics, the economy, science, and national security. It is about the kind of habitat our grandchildren will live in and the kind of lives they will be able to lead. It is about the future course of evolution.

There are a large and growing number of talented, highly professional environmental reporters available to all of the media. Yet, except when there is some sort of crisis, such as a Chernobyl or Bhopal or the Exxon Valdez or Deep Water Horizon oil catastrophes, the media give the subject relatively short shrift. Anything to do with current politics or economics; business, sports, crime, war, or diplomacy; the latest non-cure for cancer; O.J. or Monica or Brittany or Lindsay invariably gets far more space in print media and time on television than stories about potentially cataclysmic human-caused changes in the atmosphere, disappearance of plant and animal species, acidification, toxification, and irradiation of the land and people or the effects of pollution on the health of children.

In 1977, when I first became engaged in environmental reporting, the field was still in its infancy. The first Earth Day had produced a flurry of interest among the news media, but few newspapers and fewer of the electronic media had full-time environmental reporters or took the issue very seriously. *The New York Times* was more attentive than most. In the 1950s, John

Oakes, later chief editor of the editorial page for many years, wrote a regular column on environmental issues—in the Sunday Travel section of all places. Gladwin Hill wrote about the issues from Los Angeles. Ned Kenworthy did some good reporting out of the Washington bureau, particularly on the legislative battle over the Clean Air Act of 1971 and over the struggle to keep the Corps of Engineers from doing a number on the unspoiled New River in North Carolina, one of the few free-flowing rivers left in the East. A few other journalists, including Luther Carter of *Science*, Robert Cahn of the *Christian Science Monitor*, syndicated columnist Ed Flatteau, Casey Bukro of the *Chicago Tribune*, Tom Harris of the McClatchy newspapers, and Michael Frome, a writer-activist, among others, did pioneering environmental reporting. But theirs were voices in the wilderness, so to speak.

Looking back through the clips of my stories in the late 1970s, I see that I wrote far more about labor, consumer, and health care news in those years than I did about the environment. One problem that was to plague me for the rest of my years with the *Times* was that many of my editors were unfamiliar with environmental issues, were uncomfortable with them, and regarded those stories as a minor backwater in the daily flow of news. They were much more enthusiastic and supportive about articles on the other domestic issues I covered. There were exceptions, however. When Bill Kovach became bureau chief in Washington, he strongly supported my environmental coverage, occasionally incurring, while sheltering me from, the wrath of higher-ups in New York. Seymour Topping, while second-in-command of the news operation as managing editor, had a firm grasp of the importance of the environmental story and not only encouraged my reporting but also sought to widen the scope of the paper's environmental coverage. A number others, however, were abysmally ignorant and some downright hostile to stories about the environment. A few were both. Unfortunately, as I note later, they were in a position to affect my coverage and, eventually, my career.

A second problem was that, at the beginning, I was abysmally ignorant myself about how to cover the environment and even about what the environmental story really was or should be. I knew little about new laws that had been passed by Congress after the first Earth Day in an inspired burst of legislative energy. I knew next to nothing about the history and structure of the environmental movement. I had to learn a new vocabulary of unfamiliar words and terms such as dioxin, trihalomethanes, radon, chlorofluorocarbons, ambient air quality, and prevention of significant deterioration, and about programs such as coastal zone management and wastewater treatment as well as the management of federal lands and resources and of solid waste management. I had believed, naively and erroneously, that covering the environment would be largely about national parks and forests, about wildlife and trees and efforts to protect open space, which would allow me to spend a lot of time away from the office in the outdoors. Over time I did a good amount of that kind of reporting, but I found myself writing most often about toxic waste dumps, pollution from coal-fired power plants, sewage systems, pesticides, and fumes from automobile tailpipes. And politics. And economics. And ideology. I learned quickly that all environmental issues involved intense, usually nasty battles conducted in a political cauldron in which economics and ideology fumed and bubbled and frequently left a noxious odor.

In time I also learned that the environment was an issue of social justice. Although I came across a lot of evidence that this was the case, my eyes did not fully open to the reality of ecological injustice until I made a reporting trip to Robeson County, North Carolina, to look into why plans had been developed to bracket the county with two major waste disposal facilities. At one end of the county, a planned nuclear waste incinerator would have generated radioactive pollution. At the other a hazardous waste treatment plant would have dumped contaminated water into the Lumbee River, a main source of drinking water for the county. When I got there, I learned why that county had been targeted; it is one of the poorest in the United States, its median income half the national level. It was also an area badly divided by race. A third of the population was white, a third African-American, and a third Lumbee Indian. The three groups were often at violent odds over the county's scant economic resources, and the murder rate in the area was high. County residents understood quite well, however, that they were being deliberately victimized. For once they united in a campaign to resist. I attended a candlelight vigil at which black, white, and Native American men and women linked arms, sang hymns, and vowed to fight against the waste sites. The sites were not built there, at least the last time I checked. But the poor and disenfranchised continue to bear the brunt of the nation's environmental ills.

I suppose I should not have been surprised to discover that the worst insults of air and water pollution, of toxified surroundings, of an absence of open space and green and wild things are heaped upon the poor, racial minorities, and the politically neutered. I belatedly came to realize the power of the great corporations and their lobbyists and the ability of business and industry to control not only the economic and political life but also the physical condition of our nation and, indeed, the entire globe.

It was not until well into my years as an environmental reporter, however, that it dawned on me that, in my lifetime, human beings had become a force as powerful as nature itself in shaping the fate of all life on Earth; that our numbers, our economy, our technology, and our lifestyles were inflicting profound harm on the physical, chemical, and biological systems that govern our planet. In a few generations, we humans have drastically altered the processes that have fashioned the Earth and the ecological niches of its inhabitants over thousands of millennia, have sharply reduced the possibilities of evolution, and may be threatening the viability of life on Earth. I know that may sound excessively portentous, but after close examination of these issues for more than forty years, I am deeply convinced it is so.

Before my environmental education was well underway, however, I was unceremoniously yanked from the beat. After about a year, Hedrick Smith, the Washington bureau chief at the time, told me he was assigning another reporter, Charles Mohr, a highly respected former war correspondent who was sick with diabetes and who would die within a few years, to cover the environment. I was disappointed but understood the reason for giving Charlie something he wanted to do. As it turned out, Mohr decided after a few months that he didn't really enjoy the beat, and it was given back to me along with my responsibilities for covering other domestic issues. It was not until Ronald Reagan became president, and right-wing conservatives controlled much of the government, however, that I was finally given the green light (forgive me) to cover the environment full time.

Reagan was a simple man with a simple view of governance. His policies and programs followed the axiom that the least government is the best government. The country is best served, he believed, by entrusting it to the invisible hand of the market. His stated goal was to get government off the backs of the American people. In practice, however, this evolved into getting the government off the backs of business and industry by reducing or eliminating federal regulatory activities, shrinking the budgets of regulatory agencies, and seeking to transfer public lands and resources into private hands as quickly and cheaply as possible. Reagan was not anti-environment; he just didn't know or care much about it. He thought most pollution came from trees.

To carry out his philosophy in the key government agencies making environmental policies, he chose two right-wing Republicans who shared his negative view of government—but, as it soon became apparent, not his political skills. As Secretary of the Interior, and as his chief environmental policy deputy, Reagan chose James Gaius Watt, who headed a right-wing legal foundation in Colorado that represented extractive industries, developers, ranchers, and other interests that sought to exploit public lands and resources for their own enrichment. A fundamentalist Christian, Watt proclaimed that he had a God-given mission to turn public property over to private hands as quickly as possible.

I rather liked Watt personally. He was accessible, gentlemanly, completely open about his goals for his department, and often quite funny. When he was accused of assigning foxes to guard the public domain henhouse when he named representatives of industrial and development interests to subcabinet posts, he promptly adorned his office with pictures of foxes. He had the Department of the Interior official seal, which showed an American bison facing to the left, changed to have the bison

facing to the right in keeping with his own ideological orienta-
tion. He also had a penchant for shooting himself repeatedly in
the foot with off-the-cuff remarks that revealed him as a zealot
and something of a bigot. He boasted of the diversity of an advisory commission he appointed by saying, "I have a black, I have
a woman, two Jews, and a cripple." He compared environmentalists who criticized his policies to communists and Nazis, saying they pursued "centralized planning and control of society."
Some of his statements, such as calling the popular singing
group the Beach Boys the "wrong element," were even too
much for President Reagan.

While Watt headed it, the Department of the Interior followed an agenda that moved radically away from policies of
long standing by shifting from conservation of public lands and
resources to their exploitation. He put the entire Outer Continental Shelf up for oil lease, offered federal coal reserves to private companies at less than bargain-basement prices, sought to
sell off much of the federal lands in the West, declined to purchase any more land for national parks, and promoted energy
development in federal wilderness areas and wildlife refuges.
These activities provoked intense hostility and opposition from
environmental organizations that began to call for Watt's resignation within six months of his taking office.

Reagan's second key environmental appointment was Anne
McGill Gorsuch, later Anne Burford, to head the Environmental
Protection Agency. Another right-wing Republican from Colorado, Burford made no secret of her aim of lightening the burden of environmental regulation on business and industry. I
came to believe that she did want to take steps to protect the environment, but thought she could do so without bringing the
heavy hand of government to bear. Burford was clearly sympa-
thetic to the problems, real or manufactured, that the business
community had with environmental rules. She had virtually no
administrative experience before she took over the big, un-
wieldy, and controversial environmental agency. She also had a
cadre of assistant administrators, many imposed on the agency
by the Reagan White House, who came out of the very industries they were supposed to supervise and for which they were
supposed to assure compliance with environmental laws.

Burford acquiesced with a drastically reduced budget for the EPA (although eventually it became too drastic even for her) and basically stopped using the agency to enforce environmental laws, seeking voluntary compliance instead. When asked why the number of enforcement cases was down so sharply, she replied that "bean counting" did not clean up the environment. Soon rumors of favoritism and sweetheart deals by the agency, particularly with regard to a new law to clean up hazardous waste sites, began to circulate among environmentalists and journalists and on Capitol Hill. Several congressional committees launched investigations and subpoenaed documents from the agency. Burford, acting on orders from the White House, refused to turn them over. The refusal touched off a constitutional confrontation between Congress and the White House. The House began contempt of Congress proceedings against Burford. An EPA official, Rita Lavelle, the assistant administrator in charge of the toxic waste program, was found guilty of withholding evidence about agency dealings with a waste company and was sentenced to six months in prison. Morale at the agency plummeted, and its environmental protection activities slowed to a near standstill. Many able career employees resigned in disgust.

One day Burford was called to testify in closed hearings about her activities. A large crowd of reporters and photographers waited outside the hearing room. When the hearing ended, Burford came out of a back door of the committee room down the hall hoping to avoid the media, who promptly ran after her en masse. I was standing next to George Tames, a *Times* photographer since the Franklin Roosevelt administration and wise in the ways of Washington. "When they start running after you like that, you are gone," he said. He was right. A few days later, the Justice Department informed Burford that they would no longer defend her against the contempt charges because they were investigating charges of wrongdoing at the EPA and representing her would constitute a conflict of interest.

Within a week, a bitter Anne Burford handed her resignation to President Reagan.

Several months later, Watt, now clearly a political liability to the Reagan Administration, also resigned. He had only

carried out Reagan's agenda of letting industry and developers have their way with the public's property, but his bull-in-
the-china-shop style had become an embarrassment to the
administration.

For the major environmental groups, the departure of
Watt and Burford was the old joke about having mixed feelings while watching your mother-in-law drive your new Cadil-
lac over a cliff. The environmentalists had been dismayed over
the wrecking ball being used against government efforts to
protect the environment and the wholesale giveaway of public
lands and resources. For them, Watt and Buford's forced resig-
nations were a major victory, an unmistakable signal that
Reagan's anti-environmental counterrevolution, if not defeated, had been stalemated. But for the environmental groups, the
Watt-Burford era had been a time of wine and roses or, as I
wrote at the time, of Champagne and caviar. Americans do
care about the environment (or, at least, did at the time), and
one of their reactions to the Reagan administration onslaught
was to become members of and give money to the environmental organizations. In the 1980s the environment emerged
for the first time as a third-rail political issue, an issue that
government leaders at the highest level had to address to save
their own political skins. Groups such as the Sierra Club and
Wilderness Society and others saw their memberships double
and their funding increase even more. It was boom time in the
environment business.

The Democratic Party, which then still knew a good political issue when it saw one and had kept up a fusillade of criti-
cism of Reagan's environmental actions, was sorry to see Watt
and Burford go. Reagan's record on the environment was turning into one of the party's major weapons against the Republicans. Their replacements were not as easy targets. William
Ruckelshaus, the first administrator of the EPA, returned for a
second tour at the agency. He had a reputation as a man of integrity that cared about the environment, and he lived up to that
reputation even in the Reagan Administration. William Clark
and then Donald Hodel, who succeeded Watt at the Department
of the Interior, had basically the same agenda as Watt but conducted their business more adroitly.

For me professionally, Reagan and his environmental appointees were an unmitigated blessing. Early in 1981, less than a year after the new administration had started its counterrevolution, Seymour Topping, the *Times*'s managing editor, came to Washington and at lunch asked me to devote myself full time to covering the environment. Because it had become a hot political story, the environmental beat was now deemed worthy of having a Washington correspondent who covered the beat exclusively. I thoroughly had enjoyed almost everything I had done on the *Times*, but the next ten years were the most rewarding and productive of my career.

Journalists, particularly reporters for a daily newspaper who switch from beat to beat, rarely have an opportunity to immerse themselves fully in any issue or discipline. I had hopped around from business news to foreign corresponding in Europe and Asia, to labor and economics, to the White House. I used to complain to friends that my intellectual range as a journalist was a mile wide and an inch deep. But reporting on the environment for the *Times* for fourteen years and then founding and publishing *Greenwire*, the online environmental news service, and writing books on environmental history and policy, enabled me to plunge fathoms down into the subject.

As a young man, I had briefly stood at a crossroads, one branch of which would have led me to a life as an academic. I had done well at the University of Chicago, and when I received my master's degree from the Committee on Communication there, I was invited to stay on as administrator of the committee and have a free ride toward my PhD. After thinking deeply for about five seconds about the choice between journalism and a career in academia, I turned down the offer.

I have never for an instant regretted the decision to stick with my original choice of journalism but often wondered whether I would have liked a life of scholarship. Becoming an expert on the environment and doing research for books on environmental issues, gave me a taste of what it might be like. To understand the issues and to inform *Times* readers with accurate and trenchant reports, I had to learn rudiments of ecology, environmental chemistry, atmospheric physics, botany and zoology, environmental law and regulation, the economic and social implications of environmental degradation and regulation, and the many public and private bureaucracies that sought to influence environmental policy. I quickly was forced to understand the ebb and flow of environmental politics and the interactions among environmentalists, business lobbyists, Congress, the White House, and executive agencies and the states and to cultivate sources within all of those diverse groups, as well as with the scientific and public health communities.

Every day I had to sort through a foot-high or higher pile of documents, press releases, magazines, and letters and actually read a good number of them. My telephone rang an average of twenty or so times a day, and I responded to every call—any one of them might lead to a good story. I had to keep up with what other newspapers and magazines were carrying on the environment and read a good number of specialized periodicals, including the magazines published by many of the national and international environmental groups. I had press briefings and congressional hearings to attend, interviews to conduct, leads to follow—and I had places to visit.

The environment is about places. Reporting on the environment meant looking at and writing about how human activity affects those places, particularly the human and nonhuman life that inhabits those places. The environment is a city, a suburb, a factory, a forest, a farm, a wetland, a desert, a prairie, a river, a tundra, a village next to a hazardous waste dump, a school with asbestos fibers dripping from its ceilings, and even, I found, the inside of a house and its backyard. It is entire regions and countries. It is the atmosphere, the soil, and the oceans. It is the world. The environment is any place and every place. We humans are altering the environment every place on Earth, from the tops of the tallest mountains to the deeps of the oceans.

I did not really understand all that until much later. To me, the environment was simply stories and places I had to go to get those stories. Many of those places were right in Washington, where I gathered secondhand information about the environment in congressional committee rooms and the offices of congressmen and senators, in claustrophobic briefing rooms at the EPA's shabby, crumbling headquarters (the agency has since moved); in the Interior Secretary's wood-paneled office; in the crowded offices of the national environmental groups and the plush suites of industry lobbying organizations. My stories were gathered over tables in the once popular but now long gone Duke Zeibert's restaurant, which served as an unofficial lunchroom for the Gucci Gulch lobbyists of K Street, government officials, and the reporters who sought information from them and from documents leaked to me by disgruntled or outraged government employees.

Many of my stories came to me by telephone and by mail, and as they entered the workaday world, by fax and email. I was plied with information by the army of young people who worked for national environmental groups in Washington. This cadre of environmentalists kept a watchful, suspicious eye on the machinations of government, on business and industry, and on their lobbying activities and also acted as a conduit to the media from their field operatives around the country. They also served the very useful function as intermediaries between the scientific community on one hand and the media and public on the other.

I did, however, try to get out into the field as often as possible to see for myself what was happening to this environment I was writing about. Some of those places were unpleasant but highly instructive.

One such place was an isolated, impoverished community of tiny, paint-shedding bungalows and rusting, wrecked autos at the edge of Baltimore that abutted an industrial area along the Chesapeake Bay. The community surrounded a small lagoon into which some of the neighboring factories had been dumping chemicals and other toxic substances for years. The lagoon once had been a small lake where one elderly resident used to fish as a boy. Now there were no fish; no life could exist in that dark, evil-smelling body of water. Residents told me that many of the community's children were coming down with unexplained but serious illnesses and older people were dying sooner than they ought to expect. They suspected the lagoon was the source of the tragic blight, but no one had done anything about it. The Federal EPA and state agencies said they would investigate, but month after month, year after year, the lagoon just sat there, festering.

I found evidence of a different kind of environmental crime in a union hall a few miles from that community and talked to men who had worked in Baltimore's shipyards during World War II building the vessels that helped win the war. They had worked without protective clothing amid clouds of the asbestos used for fire containment on the ships. Now in their late fifties and early sixties, the men were gaunt and hollow eyed. They were dying, they said, from mesothelioma, an incurable cancer in the lining between stomach and chest caused by exposure to asbestos. Many of their coworkers in the yards were already gone. They spoke with resignation about their impending deaths, but they were bitter that the company they had worked for would not acknowledge responsibility for having exposed them to asbestos and refused to pay compensation to help their families when they were gone.

Another sad place I visited, sad in a different way, was the top of Mt. Mitchell, in North Carolina, the highest point on the nation's Eastern seaboard. Robert Bruck, a plant pathologist at North Carolina State University who had spent years investigating why trees were dying on top of the mountain, invited me there. When I reached the summit and looked around, all I could see in every direction, were dead trees—red spruce and Fraser firs—their bare, spindly branches looking like the shriveled limbs of desiccated bodies. Trees were dying, Professor Bruck had concluded, because a witches' brew of air pollution—sulfates and acid rain from coal-fired power plants in the West and nitrous oxides and other emissions from auto and truck tailpipes—had attacked the leaves and roots of the trees and left them vulnerable to natural enemies such as insects and intense cold. Prevailing westerly winds carried the pollution over the high elevations so that the trees near the top of the mountains were most exposed. More trees were dying down the slope of the mountain each year. Moreover, Bruck said, what I was seeing on top of Mt. Mitchell was happening with varying degrees of intensity along the entire crest of the Appalachian chain from Maine to Georgia.

I wrote several stories about dying trees, and they touched a raw nerve, especially among utility company officials, who disputed that air pollution had anything to do with the dying trees. Forest products companies feared that news about forest death would devalue their shares on stock markets. Some professional foresters' training had convinced them that only natural forces could cause trees to die, and of course right-wing ideologues and their political satraps wanted no government regulation of polluting industries. But, as the saying goes, facts are stubborn. Some two decades later, I was invited to contribute to a chapter of a book about massive tree deaths in Appalachia, much of it caused by acid rain and other human-generated pollution. In recent years the same groups of skeptics have continued to insist that pollution does not affect trees—and trees are continuing to die.

Covering the environment also took me to many places of great, often breath-stealing natural beauty. I looked for every opportunity to write about national parks and forests and wilderness areas, about federal wildlife refuges and rangeland and protected private areas. My travels in those years took me to every corner of the country, from Maine to Florida, to Alaska to the Midwest, and led me for the first time to appreciate the size and ecological diversity of my country. There were a couple of times while driving through the vast open deserts of the Southwest when I was so disoriented by the endless, empty space and limitless horizon that I experienced so strong a sense of vertigo that I to had to pull my car to the side of the road for a few moments.

Frequently during my career with the *Times*, I felt extraordinarily fortunate to be paid to do such interesting things and go to such fascinating and appealing places, but never more so than when I covered the environment and explored the glories of the American landscape. How many people in this world have jobs that pay them to lie under the stars in Minnesota's Boundary Waters wilderness and listen to the manic calls of nesting loons and the primal howls of a wolf pack?

One unforgettable experiences was a visit to an Audubon Society wildlife refuge on the Platte River near Kearney, Nebraska, to watch the sandhill cranes pause during the spring equinox period on their annual migration north to Canada and Alaska. The cranes are huge birds, with a six-foot wingspan, gray in color with a splash of bright red over their eyes. They look like creatures from an earlier epoch, and they are, in fact, an ancient species. Each year, some five hundred thousand of the great birds arrive on the Platte from Mexico and the Southern US sometimes reaching concentrations of twenty thousand birds per river mile. In 1987 I joined a group of Audubon Society workers, including Peter A.A. Berle, the president of the national society, in a blind near the river. The birds started to come down late on a cold, dark March afternoon. Here is the lead of my story.

> Announcing their approach with a hoarse,
> tremolo cry, the sandhill cranes return to the
> river as evening falls. At first they descend in
> small clusters of half a dozen or so. But as the
> twilight deepens, the stately birds arrive in
> waves of twenty, then one hundred, then one
> thousand , until the world seems to be filled
> with their wings and their wild calls.

As we sat in the blind, snow began to fall. It was the onset of a major blizzard that would blanket the plains with several feet of snow by the end of the next day. The cranes kept arriving through the thickening air when, suddenly, there was a vivid flash of lightning and a startling crack of thunder. The lightning and thunder continued for nearly an hour. The coincidence of the descending cloud of birds, the blizzard, and the thunderstorm fused to create one of the most exhilarating experiences of my life. Some years later, Alice bought me a large lithograph of a sandhill crane by John James Audubon. It is one of my cherished possessions, as is a small sculpture of a sandhill crane presented to me by the National Wildlife Federation at one of its annual conservation award ceremonies; it sits on a table beneath the lithograph. Every time I look at them, I think of that wild, snow-swept late afternoon along the Platte.

Are the sandhill cranes still descending on the river in such great numbers? I don't know. Even then, in the 1980s, the migration was threatened by diversion of water from the river, which, drained heavily for irrigation, contained only a fraction of its original flow. Planned dams and growing demand for drinking and agricultural water threatened to reduce the amount of water in the river even more drastically, leaving less and less for the cranes and other wildlife. Peter Berle, who has since passed on at a much too early age, warned at the time, "Humans may destroy in a single lifespan something that has been going on for ten million years."

America's public domain, nearly eight hundred million acres of national parks, monuments and forests, wildlife refuges, rangeland, seashore, and wilderness areas, is an astonishing, priceless legacy left to us by our forebears. They are often the lands left over after most of the continent had been distributed among homesteaders, miners, loggers, ranchers, railroads, military services, and others seeking land and resources for their own livelihood or enrichment. But what are left are places of great diversity, beauty, and wonder. They also continue to be battlegrounds between Americans who wish to preserve them in as close as possible to their natural state and those, both Americans and foreign interests, who wish to exploit them for their own economic benefit in alliance with right-wing fanatics who believe that all property should be in private hands. I set myself the task of being a war correspondent in those battlegrounds, traveling to wildlife refuges in the Louisiana bayous, national forests in the Pacific Northwest with their towering ancient firs and redwoods, and deserts punctuated by dreamlike pinnacles and mesas in the Southwest. Much of this land is under the dubious protection of the Department of the Interior's Bureau of Land Management, which often represents developers and extractive industries rather than the public interest. All of those lands were and continue to be under enormous economic and political pressure.

Our national parks are theoretically inviolable. The legislation that formally created the park system requires that the parks be preserved "unimpaired for future generations." The national parks have been called "the cathedrals of American civilization," and to many Americans they are sacred places. But they, too, are vulnerable to our juggernaut economy and expanding population. Visiting Yosemite, Yellowstone, the Grand Tetons, the Grand Canyon, Bryce Canyon, Zion, and other parks, I found all of them in trouble from too many visitors, too many cars, air and water pollution, noise pollution from snowmobiles, inadequate funding to pay for maintenance and for the salaries of park rangers, economic and energy development around their borders, and many other insults. This is how I began one long article on the park system:

> YOSEMITE, Calif.—The beauty of this great
> national park in the high Sierras depends less
> on the eye of the beholder than on the
> beholder's line of sight.
>
> Looking upward from the Yosemite Valley,
> the eye follows tall redwoods and cedars to
> the summits of towering granite cliffs, over
> which silver ribbons of water fall from
> dizzying heights.
>
> But at the horizontal, the field of vision is
> filled with hot asphalt, slow-moving lines of
> cars and buses, and crowds of tourists, some
> visibly irritated by the heat and congestions.

The article went on to describe the same sort of split personality in other parks and to express fears about their long-term future. But this is how it ended:

> It is still possible to find solitude at night at
> the foot of Yosemite Falls while watching the
> beams of a full moon create a white moonbow
> in the thick spray where the falling water
> booms off the rocks.
>
> It is still possible, despite the heavy
> development around it, to be surprised by the

> gossamer charm of Old Faithful as well as by
> its mystery.
>
> One can still be overwhelmed by the sense of
> sky and earth, time and distance, standing on
> the rim of the Grand Canyon.

Alaska is the most beautiful place I have ever been—and
that is saying a lot because I have seen many hauntingly lovely
places around the planet. But with its daunting, snowcapped
mountains; its countless lakes and wide, swift rivers; its bogs
and tundra; its deep valleys and lush islands; its fjords and dazzling glaciers; its blue surrounding waters; and its abundant animal and marine life, most of Alaska, although not all, is one of
the Earth's most splendid remaining fragments of a wild and
natural world relatively unsoiled and untamed by humans.

In 1980, Congress enacted the Alaska National Interest
Lands Conservation Act, setting aside more than one hundred
million acres as protected national parks and monuments, wilderness areas, forests, and wildlife preserves. It was, perhaps,
the biggest act of land and resource conservation in history. It
was also an act that aroused intense hostility among corporations that wanted a free hand to develop the state's rich resources of oil, gas, timber, and minerals, and among many
Alaskan citizens who had hoped to reap a financial windfall
from such development. But it was a historic and magnificent
gift to the nation, to the world, and to the future—if human
demographics and human greed permit the gift to endure.

In 1986 I made a ten-day reporting trip to Alaska. It was an
expensive visit; much of the travel in the state had to be done by
chartered airplane. I convinced my editors that the paper needed to take a look at how the land conservation act was working
out on the ground, and I did find a good half dozen interesting
and informative stories. But in fact, the trip was a gift to myself,
a once-in-a-lifetime opportunity to immerse myself in Alaska's
wonders, from the fjord and glacier landscape of its southeast to
the tundra and Arctic shore on the far north.

In a National Park Service plane, I flew hundreds of miles
over uninhabited valleys and mountains, empty rivers and

lakes, and endless bogs into the heart of the great Wrangell–St. Elias National Park. We finally came to Earth in the village of McCarthy, an isolated hamlet that seemed hundreds of miles from nowhere. The community was once a bustling town that served a nearby Kennecott Copper mine, now long since abandoned. Only a handful of full-time residents remain. What struck me most as I wandered the wildflower-carpeted slopes around the village was the intense silence—there was no sound except the whining of dense clouds of mosquitoes, insects so large and ubiquitous that Alaskans call them their state bird. The silence of the mountains and the sense of isolation from civilization were at once a bit intimidating and immensely exhilarating. The cool, untainted air; the profound blue of the sky; the fragrance of the pines; and the freedom of endless space affected my senses like a double martini.

I had a somewhat similar response when I plunged into the heart of the great Tongass National Forest, the continent's last remaining temperate rain forest of any size. Stretching some five hundred miles along the southeastern coast of the state, the Tongass encompasses seventeen million acres of dripping coastal forest, volcanic uplands, deep valleys cut through by glaciers, and broad meadows of spongy bog. It is more than four times the size of any forest in the lower forty-eight states. Where left untouched, the Tongass is filled with ancient, towering hemlocks and Sitka spruce trees of huge girth. The old trees rise like silent, brooding gods from some unimaginable time in distant prehistory. Unfortunately, the untouched places are dwindling. Two big forest products companies, one of them Japanese, had been granted bargain-basement concessions to log the Tongass, and hundreds of thousands of acres were leveled by clear cuts, leaving barren fields filled with tangled debris and stumps that jutted like dragons' teeth from tangled brush and debris. Much of the timber has been shipped to Japan.

The highlight of my Alaskan trip was a three-day stay on Admiralty Island, just off the coast from the state capital of Juneau. Designated a national monument in the lands act, the island is inhabited by Tlingit Indians, who make their way in the world in large part through their traditional occupations of fishing, hunting, and trapping. Its steep hills sloping to the sea are heavily forested with evergreens. The island is pierced with large streams, two of which are thick with salmon when the anadromous fish return from their ocean journey to spawn, providing a substantial proportion of the local diet. Residents were hoping to supplement their meager cash earnings through tourism, but when I came to the island, I was the only guest at the only motel, located at the water's edge in the biggest settlement, called the City of Angoon but in reality a small fishing village. While interviewing the mayor of the village, I expressed an interest in seeing whales, and he arranged for a Tlingit fisherman to take me out in his boat.

The next morning, a clear, brisk day, I set out with the fisherman, whose name was James, in his ten-foot dory. We first moved rapidly inland on a broad deep river, more like a fjord. After only a few minutes, he pointed behind me and said, "Whale!" I swiveled just in time to see massive flukes disappear into the water. We then turned around and steered into open sea, first moving toward the river's edge to look at a large grizzly bear. It looked back at us, and we did not get too close. When we were several hundred yards offshore, I noticed that dozens of trees lining the island's littoral had what appeared to be white balls in the branches. "What are those white things?" I asked my guide. "The heads of bald eagles sitting in the trees," he replied matter-of-factly. The great birds, once nearly extinct, now protected but still scarce in the lower forty-eight states, are commonplace on the island and throughout much of Alaska.

To my delight, we soon spotted a pod of five humpback whales lying on the surface of the water about a mile away like low, dark islands. As we watched they sounded and a few minutes later breached halfway between where they had been and our little boat. They disappeared again and then reappeared, this time only a couple of hundred yards away. "They're not chasing us. They're just following a school of fish. But I think we'd better move out of the way," James said, and moved the boat about a quarter-of-a-mile in a different direction. The whales sounded again and did not reappear for a while. Then James peered at bubbles coming up in the water around our boat and said, "I don't like the looks of this" and gunned the outboard motor. Seconds later the five humpbacks breached just where the boat had been, so close they looked like black skyscrapers exploding out of the water. It was a terrifying and tremendously exciting and satisfying moment.

By then it was midday. James took out his lunch, a jar of salmon chunks he had smoked himself, another jar filled with water, and a packet of hardtack. He generously shared his food with me, and it was delicious, the salmon more intensely smoked and flavorful than any fish I had eaten. After the uneaten food was stowed, the fisherman pulled out his rod, baited the hook, and dropped it into the water. Within a few minutes, the tip of the rod dipped sharply. "I think it's a small salmon," he said. "Would you like to bring it in?" I had never fished in my life, but I thought, *What the heck,* and took the wooden rod. The "small" fish fought for nearly half-an-hour, pulling the boat a considerable distance. At one point the bottom of the rod snapped off between my legs. I still shudder to think of the injury it might have caused. Finally I brought it close enough to the dory for him to slip a net under it. It was a forty-five-pound king salmon, with iridescent silver, violet, and salmon-colored scales.

I think we humans respond atavistically to wild creatures and wild places—to whales, and eagles, bears, and fish in the sea—and to deep woods and hidden valleys and other places that we have not tamed. These things fill some need within us; at least they do for me. Even the fear they sometimes inspire is invigorating and makes us more aware of being alive and gladder to be so. Our species has gained much through its conquest of nature—safety from the tooth-and-claw perils of the wilderness, security, warmth, and wealth. But we also have lost much, perhaps too much. As the wild places and the creatures that inhabit them dwindle before our onslaught, we are diminished in our sense of possibility, of freshness, of freedom, of being at home in the community of life. Thoreau warned us more than a century-and-a-half ago of the toll industrialized civilization would take on the human spirit, and he has proven to be all too accurate a prophet.

How our civilization transforms wildness and beauty to something far different was manifest when I traveled to Alaska's North Slope to take a look at the industrial activity at Prudhoe Bay, activity that sends oil flowing through the Trans-Alaska pipeline. The pipeline begins a few hundred yards from the edge of the Arctic Ocean and terminates in Valdez far to the south, where the crude oil is loaded on to tankers, then often bound for Japan and other foreign destinations.

Sitting on flat tundra that merges almost imperceptibly with the ocean, the Prudhoe settlement was an ugly jumble of faceless buildings, trailers, vehicles of all sizes and shapes, and a maze of pipes and vents that reached out like tentacles in every direction. The main housing and office facility maintained by the British Petroleum Company was a big squat structure, much of it underground, that housed a gymnasium, a movie theater, a huge dining room, and dozens of small but comfortable sleeping rooms with bunk beds. One of the nights I spent there I was awakened by shouts outside my room at about one o'clock in the morning. I went to the window and shoved aside the heavy curtains to find the shouts coming from men and women playing a softball game in bright sunlight.

Oil company spokespeople insisted that the development had virtually no impact on wildlife, an argument repeated incessantly to remove objections to their hope of opening the Arctic National Wildlife Refuge to drilling. In fact I saw a few caribou wander around amid the pipes and buildings, and at the shore there were a substantial number of nesting ducks, snow geese, and other waterfowl. But some weeks later I was leaked a draft report from a US Fish and Wildlife Service office in Alaska, which documented serious impacts on wildlife from the activity at Prudhoe Bay. The Reagan Administration had suppressed the report. My story on the report ran on the front page, and a number of people said that it was responsible for killing that year's attempt to open the Arctic refuge to drilling.

One of my chief reasons for going to Prudhoe Bay was to use it as a jumping-off point to get into the Arctic wildlife refuge. I had been reading for years about its tens of thousands of migrating caribou, its polar bears, arctic foxes, musk oxen, and other wildlife, and I badly wanted to see it for myself and to describe it to *Times* readers. The day I was to fly out, Kaktovik, which had the only airstrip near the refuge, was fogged in. So I spent another night at Prudhoe, hoping to catch a plane out the

next day. The following morning I got on a small plane that tax-
ied out on to the runway. The other passengers were three
bleary-eyed Inuits who looked and smelled as if they had consumed a lot of alcohol the night before. But when we were ready
to take off, word came that Kaktovik had fogged over again. So I
sat on the runway in the cramped plane with the three hungover
Inuits for more than an hour, waiting for the fog to lift. It didn't,
and the flight was finally canceled. I never made it to the Arctic
refuge. Many years later, *Times* columnist Nicholas Kristof visited the refuge and wrote a series of columns about it. I read them
with envy. But even if I never get there, I am glad and comforted that such a wild, magnificent place still exists. I can only
hope that, against the odds, our nation will continue to resist
endless efforts by the giant oil companies, with the connivance
of their bought accomplices in government, to break into the
refuge, develop it, and destroy it. During the administration of
President George W. Bush, who seemed determined to hand
over all of our public lands to industry, that appeared to be a
forlorn hope. Thanks in large measure to the activism of environmentalists, the refuge remains intact—as of this writing.

I returned to Alaska one more time. In 1989, a supertanker
named the *Exxon Valdez* ran into a shoal shortly after leaving the
town of Valdez and spewed millions of gallons of crude oil into
the lovely Prince William Sound. I was in bed with a bad case of
the flu but was called into the office to do a story on the emerging reports about the spill. It soon became clear that this was the
biggest oil spill in the nation's history and its effects would be
devastating.

Two days later I was flying to Alaska to report on the accident. When I arrived, I found that my baggage with all my
clothes, including the parka I needed in the chill Alaska air, had
not, so I had to spend my first hours buying clothes and then
finding a place to stay. The town was already crowded with reporters and photographers. The next morning I rented a helicopter along with two other journalists and flew over the sound to
inspect the damage. The crippled supertanker was stranded in
the middle of a dark shadow of oil that stretched around it in an
irregular circle already some twenty miles in diameter over the
beautiful body of water. Efforts to contain the spill were largely

futile. Oil lapped on to the surrounding shores and oozed up the beaches of the sound's numerous islets. The helicopter set down on one of the little isles, and along with the other journalists, I stood on its strand and watched cormorants and gulls covered with the toxic, viscous crude, vainly trying to spread their wings and fly. A few yards off, a large herd of seals stretched their heads awkwardly out of the water as they swam in panicky circles through the dark, sticky water. The oil already had moved several feet up the beach and inches down into the soil. In Valdez, volunteer workers were struggling to clean a thick coat of oil from the fur of hundreds of sea otters in a too often losing effort to keep the appealing little creatures alive. I visited several fishing villages around the sound and talked to families in despair over the loss of their livelihood because of the spill.

An inquest determined that the skipper of the *Exxon Valdez* had been drinking heavily just before the tanker left port, and that probably contributed to the accident. But there had been many such tanker accidents before and have been since. As oil is sought and extracted in ever more difficult and remote places and is transported by pipeline, tanker, and truck many thousands more miles, accidents and their despoliation of the environment are inevitable. Indeed it has by now become abundantly clear that a global economy and civilization based on the combustion of fossil fuels—oil and coal—is exacting an enormous toll upon our habitat, our health, and our economy. Such an energy economy most assuredly cannot be sustained. Oil spills and noxious, polluting exhaust from petroleum-powered vehicles and the acid rain and sulfate and lung-piercing particulates from coal-fired power plants have wreaked tragic, exhaustively documented damage on human health, our built structures, crops, trees, and wildlife. America's dependence on foreign sources of oil is the largest contributor to our huge balance of payments deficit, imposes a heavy additional burden on our military budget, and still creates endless compromises of our national security, including leading us into ill-considered and disastrous military adventures. Coal mining has ripped the tops off mountains, poisoned hundreds of bodies of water, and sickened and killed miners with black lung disease. Despite decades of efforts and some improvements, the air of many of our cities is still foul with pollution created by burning oil and coal. Most crucially, the carbon dioxide released in such burning is the major contributor toward the rapidly changing climate that threatens to disrupt the planet and the lives of our children and grandchildren and into future generations.

It seems irrefutable that from almost every perspective— our national security, our economy, the health of our citizens, the preservation of our environment from the local to the global level—an exit from the age of fossil fuels as rapidly as possible makes eminent, even crucial, sense. Yet our national policy is not heading in that direction. In fact under the administration of President George W. Bush, we were heading in the opposite direction. A draft energy policy prepared for the administration by a task force headed by Vice President Dick Cheney— composed exclusively, it appeared, of executives of the energy industry—would in fact increase our dependence on fossil fuel and substantially increase the pollution it produced. I say it "appeared" that the task force was exclusively business executives because the administration refused to disclose its composition. President Bush, who seemed to be bent on leading the country back to diplomatic isolationism before the September 11 terrorist attacks, also rejected the Kyoto treaty that would require steps to reduce the carbon dioxide emissions that rapidly are warming the planet.

With the election of President Obama, there was hope the nation would embark on a rational, sustainable energy policy. But Obama, harried by right-wing political opposition that, as one commentator noted, would rather see the country fail than him succeed at anything, proved a tremendous disappointment on environmental policy as on many other issues. As of this writing, money and politics still trump the future of the planet.

Why is the nation still clutching to such an irrational, destructive reliance on fossil fuels? The answer, I think, is that national policy, now more than ever, is dominated by business, or, more properly, business political money. The rich, powerful, oil, coal, and automotive industries, along with some of their unions, have a big short-term stake in maintaining the current reliance on fossil fuel and are able to dictate energy policy to receptive, right-wing governments and bought-and-paid-for legislators. The wellbeing of the American people, the best interests of our country, and the long-term health of the planet? Forget about it.

The year before the *Exxon Valdez* incident, Arthur Wang, the founder of the publishing house of Hill & Wang, by then a subsidiary of Farrar, Straus & Giroux, had asked me to do a book on an environmental subject for him. I had written millions of words for the *Times* but never anything as sustained as a book, and I had long wanted to try my hand at one. There is an old saying that the way to achieve immortality is to have a child, plant a tree, and write a book. By then I had planted numerous trees. I had two children, and my first grandchild was only a couple of years away. After an abortive effort to write one on the Ford presidency, however, I still had my first book to do. Wang, a cultivated, no-nonsense but good humored and friendly publisher, had left it more or less up to me to decide what to write about.

By then I had been covering the environment for more than a decade but still knew less than I should about what had given rise to the environmental movement and how it had risen. One reason for my lack of knowledge was that there was scant literature on environmental history. Samuel Hays, Roderick Nash, Donald Worster, Stephen Fox, and a few others had written thoughtful, scholarly books on environmentalism, but there were large holes to be filled in the history. So I undertook to do so with a book that eventually was to be published as *A Fierce Green Fire.* The title came from an essay by Aldo Leopold, a patron saint of the American environmental movement, who, describing "a fierce green fire" dying in the eyes of a mother wolf he had just shot, decided that leaving wolves alive was a better idea than shooting them.

A few months after returning from Valdez, I took off three months of accumulated leave time to write as large a chunk of the book as possible. The work was as intense as anything I had done in my life. I found that to write about environmentalism in the United States I first had to learn about and describe how the American landscape had been transformed since the first Europeans began to permanently settle the continent nearly a half-millennium earlier. I enjoyed the work and it went well. After I returned to the Washington bureau early in 1990, I was able to finish the first draft in a few months, writing weekends and evenings. Arthur Wang edited my manuscript himself, and under his stern tutelage, I went through several drafts before it was ready to print.

When I returned to the Washington bureau, I found my position there greatly changed. My reporting had, I was often told by outsiders, made the *Times* preeminent in environmental journalism in America. When my daughter was at law school, one of her professors told her that I had defined environmental journalism for the rest of the profession. My work had been treated with respect by editors on the paper, even by editors who really did not understand the subject and were wary of it. But now my stories were being questioned and, according to Howell Raines, then Washington bureau chief, the top brass in New York thought I was "too close to the environmentalists." They also thought, they said, that my coverage was "biased" in favor of the environment—a peculiar formulation I thought. Who is against the environment? When I asked for an example of my "bias," Raines mentioned a recent story in which I had described dolphins being accidentally "slaughtered" by tuna fishing boats instead of being "killed." Finally, he said, "New York" thought I was paying too much attention to the harm that economic activity was doing to the environment and not enough to the harm that environmentalism was doing to the economy. Funny, when I was writing on national economic issues, no one asked why I wasn't paying more attention to the harm economic activity was doing to the environment. I had covered the environment in exactly the same way I had covered everything else I wrote about for the paper, but the environment was somehow different.

The "New York" that was questioning my work, it appeared, was mostly the national news editor at the time, a woman named Soma Golden, whom Max Frankel had first brought to the *Times* from *Business Week* magazine as an editorial writer when the paper was making an effort to remedy its reprehensible neglect of women journalists. When Frankel became executive editor, Golden was appointed editor of the Sunday Business section and then as national editor. She had little experience with daily news writing, and I thought her to be one of the least competent editors with whom I had ever worked. As far as I was concerned, she hadn't a clue about the environmental story. But she knew what she didn't like, and that was my reporting. I think she looked at the news through the prism of her background in business reporting and may have heard from corporate executives who were annoyed at my reports about the effects of their activities on the environment. At one point she wrote me an insulting letter complaining about a news article I wrote that stated that the Environmental Protection Agency had decided to allow a certain chemical to remain on the market even thought it had determined the substance was a potential carcinogen. I was simply reporting what the agency had announced, that the chemical was allowed to remain in production because the EPA had decided its benefits outweighed the risks. But Golden wrote that I was being unfair to the agency.

Nonplussed, I called the agency's chief public affairs officer, who said that my story was completely accurate and carried the message that the agency had wanted to convey. I then wrote an angry reply to Golden. It was injudicious, perhaps, in an institution that often treated editors, even incompetent ones, like high-ranking military officers and reporters like enlisted women and men, but I felt I had a long record of accomplishment on the paper that deserved a modicum of respect. The exchange of letters was the beginning of the end of my career at the *Times*.

I was soon removed—perhaps "shoved" is a better word—from the environmental beat after having filled it for fourteen years. I was not immediately replaced but subjected to a series of petty indignities, such as not being permitted to cover the celebrations of Earth Day 1990, to demonstrate my position. There was no point appealing my treatment to Frankel because Golden was his protégé, and he seemed to share her views about my environmental reporting. After a while I was reassigned to write about the Internal Revenue Service. Sure enough, my successor on the environmental beat was soon writing front-page stories about how environmental threats had been exaggerated and about the alleged toll that environmental regulation was taking on the economy.

It was clear that the time had come to leave the paper. I would have resigned immediately after my reassignment, but the Newspaper Guild was negotiating a severance package for senior reporters who opted for early retirement, so I hung on a few more months until that came through. I had already begun to prepare for the next stage of my career. Doug Bailey, head of the American Political Network, which published a well-regarded daily, online political report called the *Hotline*, asked me to join his company to develop and publish a similar online environmental report. My contract called for me to give only half my time to the new publication, which would enable me to continue with my own writing. I had already begun work on my second book, *A New Name for Peace*, which examined the interface of international environmentalism and economic development by focusing on the 1992 Earth Summit. Joan Martin-Brown, a friend who then ran the Washington office of the United Nations Environment Program, had put me in touch with Maurice Strong, a successful and extraordinarily energetic Canadian businessman and diplomat who had been named secretary general of the summit. Strong invited me to join his secretariat as public affairs officer and offered me full access to the entire process for my book. I declined his invitation, not wanting to be part of the story I would write, but Strong granted me the access anyway.

I resigned (officially I retired) from the *Times* on May 1, 1991, after thirty-two years with the paper. The landing was a soft one. I had taken some additional leave to begin to prepare for publication of *Greenwire*, the name we had chosen for the online environmental report, so it was ready to go the day after I quit. I received a good, if not overly generous, severance from the paper as well as my pension in a lump sum. I also had raised substantial funds from several foundations, including the Ford and Joyce foundations, the Carnegie Corporation, and Rockefeller Family Services, to support the research and writing of my book. I accepted a number of paid speaking engagements, something I never had done while working as a reporter for the *Times*. I joined the Dow Chemical Company's corporate environmental advisory council, thinking it was worth a try to help that company, often the object of environmentalists' wrath, become a good environmental citizen. I became a juror for the Heinz Family Foundation's annual environmental awards, given in the name of the late Senator John Heinz and presided over by his bright, attractive widow, Teresa Heinz. My income was now appreciably higher than it had been as a reporter.

Still, it was a difficult, emotional period. The *Times* had been my professional life. It is a great and unique institution (I could never use the word "unique" as a reporter). In an age of scandal mongering and "infotainment," it is one of the few remaining sources of serious, solid, and impartial journalism in this country (though it has added a considerable amount of frivolity to its pages since I joined the paper in 1959. The "Gray Lady" now includes an array of brightly colored outfits in her wardrobe.) Writing for the *Times* had been my goal since childhood. I had done it and succeeded at it. I missed my colleagues, the daily routine, the virtually unlimited access to sources, and, I must admit, the prestige and the small power that came with being a *Times* correspondent in Washington. Most of all I missed the ability to find and give my fellow Americans the information they needed to act as engaged citizens of our democracy.

Now I had left that behind. I was not adrift; I had found new anchors. But it was long before I could shake off a feeling that I had lost something important. Two decades after I left, I still have flashes of anger at those editors who were too dense and, yes, biased, to understand what my environmental reporting had brought to the paper.

Publishing *Greenwire* was a lot of fun but also difficult and often frustrating. Our offices were a pair of rather small rooms in a big old frame house rented by the American Political Network in Falls Church, Virginia, about a twenty-minute drive from my home in Chevy Chase. It was a pleasant-looking place, with a park out behind it, but overcrowded with young men and women working on the various publications. The air was close and sometimes foul with lavatory smells, and the downstairs rooms were occasionally infested with swarms of insects.

At the beginning, with a staff of three, including a talented, very young editor named Pete Nelson, I started at six in the morning to prepare a twelve-page report that would be available online by ten a.m. Pete, like almost all who would work for me, was a year or two out of college. Our budget permitted only miniscule salaries, and we could attract, therefore, only kids at the start of their journalism career who would work for next to nothing to get a foot in the door. Most of my reporters and editors were bright and energetic but almost totally without work experience and the discipline such experience brings. Bailey kept up morale with frequent parties and free food, as well as pep talks at staff meetings. It was more like a college dormitory than a professional newsroom. I was in my late fifties by that time, and I found the energy of my young staff invigorating. All of them knew far more about computers than I. But sometimes I felt like a babysitter instead of a publisher and often found that my staff was unable to accomplish some of my goals, such as doing original reporting and writing. *Greenwire*, like the *Hotline*, was largely a summary of environmental news from other sources—newspapers, television, and magazines. I wrote most of whatever original content we had.

At first it seemed likely that *Greenwire* would fail. Doug Bailey had assumed that corporations would pay premium prices for daily environmental news just as political professionals paid such prices for his *Hotline*. But corporations did not really care about environmental news, and many were averse to it. The national environmental groups liked it but could not afford the annual subscription cost. Our marketing director had no experience in marketing, and we had no advertising budget. I knew nothing about marketing and had little aptitude for it. On top of that, the administration of the American Political Network was chaotic. The number of publications it put out expanded quickly, but its administrative staff and expertise did not. Bailey, a Republican political consultant, was a creative and charismatic leader, shooting off ideas like fireworks, but he seemed not to be that interested in the details of running a business organization. At one point I told Bailey that *Greenwire* needed to lower prices and get a professional marketer in order to start turning a profit. I also said that something had to be done to improve the administration of the company.

After about a year with *Greenwire*, I spoke to my friend Alan Wurtzel, then chairman of Circuit City, who had built his family business into a multibillion-dollar enterprise, about the

problems at the American Political Network. He offered to
help, and after the two of us met with Doug Bailey, he agreed
to become a director of the company and sent over one of his
assistants at Circuit City, Ed Kopf, to be our company's chief
operating officer. Kopf quickly brought order and financial
discipline to the company. But he also decided that *Greenwire*
was losing too much money and started to suggest that it
might have to be shut down. The executive that my friend had
sent over as a favor to help make a go of *Greenwire* now wanted to kill it!

I was not willing to give up after only a year. I raised a substantial amount of money from foundations that regarded
Greenwire as a valuable product and that gave us grants to give
the report away to universities and journalists. That funding
kept us going until we were able to get a foothold. Bailey agreed
to hire a professional marketer and to lower prices, and our
sales began to jump. The parent company hired a co-publisher,
Dale Curtis, with more aptitude than I for selling. *Greenwire*'s
reputation spread, and we soon were selling subscriptions to the
White House, the House of Representatives, and to federal and
state environmental agencies. Advancing technology enabled us
to provide hypertext so that subscribers could click to the original articles we were summarizing, making our product even
more attractive. *Greenwire* had made it.

In the mid-nineties, the *National Journal*, then a subsidiary of
the giant Times-Mirror Corporation, bought American Political
Network and its publications. They had their own editors and
publishers, so I and other executives of APN were not needed. A
couple of years later *Greenwire* was sold to another publisher.
Today, more than two decades years after its first publication, it
is still going strong.

At that point, in my sixties, I wanted no more of daily journalism. I was working on a third book, this one about the future
of American environmentalism and published by Island Press as
Earth Rising. I was also getting sick of Washington. The political
discourse and partisanship in the nation's capital had turned
increasingly nasty. Vicious ideologues and free market fanatics
dominated the political life of the city. Congress was in the
hands of win-at-any-cost gutter fighters like Tom Delay, Newt

Gingrich, Trent Lott, and hypocrites like Henry Hyde. Bill Clinton, with the intelligence and political skills to be a great president, undermined his presidency with his own weakness of character and barely survived the long knives of his political enemies. Elected officials became increasingly for sale to the highest bidder. The city reeked of corruption.

I badly wanted to get away and clear my lungs of the stench. Above all I wanted to spend more time with my children and expanding brood of grandchildren. Alexa, with her husband, Roger, and children, Adam and Sophia, lived in the city of Newton outside of Boston. Alexa had been a legal services lawyer and now was an assistant dean and director of the Office of Public Interest Advising at the Harvard Law School. Roger practices law with Harvard's legal services firm and teaches clinical law to its law students. My son, Peter, had returned from Paris where he had worked for years for the French office of a large New York law firm and then joined the firm in Manhattan. He lived in a high-rise with a spectacular view of the East River with his wife, Deborah, and his identical, model-handsome twin boys, Edward and Alexander. He soon left the firm to join a client company that invited him to become a partner. A few years later, he founded his own multimillion-dollar investment company. Peter and his family now live in Greenwich, Connecticut, with a third son named William, in a big, comfortable old federal house.

Living in Chevy Chase, we saw our kids and their families only a few times a year, and that was not enough. We were a close family when our children had been growing up, and we wanted to restore that relationship. With some hubris, I even dreamed about becoming the patriarch of a big extended family of the kind that had surrounded me as a child.

Sidney, my father, had died a few years earlier. He was a hearty, independent man even in his mid-eighties, with his own active social life. But then his health began to fail. He went through surgery for colon cancer, which was successful but diminished his control of his bowels and he had to wear diapers. One night soon thereafter, he stood on his bed to swat a fly, fell off, and broke his shoulder. He was in considerable pain and was unable to care for himself. I found myself having to change my father's dirty diapers, which I found emotionally devastating. His doctor recommended he be put in a nursing home until his shoulder recovered. When we did, however, Sidney became suicidal, thinking he was going to be warehoused there, even though we assured him repeatedly that his stay there would end as soon as his shoulder healed. He grew calm again when he returned to his own apartment but could not manage for himself. Alice and I were both working full time, so we hired a nurse to spend the daytime with him. He was alone at night, however, and growing increasingly disoriented. One morning I came to check on him, and he was nowhere to be found. He had felt sick and panicky and had called 911 for an ambulance to take him to the emergency room. When I asked Sidney how he felt, he said, "I feel like death." A few weeks later the same thing happened. We found a small assisted living facility in a private home in a leafy suburb not far from us and brought my father there. Two days later the manager of the facility said my father was too sick to stay there and that we needed to put him a nursing home. The next morning the manager called to say my father had collapsed and had been taken to the hospital. I left work and rushed to the hospital, but Sidney was already in coma. He died of kidney failure the following morning.

We decided to move to the Boston area for several reasons. We ruled out Manhattan because there we could not afford the ample housing to which we had become accustomed. Another was that my grandson Adam, a beautiful, intelligent, and affectionate boy with a wonderful sense of humor, suffered from attention deficit and hyperactivity syndrome (ADHD), which created additional work and stress for his parents. If we lived near them, we could act as reinforcements when necessary, and we often have and enjoy it. His younger sister, Sophie, a blonde-haired, blue-eyed, snub-nosed, freckle-faced prototype of a corn-fed Iowa farm girl (our son-in-law, Roger, is from Iowa), filled to the brim with life and joy and music (except in her teenage years), was a big bonus for us. Living in Newton for two years—and now Brookline—let us drive to our place in the Berkshires in two hours. Finally, I loved New England. I loved its landscape and its history. Even as a child, reading about the Pilgrims and the Indians; about the Adamses, Paul Revere, and

222

the other patriots; about the rocky coasts and little harbors; about its fishermen and farmers; and its Norman Rockwell villages, I was captivated by the idea of New England. Visiting my father's family in Norwich, Connecticut, when I was a child, I felt, for no good reason, I suppose, that this was more the *real* America than the Bronx. My aunts and uncles and cousins there often talked casually about "going up to Boston."

Was it Willie Morris who wrote a book titled *North Toward Home*? That is how I felt when we moved into half of a big two-family house built at the beginning of the twentieth century in Newton Center, a ten-minute drive from my daughter's home in West Newton. Alice didn't care for it that much, so two years later we moved closer to Boston to a lovely, large apartment in Brookline, on a reasonably quiet street just around the corner from shops and restaurants and a two minute walk to the T, Boston's subway system. Alice misses her close friends in the Washington area and sometimes wonders about our move, but I have not regretted it for a second.

I do sometimes miss my daily immersion into the environmental story. It was always interesting and often exciting. I felt I was doing something useful to help point society toward a more rational and sustainable way of living on this planet. I also believed I was among the first and the few to chronicle the emergence of a major new cultural force in this country and around the world—the environmental movement. That movement arose out of the inescapable recognition that human numbers, human activity, and human technology are wreaking serious harm on our habitat and to our bodies and the potential future life on earth. We would be in far more difficult straits today if environmentalism had not emerged as a mass movement in the twentieth century. We could be in desperate straits in this century if the environmentalists do not succeed in altering, to a degree at least, the unsustainable course of modern civilization.

When the corporations and right-wing ideologues resumed their efforts to roll back progress in protecting the environment during the Newt Gingrich "Contract With America" period and again when the second Bush administration began its stealth attacks on the environment, I was no longer with the *Times*. It got even worse when the Tea Party extremists took control of the Republican Party and imposed their anarchistic antigovernment agenda on a perplexingly weak Obama administration. Despite having written four books on environmental subjects, I have had periods of deep frustration and feelings of impotence at not being able to arouse the public to what industry and their paid-for government are doing to the environment and how it will affect them.

I was not sorry to leave Washington. The virulent partisanship, particularly by the ascendant right wing of the Republican Party, combined with rising control of corporate money over the political process and its outcomes, had turned the climate poisonous. For someone like myself who had grown up with a government that largely—although not entirely—honestly served the interests of the American people, the culture of greed initiated by the presidency of Ronald Reagan was hard to take. And its consequences have been devastating for America. The distribution of our country's wealth has become intolerably inequitable. The nation's manufacturing base has been shattered. Our treasure is being systematically transferred to China and other countries to further enrich a few Americans. The labor movement has been worse than decimated. Pressing environmental threats such as global warming and the toxification of our habitat are unaddressed. The list goes on. I, like many others, had hoped the nation's trajectory would change with the election of President Obama, but any hope for meaningful change has been dashed by the determination of the Republicans, now a radical right-wing party, to block any progress by the Obama administration. Their goal? To return to power, no matter the cost to the nation.

In one way I do miss being a *Times* reporter in Washington. In that position I was able to have a miniscule but real influence on events there. A local business magazine once listed me as one of the one hundred most influential nongovernmental people in the city because of the effect my articles had on the legislative process.

Since I left, though, I have been able only to be an impotent distant observer as the country is being torn apart. I still, however, continue to write about the environment, to do what I can to defend the habitats that sustain my family and all of the human family.

I should not end my tale of environmental journalism without noting that my reporting brought me into regular contact with many extraordinarily talented, bright, dedicated, and decent women and men who labored for the environmental groups at the local, regional, national, and international level. These people could have made themselves rich by working for corporations and law firms, or secure and honored in academic institutions. Many of them did go on to other pursuits, but they served the broadest public good, often against difficult odds, to protect us, our land, our air, our water, and our biological legacy. Often dismissed as tree huggers and birdwatchers, they significantly have altered global consciousness regarding our environmental dilemma. Those who call the environmentalists "special interest" groups are either cynical corporate lobbyists or right-wing ideologues or speak out of rank ignorance. The environmental activists serve everyone's interest in a clean, healthy, safe, and pleasant environment.

If we manage to save ourselves and what is around us from ourselves, it will be in good measure because of the efforts of environmentalists, abetted by many dedicated public servants in government at all levels, by my fellow journalists, and on rare occasion, by farsighted business men and women. I could not possibly begin to list them all, much less describe their contributions. But I wish here to honor the great and critical service they have given to their countries and to the world.

CHAPTER 12

A POTPOURRI OF PLACES

THE PLACE WHERE EDEN WAS LOST
The Rift Valley, Kenya

In the early 1980s, while in Nairobi covering a United Nations conference on the global environment, some friends of mine, a married couple, suggested we take the weekend break from the meeting to visit a safari camp in the Masai Mara, one of East Africa's great wildlife preserves. As I had promised an article on Africa's disappearing black rhino population for the *Times* Science section, I thought this might be an opportunity actually to see one of those increasingly rare animals. We rented a Land Rover, packed a picnic lunch, laid on a couple of jerricans of extra gasoline for possible emergencies, and set out in mid-morning for what we expected to be a two- or three-hour drive.

Driving down a narrow road on the side of a steep escarpment with a sheer drop-off a few inches from the edge of the car, while trucks passed us at breakneck speed, we came after twenty or so white-knuckle minutes to the floor of the Rift Valley. The valley is a long crack in the Earth's crust that extends nearly four thousand miles from Mozambique in the south to Lebanon in the north. In Kenya, the crack divides the country neatly in two. We drove through a gently rolling green-and-light-brown savanna punctuated by isolated stands of acacia trees. In this valley, the remains of some of the earliest humanoids have been unearthed.

As we came around a curve, we saw in the distance what looked like some kind of protuberances above a clump of acacias. Coming closer we realized they were the necks and heads of three giraffes browsing on the leaves. Grazing nearby was a small herd of zebras. We pulled over to the side of the road and got out of the car to look. This was not a zoo; these were wild animals in their natural habitat. After a few moments, I was surprised to feel tears rolling down my face. I clearly was having some kind of emotional response to seeing these wild creatures, but I did not understand why. I have thought about that moment many times over the years, and I have come to believe that what I experienced was briefly regaining the sense of being deeply a part of the old natural world, of intimately sharing a habitat with untamed, nonhuman creatures. It is something I and most other modern humans rarely achieve, and a feeling of irreparable loss may have triggered my tears. By our estrangement from the natural world, we humans have become, in effect, aliens on our own planet.

We continued to drive for another couple of hours until the gas gauge showed an almost empty tank, so we stopped to empty one of the jerricans into the tank. It was getting to be late in the afternoon, and as we looked around the empty savanna, it became apparent we had taken a wrong turn somewhere. As the sun began to go down, we kept driving on what was more track through the grass than road. With night coming on, we were probably lost in a place filled with lions and other predators and nothing between us and them but the cloth top of the Land Rover. The experience was unnerving but also exhilarating.

Just as dusk was gathering, we came to a bridge over what we learned was the Mara River. The bridge was guarded by two park rangers who gave us directions to our camp, which, they said, was only a few minutes away. They were right. We soon came to a series of tents along the river and were greeted by a hostess, who led us to where other guests were sitting around a blazing campfire and took our order for drinks. Getting into the spirit of colonial Brits, I ordered a Pimm's Cup. It had cucumber slices in it, but I drank it anyway. A few minutes later, we were ushered into a large dining tent with tables covered with white linen and good flatware and served a sumptuous meal. From primal fear to pampered civilization in about an hour's time! That night I slept in a comfortable bed in a tent with rugs on the floor, waking occasionally to the snorting of hippopotamuses (hippopotami? hippos?) in the river.

Just after sunrise the next morning, we went with a guide in the Land Rover to see the wildlife. There was a lot of it. Only a few minutes out, we came to a small pride of lions lazily picking at the remains of its night's kill. We parked almost next to them, but they paid no attention to us. We saw quite a few lions that day, including a lioness slithering through the tall grass, belly close to the ground, stalking a warthog. For some reason she gave up after a few hundred feet. Perhaps she wasn't hungry. We saw elephants, many giraffes and zebras, gazelles, kudus, wildebeest, and hippos and crocodiles in the river. We even spotted a few ostriches. Late in the afternoon, the guide pointed to a dark patch near the top of a low hill. "Rhino," he said, handing me his binoculars. There, unmistakably, was a large black rhino with a small calf huddled alongside. We could not approach closer because of the rhino's protected status, but I felt privileged. The air over the sun-washed plain was mild and fragrant. The golden savanna stretched out into a hazy infinity, its silence slightly broken by the whisper of an easy breeze.

Was this the Eden from which humankind, tasting fruit from the tree of knowledge, had been cast out?

Ten years later, while on a reporting trip for a book I was writing about international environmentalism, I again visited the Mara, this time bringing Alice with me. It was much changed. The Kenyan government had opted for an economic strategy of high-volume, relatively low-cost tourism, which had put unsustainable pressure on ecosystems such as the Masai Mara. Everywhere we went on our search for wildlife, the savanna was deeply rutted from heavy traffic by four-wheel-drive vehicles. Some places were so torn up they looked like moonscapes. Animals were scarce. We crisscrossed the land repeatedly, looking for lions. Finally, toward the end of the morning, we came across a solitary, weary-looking male lion, already surrounded by three other Land Rovers.

This economic strategy undoubtedly brought in large volumes of cash, but most of the tourist operations were owned by foreigners who promptly shipped the money back out of Kenya, with the tacit permission of the then highly corrupt government, whose leaders no doubt received a substantial return.

It was the old story. The natural world and its wild inhabitants are no match for human greed. Primeval places have all but disappeared. The flaming swords set before the garden to prevent Adam and Eve from returning are now extinguished. Their descendents have reoccupied Eden and are tearing it to pieces.

I have no desire to return to that place.

A PLACE LOVED THROUGH LITERATURE
OXFORDSHIRE AND THE COTSWOLDS, ENGLAND

Is it possible to be homesick for a place one has never seen? I believe I was sick for the English countryside long before I ever went there. I was infected by books. I grew up reading the eighteenth- and nineteenth-century English novelists and continued to read them throughout my life. I have lived vicariously but deeply among the meadows and moors, woods, farms and gardens, pubs, cottages and great houses, villages and towns portrayed in enchanting detail by Smollet, Fielding, Austen, the Brontës, Thackery, Trollope, Gaskell, Eliot, Hardy, and so many more. My desire to experience those places sharpened when I read Flora Thompson's *Lark Rise to Candleford*, with its artfully evocative description of farming hamlet and small-town life around the Cotswolds in the waning days of Victorian and Edwardian England.

Dickens, too, of course. But I more or less slaked my thirst for Dickensian places with a number of trips to London when we lived in Germany. We used to travel there every year around Christmas, usually by boat train, to buy books and clothes and to speak English instead of German for a few days. What I liked best were the older places—Shepherd's Market, the Inner Temple, the Embankment, pubs with the low ceilings and fireplaces, the graceful curve of Regent Street. However, my longing for the habitat of Emma and Heathcliff and Jude and the good folk of Barchester and Cranford and all the other companions of my long lamp-lit evenings with a book on my lap remained unrequited.

Then, when Alice and I were approaching seventy, we decided the time had come. Searching online house-swapping sites, we found a place that sounded ideal—an eighteenth-century thatched-roof house in a small village called Bucknell in Oxfordshire. Its owners, a warm and hospitable professional couple named Neil and Pauline Wainman, agreed to let us live there for a month while they stayed at the Barn. Alice's sister, Susan, came too. It turned out to be a month that matched my storybook expectations.

One of the Wainmans' friends, Malcolm Dorrington, met us at Heathrow and drove us to Bucknell. Malcolm, a teacher and artist and a companionable, bearded bear of a man, immediately became our friend, our guide, and our expert instructor in church architecture, the best pubs, and English life as we drove around Oxfordshire and beyond.

Bucknell is a small cluster of old and newer houses, a stone church with a square tower, a general store whose proprietor also served as the postmistress, and a perfect pub called the Trigger Pond. That was it, and it was just what we had hoped for. Our thatched house, named, strangely enough The Thatches, was spacious, comfortable, and well appointed. It had a large patio and larger garden, nicely landscaped by Neil and Pauline, in which we drank our evening whiskies and ate many of our meals when we were not patronizing the Trigger or other pubs in the area. The house came with a large, friendly cat named Tobias that brought in mice from the surrounding fields and once proudly deposited a bloody rabbit on the living room rug. Bucknell also had the additional attraction, for me, of being only a few miles from the village of Fringford, which was the model used for the fictionalized village of Lark Rise.

We also had exchanged cars with the Wainmans and, with Malcolm's jolly company and knowledgeable guidance, at first explored the surrounding Oxfordshire countryside. We duly visited a clutch of old churches and stately homes, including Blenheim Castle, where Winston Churchill was born. We found its zillions of beautifully furnished rooms and its hundreds of acres of manicured grounds with lakes and fountains and statuary and topiary magnificent in an over-the-top kind of way, but we preferred the smaller but still stately manor houses that looked like real homes (for really rich people). We were especially enamored of the lovely lawns and gardens that surround these places. They called to mind the old saying that the way to have a nice lawn is to plant grass and then tend it carefully for three hundred years. But it was the flower gardens that knocked us out. Some were formal spaces filled with bright flowers aligned in military precision, without a weed in sight. Others were more like cottage gardens, with a profusion of blossoms crowded together in a cheerful growing mass. The rose gardens especially entranced me with their seemingly endless variety of red, pink, white, and yellow blossoms exuding delicious, complex aromas we could almost float on. In a short time I was suffering a bad case of rose envy. I have only partially ameliorated the condition by creating my own rose garden at the Barn. The thin soil and frigid winters of Becket Mountain make a mockery of my feeble attempt to create a facsimile of an English rose garden. Nevertheless, I bring what roses I can into the house all summer long.

The landscape of Oxfordshire, and particularly the Cotswolds, looks as if it emerged straight from the pages of Lark Rise. There are green fields and meadows, small streams traversed by arched stone bridges, villages and farms, honey-colored stone cottages, market towns with small shops that feel as if they have been there for generations, and of course the ubiquitous pubs, each featuring beer and ale from a specific brewery, often local. With Malcolm leading the way, we managed to sample at least one pub a day, usually managing a nice meal— nice if you happen to enjoy things like shepherd's pie, mutton chops, or fish and chips, as we do.

British custom, as well as law, permits walking across private property, and we did so in many areas, including around two charming villages called the Slaughters. In Lower Slaughter, we watched a shepherd and two dogs move a large herd of sheep across a velvety green meadow as if they were conducting a close-order infantry drill. In Upper Slaughter, we ate lunch at a sweet little hotel surrounded by a manicured lawn, old trees, and a small pond. A gaggle of geese moved with proprietary authority around the pond.

Many of these fields and villages are preserved from development, often by Britain's National Trust. In Oxfordshire, at least, the best of the past is preserved without turning the landscape into a museum. Past and present seem to intermingle comfortably, creating a lovely, livable habitat. In the United States, we rarely get it right with settled places. We do fairly well with wilderness areas and our national parks are spectacular creations. But the fate of our farms and pastures, villages, and small towns, as well as many of our big cities, are left to the rough hands of the market and the speculations of developers. Those places have not fared well over the last century or so.

The city of Oxford is one of those places where past and present blend nicely. It is a modern city with a bustling center filled with shops and lively cafes and restaurants where students and tourists hang out. It is also the city of Mathew Arnold's "dreaming spires," the tradition-encrusted ancient buildings of the Oxford colleges, some dating back to the twelfth century. Some years later, while spending a month at the Rockefeller Foundation's study center at a villa above Lake Como in Italy, I became friendly with Peter Hacker, a witty, erudite philosophy don from Oxford's St. John College. He invited me to join him at lunch at the faculty "high table" if I chanced to visit the city again. I still hope to do so.

My preconception of the city came not so much from books as from the BBC's Inspector Morse television series on its *Mystery* program. Oxford, however, has produced many noted authors. Alice, Susan, and I signed up for a literary tour of the city sponsored by Blackwell's, the old and much-loved bookseller. It was a long walk. The writers associated with Oxford are legion, from John Donne, Percy Bysshe Shelley, and Samuel Johnson, to Oscar Wilde, Lewis Carroll, and Aldous Huxley, to J.R.R. Tolkien, V.S. Naipul, and Philip Pullman, to name just a few.

One of the most memorable events of our Oxford visit was a *tour de force* or, rather, a *tour* à *manger* pulled off by Alice and Susan. We had stopped for what the Brits call a cream tea at an elegant little hotel just across the street from the city's venerable Ashmolean Museum. The waiter set down a silver pot of tea on the crisp linen tablecloth and next to it, a kind of tower, also silver, piled high with scones, pastries, and biscuits. Next came little jars of fruit preserves and honey, then a bowl filled with thick Devonshire cream. It looked like enough food for a team of hungry football players. I took a scone, covered it with jam and cream, finished it off with a cup of tea, and was happy. But Alice and Susan, both small, slender women, proceeded to demolish the entire mound of confections, scone by scone, pastry by pastry, biscuit by biscuit, each covered with layers of jam and cream, until not a crumb or dollop was left. I watched in incredulous admiration. We left Oxford shortly thereafter, with the sisters riding a sugar high.

Venturing farther afield in the Wainmans' little car, we zipped through Cornwall, Devon, and Dorset, overnighting at bed and breakfasts and spending a couple of nights at an organic farm where the chicken coop was cleaner than the farmhouse in which we slept. We saw cathedrals and megaliths (but not Stonehenge), moors, museums, and manor houses. We hiked rugged coastline trails and ambled across Thomas Hardy-esque heather-covered heaths. We went to Bath and drank the water in the Pump Room where Beau Brummel once mingled with the gentry and aspiring gentry, then walked around town admiring its stately Regency homes. We took a day in London to see the then new Tate Museum of Contemporary Art in its cavernous former power station and to take in a play at the reconstructed Globe Theatre. The play was by Fletcher, not Shakespeare but the Bard is said to have helped with its writing.

We returned to Bucknell and The Thatches, visited a few more churches and gardens, spent a few more pub evenings with Malcolm, and then returned home to America. My bookish thirst for the English countryside had been slaked but not extinguished. The actual rural England was almost, if not entirely, as enchanting as the novels had led me to envision.

The Brits may have lost their empire, but they still have their "sceptered isle...other Eden, demi-paradise." How long they can keep it preserved from the juggernaut of the global economy and the corporate oligarchy remains to be seen.

I just took a break from writing this today to look at my e-mail. There was a message from the Wainmans saying that Malcolm had been diagnosed with a very aggressive form of cancer and that he did not have long to live. It was a tremendously sad coincidence. We had thought about visiting England again this year but decided instead to go to France to see one of our grandsons, who is studying there this year. Malcolm had come to stay with us at the Barn a couple of times and we thought we would enjoy his lively companionship for years. We are far enough advanced in years to expect friends to start departing. But Malcolm was ten years younger than we. It is hard to accept. Our lives touched only briefly, but he was a bright candle in ours.

(A week after we first heard about Malcolm's illness we received a second e-mail. Malcolm had died. We are only slightly comforted to know that the Wainmans managed to read him a goodbye message from us before he went.)

A CIVILIZED PLACE
Paris

There probably is not much more that can be said about Paris. It seems that everyone who has been there and can write has written about the City of Light. But because it is Paris and it is a place I have happily experienced, and because it is the archetype of a civilized urban habitat, my book about places should at least give it some small but due attention.

Alice and I probably have spent more time in Paris than any other city in which we did not live. We went there several times as tourists when we lived in Germany. We went there when I was gathering material for a book. We went there for weeks at a time, four years in a row, to visit our son and his family when he worked as a lawyer in the Paris office of a New York law firm. Recently we spent several days there on the way to visit one of our grandsons who had taken an academic year in Brittany.

When I think of my times in Paris, it is always with pleasure. It is a place whose physical spaces and culture have evolved over many centuries to provide its inhabitants, and visitors, with unmatched physical comforts and aesthetic delights. Montaigne had it right. Paris, he wrote, is "great in population, great in the felicity of her situation, but above all great and incomparable in variety and diversity of the good things of life." There are, of course, endless magnificent places to visit in the city. On our last trip, we entered for the first time Sainte Chapelle, the splendid little Gothic church built by St. Louis, and were stunned by the glowing beauty of its wall of blue stained-glass windows.

What Alice and I like best is just to absorb the city and be absorbed by it. We do it by walking and looking and listening, and breathing and feeling and, of course, eating.

The last time I saw Paris (I had to get that in. It is a great song and a terrible movie), we spent nearly all day every day walking around the city. It was not entirely because we wanted to. Our visit was during holy week, and the place was crammed with mostly French tourists; long lines formed outside all the major tourist places. I had wanted one more—and probably last—ascent of the Eiffel tower, but the queue wait for the elevators was a quarter-mile long at nine in the morning. Same with the Louvre and the Orsay. So vigorous septuagenarians that we are, we walked around the city virtually all day every day we were there. There was something to enjoy around every corner—a small leafy square with a carousel in its middle; a panoramic view from the steps of Sacre Coeur; the elegant Place de Vosges with its double rows of chestnut trees in bloom; the small park at the back end of Notre Dame; the narrow streets and bustling street life of Montparnasse; the bridges over the Seine, their sides studded with hundreds of locks etched with the names of lovers; the book and print stalls along the embankments; coming unexpectedly upon the Odeon; the expensive shops along the Fauberg St. Germain; the Belle Epoque décor of the Galleries Lafayette; the brasseries and bistros and cafes on every block, most them filled young people talking, smoking, drinking eating, and wooing.

We seem to have a different experience every time we go to Paris. The first time was when we drove overnight to get to Paris on a three-day pass from my Army base in Germany. We found a grubby little hotel and a room under its roof that seemed just right. The next morning we sat down at a sidewalk table of a nearby cafe, and I ordered croissant and café au lait in my best high school and college French. The waiter looked down his nose at us and said, "It's all right, *monsieur*. I speak English." (I said I loved Paris. I didn't say I loved Parisians.) We made our first visit to the Louvre, which was not crowded then in the late 1950s, where I developed a hopeless crush on a beautiful, ethereal blonde Virgin by Filippino Lippi. We strolled along the Seine and bought a Japanese print at one of the stalls along the river. It now hangs in our Brookline kitchen more than fifty years later. In the evening we sat outside Les Deux Magots, the cafe once frequented by Hemingway, Camus, Sartre, and others we had been reading for years. We sipped our aperitifs and contentedly watched the stream of pedestrians along the Fauburg St. Germaine. Alice had on a bright red sundress, and she wore her hair coiled in braids around her head. She was twenty-three years old and in my eyes utterly lovely. A mild late-spring dusk gathered around us. I don't think I have ever been happier—well, maybe when my children were born.

Many years later, when my son lived in Paris, we spent a lot of time in the Luxemburg Gardens with his new twin sons, Edward and Alexander. The gardens were close to his home, a spacious apartment on the Rue de la Sorbonne, whose tall windows looked directly down at the Cluny museum, with a full view of Notre Dame in the middle distance. Pushing the baby stroller around the gravel paths of the garden, frequently stopping to let passersby exclaim over our beautiful little *jumeaux*, we felt we were now part of the city instead of merely visitors. We bought charcuterie, cheeses, bread, and vegetables at the outdoor markets. We window-shopped the too expensive stores along St. Germaine. We chatted as best we could with the nice woman behind the counter at the *boulangerie*. We complained about the pollution from the choking traffic. If only for a few weeks, we were Parisians!

Last summer we were back in Paris on our way to visit our then seventeen-year-old grandson, Edward, in Brittany. We were joined by our friend and honorary granddaughter, Emma, who was studying at the prestigious Sciences Po University. The three of us walked and walked for hours talking, mostly about the city but also about the young man Emma had fallen in love with. Emma, who had been living in Paris for nearly a year took us on a tour of her favorite haunts, including the bridge on which her *bien ami* had placed a lock engraved with their initials. Toward evening, we stopped at a *boîte* in the Tuileries, where I had a whisky, and Emma and Alice wine. We sat there for an hour watching the sun go down. Then we walked to a recommended restaurant, had a superb meal, and bid Emma goodbye. The next day we said adieu to Paris, perhaps for the last time. Perhaps not.

AN OLD FASHIONED PLACE
Norwich, Connecticut

My father Sidney was born and grew up in Norwich, a small city on the Thames (pronounced as in "names" not "tems" as they do in England) River. Although he lived for most of his life in the Bronx, Sidney was happiest during his frequent visits back to his place of birth. It was his natural habitat.

Norwich was a gritty old mill town already growing seedy in the late '30s when he took Sylvia and me to visit his large family, who continued to live there. It was a city of some thirty thousand residents, but it had a small-town feel. We stayed in the same house he had grown up in, a large, two-family shingled home on Pearl Street, on the wrong side of town. Sidney's family never had owned the building, but his oldest sister, Ida, continued to rent the second floor. It was a dark, cavernous space, though lit up by Ida's gentle, bustling nature. Ida was a superb cook who turned out delicious stews, roasts and pies from the big coal-fired stove that dominated her kitchen.

Whenever we visited, Sidney's entire clan would gather at Ida's house. The family included his two other sisters, Rose a spinster, and Lena, whose husband, Ben, a loud, red-faced bully of a man, often abused her verbally. Sidney's brother, Willy, a carpenter who had been a doughboy in World War I, was a quiet presence until he was badly injured when he fell off a roof he was working on and died a few months later. There was also a gaggle of cousins, including Ida's three handsome daughters, already in their twenties, and Lena's pretty little blonde daughter, Barbara, who was a year or so younger than I. These gatherings started amiably, but frequently broke into squabbles between feuding members of the family.

I said earlier that I thought they were an odd lot but they probably were no odder than other families in the community. There was an alcoholic uncle and a mentally ill cousin, but by and large, I recall them as archetypical small-town Americans, with the slight variation of being marginally Jewish. I guess I thought them odd because they did not sound like New Yorkers and their outlook on life seemed more parochial, more in-grown than what I was used to in the big city.

Often, when my boredom at what seemed endless hours of family and local gossip became unbearable, I escaped outside to entertain myself. One time I began to play with matches and dropped a lit one on the dry grass, and soon half the street was experiencing a miniature brush fire. (On another memorable Norwich occasion, while at a neighbor's house for Fourth of July fireworks, I dropped a match into the box containing the fire-crackers, roman candles, rockets, fountains, and cherry bombs and set off the whole collection into an impressive whizz-bang blaze. The neighbor, who correctly disbelieved my protestation of innocence, was not amused. The incident slightly dampened my pleasure at playing with fireworks, which were illegal in New York City.)

Everyone seemed to know and like Sidney. When we walked through town, visiting his old haunts, it was a constant stream of "Hi, Sid. Hi, Sid. Hi, Sid." He paid calls on his old buddies, one the town's kosher butcher, another a proud pro-prietor of a grocery store. Both stores had sagging wooden floors, brass cash registers, and a smell that told that those spac-es had inhaled the aroma of their goods for many decades. He showed me the Norwich Free Academy, the high school he had attended for only a couple of years before dropping out, and which his cousin, Edwin Land, the inventor of the Polaroid camera, also attended. We walked to the down-at-the-heels town center at Franklin Square with its many closed shops and to the dilapidated old mills along the riverfront. The entire town had a patina of age, rather like those old sepia photographs.

I suppose Norwich in the '30s and '40s was a fading place, but I liked it a lot. It was redolent of the nineteenth century, when my grandparents Philip and Bessie first had arrived in this country. It was a place where my father had been a boy and where he was still boyish in middle age. It made me think of those Hollywood movies like *Meet Me St. Louis,* where big families lived in big old houses and young girls fell in love with the boy next door. To me it was authentic America, although why it was any more authentic than the Bronx I never could puzzle out.

The last time I was in Norwich was more than a quarter-century ago for my father's funeral. He was buried next to my mother in the area's only Jewish cemetery. The interment took place during a driving rain, but a surprisingly large number of people showed up, many of whom I had never seen before. They all remembered Sidney fondly from his youth and young manhood in the city. Since then, the Mohegan Indian tribe, with other investors, built a gambling casino not far from the cemetery.

Perhaps the casino has brought a measure of prosperity to Norwich. More likely it has fallen victim, like so many small cities and towns in New England and the Midwest rust belt, small businesses like New York City's garment lofts, and small farms across the country, to the globalization and corporatization of the economy. Globalization and the drive by corporations to find the cheapest sources of labor, and to maximize profits and the personal income of their managers, has been debilitating, demoralizing, and, in too many cases, destroying these places, these small businesses, these small farms. More than jobs and prosperity have been lost in this process. The rise of corporate power also has eroded the sense of community in too many places and devastated a way of life for the people who dwell in those communities.

A SPRINGTIME PLACE
Irvington-on-Hudson, New York

When I was discharged from the Army in 1959, Alice and I rented a small apartment in the Flatbush section of Brooklyn. It wasn't much, but we could afford it on my miniscule starting salary as a newsroom stenographer at the *Times*. Though it had two bedrooms, it was a cramped space, particularly after both my children were born within two years. The apartment looked out on an airshaft, which often was filled with blackened debris from the building's incinerator. I always felt slightly claustrophobic while living there.

The neighborhood was deteriorating but still not bad. The Brooklyn Dodgers recently had departed for Los Angeles, and their beloved Ebbets Field was being torn down nearby. Flatbush Avenue was a bustling thoroughfare of shops, including delicatessens and appetizing stores that catered to the dwindling Jewish population of the area. Prospect Park and a playground for my small children were only two blocks away. Inexpensive restaurants and movie houses were within walking distance.

But there wasn't much of springtime. Living in an urban environment offers a cornucopia of pleasures and conveniences, but experiencing the change of seasons is not one of them. A tree may have grown in Brooklyn, but not on the street where we lived. Prospect Park was okay for playgrounds, trees, and grass but not much for flowers. Winter seemed to merge, with only a brief pause, into a hot, humid summer.

It was the same in the Bronx when I was growing up. The maple trees on the Grand Concourse would leaf encouragingly in due course. Down the block, the Catholic Home for the Blind had a flowering magnolia behind a high iron picket fence that magically puffed out with pretty white and pink blossoms. However, that was pretty much it. For me spring was notable chiefly because it was getting warm enough to begin practice for the baseball season—that and the fact that summer vacation was no longer in the impossibly distant future.

After three years in Brooklyn, Alice and I decided we needed more breathing space. We assiduously studied the *Times*'s classified real estate ads and one day spotted one for a three-bedroom co-op apartment in a place called Irvington-on-Hudson, in Westchester County, at a price we could afford on my rising salary as a cub reporter. We drove up to see it and liked it immediately. It was a garden apartment development of two-story brick houses built on the verge of the Hudson River. The apartment itself was in an end building and offered a full view of the Tappan Zee, the widest part of the Hudson, and the

Palisades of New Jersey on the other side. The tracks of what was then the New York Central Railroad ran along the river about twenty feet below us, and the roar of the frequent trains passing by drowned out conversation.

It was a small price to pay. Our world suddenly became more spacious. The rooms were bright and cheery, and we had a small patch of garden where Alice began her lifelong practice of planting every flower she could cram in. The air was clean, and fresh and the surrounding neighborhood was dotted with lovely homes. The winter was pretty, with snow that remained white, unlike the snow of the city, which became covered with an unpleasant layer of soot and garbage in a day or so. Best of all was the coming of spring.

In Irvington I experienced, I think for the first time, a real spring, a *primavera* that awakened all of my senses and embraced me like a soft young woman. I first noticed it, to my surprise and delight, while walking to and from the railroad station, about fifteen minutes away. The lawns in front of the houses were alive with crocuses, hyacinths, tulips, and daffodils, like masses of bright jewels. I may have seen flowering azaleas and rhododendrons before, but as I walked, it was like discovering an enchanted new world. The fragrance of the flowers, the intensely green grass, and the newly softened earth, and the mild clean, air was an experience so palpable I felt I could float on it.

Even standing on the platform of the station waiting for the train that would take me to Manhattan was a new pleasure. On the slope above the platform stood a huge forsythia in full bloom, an intensely yellow globe that I stared at almost hypnotically. Can a plant communicate with a human? I felt I was in contact with that glowing shrub. I even enjoyed the hour-long commute to the city. The train hugged the river for most of the trip, offering an expansive view of the Palisades on one side. Out the opposite windows, I could see the little towns of Ardsley, Dobbs Ferry, and Hastings-on-Hudson, a pleasant little journey until we came to the beginning of the grubby metropolitan area along the tracks beginning in Yonkers and Upper Manhattan. I alighted in Grand Central Station, one of the world's most beautiful architectural spaces, walked or took the subway shuttle to Times Square and the *Times* building, then headed down West 43rd Street.

Springtime was suspended until I returned to Irvington in the evening.

Urbanization has done much for the human species. It has made possible the creation of markets and wealth, molded a middle class, added immeasurably to the flowering of the arts, nurtured science and education, and provided city dwellers with a measure of warmth, security, and comfort. City life promotes social cohesion and facilitates political organization. Indeed, without cities, civilization as we know it could not have come into being.

Cities were first created by the ancients as places for commerce and for protection—protection not just against human enemies but also against tooth-and-claw nature. Modern warfare and weaponry has eliminated their function as fortresses, but cities have been all too successful in keeping nature at bay. Distance from the natural world is the price we pay for the opportunities and excitement of urban existence. Missing the experience of springtime is a heavy price. If, as Thoreau wrote, wildness is the preservation of the world, there soon will be little left to preserve and our lives are the poorer for it.

The suburbs, places like Irvington, would seem to be a compromise between the city and the countryside. Those places, however, have become increasingly urbanized, with attendant problems such as congestion, crime, pollution and the preemption of the landscape by developers.

My wife and I have found an imperfect but usable solution to this conundrum. We now live in the Boston area—actually in Brookline—for a little more than half the year, from mid-October to mid-May. The spring, summer, and early fall months, we spend in the Berkshires. Our dual residences require a lot of driving, lifting, and shuffling—and expense—but it kind of gives us the best of both worlds. We moved to the Boston area to be near my daughter and her family, and it has proved to be a pleasant, comfortable place to live, with great museums, the Boston Symphony Orchestra, and plenty of other good music, theaters, restaurants, parks, and a lot of visible history. In winter it is cold and dark but not a bad place to hibernate.

Best of all, we are now only a two-hour drive to the Barn. It is our special place, a place that lifts our spirits even as we grow old and move toward the end. Springtime is lovely there.

CHAPTER 13

THE LAST PLACE

If I am very lucky, the last place will be the best place, here on Becket Mountain.

I am in reasonably good health and shape, and I probably will be around for a few more years. But I am also approaching eighty, so I know I cannot have that much time left. So recently I have been thinking more about death and dying. Last autumn, for example, I was carrying a load of firewood to the car for our winter home in Brookline when an unexpected gust of wind brought a swirl of bright red and orange leaves off the maple tree next to our little parking area. *That is life*, I thought—a colorful, quick, inevitable downward spiral to the Earth.

We humans are the bravest animals. We are the only beasts who bear the knowledge throughout our lives that we cannot win—that ultimately we cannot escape death. Yet we live our lives in that vibrant downward swirl.

I have not been thinking of death in a morbid way but rather how I may go about it. If I have any choice in the matter, I want to spend my last hours surrounded by the flowerbeds we have worked over with such inexpert care; the music of our songbirds, which I have never learned to identify; the clean air of our mountaintop and the lilac bush we planted when we first built this house nearly forty years ago, which still bears its deliciously fragrant blossoms each spring; and, of course, by my embracing trees. I would like a last look at some of my favorite trees: the big ash; the gnarled old pine, which I always think looks like an overgrown bonsai; and the young white birch, permanently bowed into an arch by a heavy wet spring snow a few years ago. It is of some solace to know these trees will continue to mount guard around our home after I have left. If I am extraordinarily fortunate, I will depart on a mild day in late spring or summer or early autumn, sitting in one of our Adirondack chairs on the back lawn, with my wife and children sitting with me, looking down the slope I cleared with an axe so many years ago to the pretty little pond we call the center of the universe.

This is an unlikely final chapter, I know. My hour may come in the middle of winter when our long driveway is covered by feet of snow, the Barn is shut until spring, and I am many miles away in Brookline. It may come suddenly, perhaps in an ambulance speeding to the hospital. I do not think I will mind if my last hours are spent in my own room in our pleasant apartment in Brookline. But I would like to die surrounded by life, not in one of our society's waiting rooms for death: hospices, nursing homes, assisted living facilities. What I truly dread is the thought of slowly fading while lying insensate in a sterile institutional room with needles in my arms and tubes in my nostrils. So the last place is important to me; although when the time comes I may think differently—if I will be able to think at all. I would guess that to understand final thoughts about death, you have to be there.

As I said, I am not thinking about my death in a morbid way. I do not fear my end. I have learned to think about dying as a part of life, along with birth perhaps the most normal part of life a living organism experiences. I do not expect any punishment for my misdeeds or any reward for whatever good I may have done in the world. A time to leave and make room for succeeding generations has come for every human who ever lived. I have not been cheated by a short life as my mother was; I have surpassed my allotted threescore and ten years by a substantial margin already. I take much comfort knowing that my ashes will be scattered among these trees and these flowers, which have provided me with so much pleasure and contentment.

Of course I do not want to leave the beauty and unfailing fascination of this world, to leave my wife and children and other family and friends, to abandon into the void all the knowledge and music that I have accumulated and hoarded in my head. I do regret the world I will not have encompassed—all the places I have not and will never visit, all the books I will not read, all the people I will not know, all the future I will not see.

It is difficult to get used to the idea of death; life is so familiar. It seems to me, however, that death is hard not as much for the dying as for whom they leave behind—and not just for family and friends but for all who were touched by their lives. The other day, for example, I was listening to a CD of Louis Armstrong, and when he sang his signature, "What a Wonderful World," I found myself wishing that Pops were still around making me smile every time I heard his raspy voice.

I will depart with only those few regrets about what I have failed to take from life. In large part because I was born in the right place at the right time, my life has been a miraculously safe passage through what for many of my coevals born in the twentieth century was a dismal, dangerous labyrinth. I somehow evaded almost all of the wrong turns on which fate might have led me. For one thing, I did not have to fight in any of the wars in which my country engaged in the twentieth century. Nor did my father or my son have to experience the trauma of armed combat. I might have been born in Europe instead of America and, like so many, many Jewish children, perished in a Nazi gas chamber. Although I entered the world in the middle of the Great Depression, I lived most of my life in a period of unparalleled prosperity in the world's most affluent nation. While I never sought wealth or became wealthy, I was able to live in far more than comfort and even luxury with my family than I had any right to expect when I was growing up in the Bronx.

My health has been generally good, and when it has not, the amazing progress in medical care over the past century pulled me through nicely. I have had a long, happy (with the inevitable rough patches) marriage to a bright, sweet, and sexy woman who relieved me of many of the mundane tasks of daily life while pursuing her own career. My own children were a joy to raise; suffered none of the chronic illnesses that afflict so many kids today; grew up to be successful, decent, and caring adults; and in middle age remain our close friends. I was able to pursue the career I had hoped for as a young boy and was moderately successful at it. My years have been filled with music, good food, good whisky, books (both good and bad), thousands of movies (both good and bad), friends, conversations, ideas, and much laughter. My job with the *Times* and my later occupation as a writer of books enabled me to meet and question interesting, often colorful men and women; made me an eyewitness to fascinating, occasionally historical events; and above all took me to often beautiful, strange, and unforgettable places in the United States and around the world. I have a book titled *A Thousand Places to See Before You Die*. Just for the fun of it I stuck yellow tabs next to all the places I have seen. The book is a forest of tabs—at least half the places are posted. I wish I could have seen all of them.

I spent my early years in a relatively fresh, un-crowded, less degraded environment, where human numbers, a mass consumer economy, and explosive technology were not yet overwhelming and degrading the natural world. When I was born, the population of the United States was less than one hundred fifty million, and the world population less than two billion. Now, in the early years of the twenty-first century, in just my not-yet-over lifetime, there are some three hundred million Americans and some seven billion people, heading to nine billion, on the planet. When I was growing up, there were more empty places, more quiet places, more places where the heavy, coarsening hand of development had not touched. As I wrote that last sentence, it called up a memory nearly seventy years old of driving with my family on a sunny summer day from our cottage in the Catskills to the town of Ellenville, past empty meadows and small copses without seeing another car or another human along the way. The only sound was the whisper of wind through the open windows.

For much of my life, there was no heavy buildup of carbon in the air above me threatening to alter the Earth's climate drastically. Global warming, if not addressed soon—and as I write this it appears that it will not be addressed soon because of criminally callous and selfish political and corporate opposition—will force my grandchildren and their children to live in a hot world of rising waters, drought, and disease and could make life difficult and uncertain enough to disrupt civilization. For much of my life, the massive combustion of coal and other fossil fuels had not yet acidified the rain, killed life in our lakes and streams, and wiped out entire forests on our highlands. The air, the water, the Earth, our bodies, and the bodies of our children had not yet been sullied by the torrent of chemicals, heavy metals, and radioactive waste that industry poured into the environment after World War II. Every human on Earth now has toxic molecules in their bodies. The Inuit people, who live around the Arctic Circle, far from any industrial activity, have some of the heaviest loadings of poisons because they subsist on seals, fish, and other animals on the top of the food chain that bioaccumulate these toxic substances. The umbilical cords of every newborn baby tested now are found to contain multiple chemicals.

Only gradually did our seemingly insatiable consumption produce the mountains of garbage that overwhelm our landfills, degrade our coastlines, and sully our oceans with human detritus. Our unending thirst for oil has drawn us into unwinnable wars, drained our wealth, and endlessly degraded our landscape and our waters. Many years ago I went to Alaska to cover the *Exxon Valdez* oil spill and saw with sorrow the damage it inflicted on lovely Prince William Sound and to the life within it, the sea otters, seals, birds, and fish trapped in the toxic slick. The sound has still not fully recovered, but before I wrote this, another catastrophe, the explosion of the *Deepwater Horizon* oil rig, killed wildlife in and along the Gulf of Mexico, degraded coastal wetlands, and harmed the lives of humans who earn their livelihood on the gulf's periphery.

Until I was an adult, there was no interstate highway system paving over great swaths of the countryside and imposing a dulling sameness on the landscape around each of its cloverleafs and, along with mass media and the rise of shopping malls and chain stores, erasing the regional facets that inspired our many-jeweled American culture. Our endless virgin prairie had been transmuted into farms and cities, but it had not yet been compacted and poisoned by industrial agriculture with its monocultures and inundations of pesticides and synthetic fertilizers. Most cows, pigs, and chickens were still raised on family farms. Now the great majority of small farms have given way to vast factories where the animals are given antibiotics or arsenic to keep them alive and pumped with hormones to make them bigger and more productive, and where their wastes are collected in enormous, reeking lagoons that foul the air and seep into streams and underground water supplies.

By the time I was born, most of the original forest cover of the United States had been stripped to provide wood for homes and railroads for a growing nation. In some places, such as my Berkshire Hills and other parts of New England, the new-growth forests are coming back as farmland is abandoned. However, those old forests that remained, chiefly on the West Coast and Alaska are now being harvested at an unsustainable rate. But the most damaging deforestation is now taking place in the once mysterious, impenetrable Amazon, where the vast forest is being removed to make room for ranches, farms, and gold mines. Other once virgin forests in Southeast Asia and Siberia are rapidly thinning to provide wood for China and Japan. These forests are critical lungs of the planet, generating life-sustaining oxygen.

As my life winds down, I find it distressing to contemplate the enormous toll that human numbers, economy, and technology are taking on other life with which we share the planet. More than twenty-five years ago, a group of scientists reported research that showed that human activity—growing and consuming crops, raising cattle, cutting down or burning forests, building cities, suburbs and highways, and otherwise removing vegetation from the surface of the planet—was using up some 40 percent of the biomass produced by energy from the sun each year. The rest of Earth's living creatures had to make do with the remaining 60 percent. In the intervening quarter-century, human numbers and economic activity have accelerated tremendously, and our claim on global biomass has undoubtedly increased accordingly.

Because of our preemption of so much of the Earth's resources—and the pollution we pour into our surroundings and the economic development that leaves no room for biological life—we humans are wiping out animal and plant life at an alarming and accelerating rate. We are now in the midst of one of the few great spasms of mass extinction of organic life that has occurred over the eons. As the biologist E. O. Wilson has pointed out, humans are causing this spasm, not natural forces.

The other day I read an article in the *Times* that said there soon may no longer be any wild fish for us to eat. A couple of days later, there was a story that warned that there are growing dead zones in the oceans, as their oxygen is being depleted by agricultural runoff of pesticides, fertilizers, and other causes.

Like an alcoholic or drug addict, we seemingly are unable to halt our destruction of the natural world. I am increasingly astonished by the indifference of Americans, indeed of peoples all over the world, to the full implications of what is happening to the environment. We are, after all, talking about the systems that sustain life. Piecemeal we are destroying the planet, the only place on which we can live. If things go on as they have, our posterity—our near posterity—will live lives of heat, hunger, and disease and face the irrevocable loss of the beauty of this Earth. They will witness an abrupt constriction of the course of evolution. Yet our economics and politics utterly have failed to address the approaching calamity. Our free market system places no value on the natural world it is ripping apart. Our politics are held hostage to the money that the system generates.

I am not being Chicken Little here. What I have described is not alarmist—it is alarming. Very. Leading scientists from around the world, convened by the United Nations for a millennium report on the state of the world, concluded that human activity is putting into question the ability of the Earth to sustain life into the future. When I think about the apparent unconcern of people about what we are doing to our only home, it seems we have left the age of reason behind and are retreating to a darker age of ignorance and superstition and, indeed, collective insanity. Is it not madness that our economy and our civilization are sustaining themselves by destroying the habitat that provides us with sustenance? We are, en masse, acting out the tragedy of the commons. By our individual and corporate acts of enrichment and self-aggrandizement (and for some, survival), we are destroying the bounty and life-sustaining capacity of the natural world that we inhabit and use in common.

What is the cause of this madness? The answer must be enormously complex, but surely one reason is that we as a species have in many ways turned our attention—and our love— away from nature. It started with the industrial revolution, and then, in the twentieth century and continuing into this one, we have become so bedazzled with technology and enmeshed in human behavioral and cognitive concerns that we have to a large degree turned our backs on the natural world. Freud, a false prophet of the last century, preached that nature is the enemy of humankind, when in fact humankind was already the enemy of nature. Of course, nature still can put us humans and our hubris in place with the overwhelming might of its earthquakes and tsunamis, hurricanes and tornadoes, and violent storms, floods, and droughts. Human technology is puny in the face of these primal forces. Human activity only can intensify these catastrophes, as witnessed by the nuclear disaster set off by the earthquake and tsunami in Japan in 2011.

In her book *The Power of Place*, Winifred Gallagher notes that more than two thousand years ago Hippocrates had observed that our surroundings affect our wellbeing and that knowledge became embedded in Western medicine. Now, she says, in an age of psychiatry and psychoanalysis, much of the human community looks inward or to drugs for inner peace.

Filling our lives with consumer ephemera, has taken primacy for many or most of us over our engagement with trees and lakes, fields and mountains, sea and sky. The arts turned away from nature and ventured into abstract expressionism in painting, atonalism in music, and minimalism in literature. Screens are replacing our direct encounter with reality. But places are not virtual. Once degraded or destroyed, they cannot be replaced by a quick trip to the Apple store. Yet as virtual reality takes over more and more of our lives, we desperately need the elemental reality of nature.

In our seemingly insatiable getting and spending and our unrelenting quest for security, we are losing much more than nature. Although we human primates are social animals, our sense of community is ebbing away, and as many observers have pointed out, replaced by virtual communities. We also are ceding our liberty to the great corporations, which are increasingly ruling not only our economic lives but also our political and social lives. For the sake of profit and personal wealth of its executives, these corporations play a predominant role in the degradation of the global habitat. Americans, at least, complain about too much government, but in a democracy, the people have a major if declining say in who runs the government. We do not, however, have a say in who runs the corporations, which are increasingly able to dictate who rules us. The notion, propounded by conservative economists, that all are equal in a free market system, is increasingly risible in the face of concentrating corporate power and the rapidly widening gap between rich and poor. Yet we continue to elect public officials who are bought and sold by the corporations and the very wealthy among us. In America we are passive in the face of the great and growing economic disparity among our citizens, and most of us are seemingly indifferent to the lethal poverty in many other parts of the world (although the Occupy Wall Street movement, may be the first sign of an awakening. A year after it appeared, however, there is little sign of its energy or influence).

On my first date with Alice many, many years ago, we rode across Lake Otsego from our camp to Cooperstown in a little outboard motorboat. After dinner at a restaurant and sheltering from a rain squall in a small barn, we sat on a bench at the lakeshore and talked. She asked me why I wanted to be a journalist, and I told her it was important to get information and truth to people so that they could make democracy work by being informed voters and good citizens. It was a grandiose and naively idealistic statement by a college boy, but I meant it. In fact, that goal was an undercurrent throughout my long career as a reporter, publisher, and author of books on environmental issues. I thought I was making a small contribution to a more rational world.

I was, it now appears, indeed naively idealistic.

So it seems luck has run out, not so much for me as for my children and grandchildren and all those who will inherit the future. It is beginning to look, as I have noted, as though we homo sapiens may be a failed evolutionary experiment. The planet probably will survive human greed and selfishness and ferocity toward nature, but if we continue on our present course, the human race may not.

There is still time—not much—for us humans to redeem ourselves. The circle is closing, as the scientist Barry Commoner warned a half-century ago, but it has not yet closed. We know what to do, but so far we cannot bring ourselves to do it. Despite the rationalizations of religious groups and others, it is clear that to ease the pressure on the Earth's systems and resources, we must not only slow population growth but also reverse it. We must earn our living with an economy that works with the natural world, not against it. That means an economy that does not depend on perpetual growth, unending consumption of material goods, or reckless depletion of the world resources and creation of waste. It means replacing technologies that degrade, poison, and destroy the air, the soil, the water, and the bodies of our children. It means leaving enough room for all life to share the planet with us in sufficient abundance.

We need to mend our cracking civilization in a hurry. Power over our government must be taken from the corporations and the very rich and returned to our citizens if we are to have a healthy democracy that will bear us to a safe future. Legal precedent that recognizes corporations as persons with equal rights as individual citizens is bad fiction that gives them ever-growing control over our lives. Our education system must be repaired if we are to have an informed, intelligent electorate that is not seduced and misled by media demagogues and amoral political opportunists. Our science must be taken from the service of mammon and returned to the disinterested service of the common good. We must all of us lift our line of sight beyond merely our own self-interest and live our lives in ways that serve the wellbeing and health of our communities, our society, our fellow humans, and our habitat.

Having spent a lifetime as, in effect, a professional observer of how the world works, to me all of this seems to be self-evident. If nothing else, our instinct for self-preservation should lead us to demand a drastic change of course. That experience also tells me, however, that there is virtually no chance that such change will take place until the inevitable catastrophe. As individuals, as national and global societies, we are too preoccupied with the immediate, too skeptical about the warning signals, too mired in incredulity and inertia. Warnings about fundamental threats to the environment are dismissed as alarmist; proposals for a fundamental change of course are derided as utopian; concrete steps to meet the challenge are scuttled by corrupt or inept politicians. As individuals, most of us give our attention chiefly to self-enrichment and self-fulfillment, not to the collective needs of our society and shared habitat. Too many of us live lives not of quiet desperation but of noisy obliviousness.

As I walk around the Barn, however, checking out the last few roses and the American elm tree we just planted, surrounded by the blazing colors of the maples, watching a late hawk riding the thermals and filling my lungs with the crisp autumn air, I cannot be despairing or even unhappy. I feel, rather than think, that it is good to be alive. Right now. Right here. At this place.

WITHDRAWN

CPSIA information can be obtained at www.ICGtesting.com
Printed in the USA
LVOW07s2218120114

369156LV00001B/222/P